"Chances are, if this book has found its way into your hands, you are supposed to read it. Synchronicity is a topic that carries a vague sense of rightness about it, but most of us know little in depth. Robert Hopcke's book shares many examples and gives shape and form to this wonderful phenomenon."

—THE REVEREND DR. LAUREN ARTRESS,
author of *Walking a Sacred Path*

"Hopcke's book articulates and clarifies the oracular nature of synchronicity—one of the most compelling concepts of Carl Jung—for those of us awakening to the enchanted, psycho-physical nature of reality."

—DAN MILLMAN, author of
The Way of the Peaceful Warrior

"Hopcke is a gifted writer of short stories. His vividly narrated examples communicate how the coincidences of everyday life may mark the significant points of transition in our love life, our work life, our spirituality."

—CHRISTINE DOWNING,
author of *The Goddess*

"*There Are No Accidents* is a delicious slice of all those juicy, unexplainable events that shape our lives. Not only is each story riveting in its wondrous complexity of synchronous events, but Hopcke's thoughtful study of the principles behind seemingly chance occurrences is immensely helpful in guiding readers to understand—or even attract—their own synchronicities."

—CAROL ADRIENNE, coauthor of
The Celestine Prophecy:
An Experiential Guide

"While synchronicity has gotten a lot of play in psychological and New Age circles, skeptics remain. Hopcke's lively, accessible interpretations of a plethora of real-life events will make their doubts difficult to maintain."

—*Publishers Weekly*

There Are No Accidents

Synchronicity and the Stories of Our Lives

Robert H. Hopcke

Riverhead Books, New York

To Lena Drusback and Emma Hopcke,
my grandmothers,
for their faith in me and in my gifts

Ruht in frieden.

RIVERHEAD BOOKS
Published by The Berkley Publishing Group
A division of Penguin Putnam Inc.
375 Hudson Street
New York, New York 10014

Copyright © 1997 by Robert H. Hopcke
Book design by Ralph L. Fowler
Cover design by Isabella Fasciano
Cover illustration © by Rafal Olbinski/SIS

First Riverhead hardcover edition: June 1997
First Riverhead trade paperback edition: July 1998
Riverhead trade paperback ISBN: 1-57322-681-5

The Penguin Putnam Inc. World Wide Web site address is
http://www.penguinputnam.com

The Library of Congress has catalogued
the Riverhead hardcover edition as follows:

Hopcke, Robert H.
There are no accidents: synchronicity and the stories
 of our lives / Robert H. Hopcke.
p.   cm.
Includes bibliographical references and index.
ISBN 1-57322-053-1 (ALK. PAPER)
1. Coincidences—Psychic aspects.   I. Title.
BF1175.H66   1997   97-3853 CIP
133.8—DC21

Printed in the United States of America

20   19   18   17   16

Acknowledgments

Each book has its own path to completion, some hard, some easy, yet all require the efforts of many, many people besides the one whose name appears on the cover as the author. To them!

Having long imagined this book, I owe a great deal of thanks to my agent, Candice Fuhrman, who, synchronistically and intentionally, helped me to see what it was I wanted to do and how to do it. Her assistant, Haden Blackwell, also deserves much thanks for his attention to all the pragmatic details in the business of publishing, details that few know about but which are of vital importance to authors.

To the staff at Riverhead an equal measure of gratitude is due, particularly to Susan Petersen, Dolores McMullan, and Tim Meyer, whose thoughtful comments and editing on the manuscript helped me shape this book. However, I would like to extend my special appreciation to my editor, Cindy Spiegel, whose intelligence, thoroughness, and encouragement were precisely what I needed to revise and revision this book. I count myself extremely fortunate to have had the experience of working with some excellent editors who in the best of circumstances are able to be therapist, writing teacher, debating partner, and friend all at once. Cindy was all of those, and I will long cherish the memories of the many afternoons of discussion I had with her, in person or in the margins of the manuscript; my own thinking about synchronicity was refined and improved through knowing her. She is a gem.

To the many people who took the time to tell me their stories and to my clients who consented to let their work with me help others in turn, I extend my greatest appreciation. I feel quite privileged to have been entrusted with such intimate and often amazing pieces of your life stories, and I hope you feel that my retelling has done justice to the significance of what you shared with me.

And as always, to the people with whom I share my everyday life, who keep me balanced, connected, sane, and encouraged, *baci ed abbracci:* my parents and my sister, Carolann; Tanya, Jurgen, Padma, Freya, and Nimbus; the Ritrosani; the Camptons; the Castillos; and the Schwartzes, one and all; Phil La Tona, the older brother I never had until now; and, of course, my own gracefully aging family, Paul Schwartz, Bianca Neve, and Minou.

Contents

There Are No Accidents

The Stories We Live, The Connections We Make

It is wrong, then, to chide the novel for being fascinated by mysterious coincidences . . . but it is right to chide man for being blind to such coincidences in his daily life. For he thereby deprives his life of a dimension of beauty.

MILAN KUNDERA, *The Unbearable Lightness of Being*

The origin of this book is a single, simple question I asked myself following the very peculiar sort of dream a person only has every now and again. In the dream, I had become trapped in a story that I myself was writing, unable to convince my characters that I was their author and didn't really belong in the plot. Both frustrated by being unable to get out of my own story but at the same time amused by my predicament, I woke up. As a writer, a reader, and a therapist, my life is full of stories. I tell stories. I read stories. People tell me their stories. And so, on that particular day, as this vivid dream stayed with me, I was thinking about stories and the role they play in our lives.

Everyone's life is based on story-telling. You come home from work and the first thing you're asked is, "How was your day?" In other words, "Please tell me the story of your day." Or you meet a friend for lunch and before you've even reached for the napkin, she's asking, "So what's new?" In other words, "Tell me a story." If you have kids, you rarely even have to ask for stories from them. Children live their lives in the land of stories, and like it or not, you're going to get those stories told to you, often in mind-numbing detail.

Given this truism, therefore, the following question popped into my head: "What if the dream had been true? What if I actually am a character in a story?" In one way, I already know that I am. If you were to ask my parents about me, you would have definite confirmation that I am indeed a character in many stories—only the stories happen to be theirs. Likewise, ask my friends, my clients, my co-workers—they'll all tell stories about me.

But that isn't what I meant by the question. What if I—or you—*were* a character in a story? What if what we experience as our life was indeed a work of fiction? How would we know? How could we know? Assuming the story is coherent and the characters and their lives make sense, how would a character in a story know that he or she were in a story? Clearly, only something outside of the story, something introduced from beyond, might draw a character's attention to the nature of the story he or she were living. And yet, whatever that extraordinary occurrence was would need to be itself a part of the story: it would need to make sense, or have meaning, given the characters, the plot, the beginning, middle, and end of the story, wouldn't it?

Nearly every day a certain kind of event, which we call a coincidence, occurs in our lives. Two things happen, and the way they are connected gets our attention for one reason or another. Some of these coincidences do not seem to have much of an effect on us, either emotionally or intellectually; that is, they do not seem to have much significance for our lives. They are, in our usual way of speaking, "just a coincidence."

However, all of us, if we pay any kind of attention to the effect of events on us, have experienced a different kind of coincidence, a confluence of events that shakes us up. The moment such a coincidence occurs we know something quite important, something very meaningful, is happening to us. We can see and feel a significance in the randomness. While to others this second kind of coincidence may look like pure chance, or "just a coincidence," our own experience tells us that something categorically different is happening. It is this second sort of meaningful coincidence which Swiss psychologist C. G. Jung called "synchronicity."

My idea, and the basis of the book which you are about to read, is that indeed our life is a story and that synchronistic occurrences make us aware of this fact. Let me tell a story to make clear what I mean.

My friend Ann at one point in her life had a penchant for getting involved with married men. Divorced for a while and not wanting much commitment, she had a number of somewhat lengthy sexual relationships with men who were emotionally estranged from their wives. At the time, the position of "other woman" suited her. One of these relationships began on a vacation in Mexico with a man named Dan, who had recently separated from his wife and had taken his boat down south. (As her confidant, I got all the details.) The romance was intense, as vacation romances tend to be, and, although the two lived ninety miles apart, they continued the relationship even after the vacation had ended. He was handsome and financially comfortable. The sex was great. Ann fell in love. And on it went for about a year, with him driving at all hours of the day and night to her house for visits and overnights. Then slowly it seemed that his feelings began to change. The separation weighed more and more heavily on him, and he realized that however much he cared about Ann, he belonged with his wife of many years. Thus, their intense connection slowly and painfully came to an end.

A year passed, and Ann, who has a very mature attitude about the affairs of her heart, healed her wounds and went on with her life. Every once in a while she wondered about Dan, but time after time she realized that calling him wouldn't do much good and in fact would just complicate things unnecessarily. Then a girlfriend suggested they take a day trip and drive down to the coastal town where Dan lived. Ann hesitated, wondering what it would feel like to be wandering around the town where he lived with his wife, kept his boat, and ran his business, but nevertheless she went.

It was a glorious spring day, the kind that makes you feel as if you're in love, even if you're not. And as one might expect, Ann felt her former lover's presence everywhere, though she resisted at every step of the way the strong temptation to phone him, or to go by his house, or to see the dock where he kept his boat. In any case, she had never visited the town before and finding him or his boat would have required a fair bit of sleuthing. So she and her friend went sightseeing, shopping, had lunch overlooking the bay, and watched a beautiful sunset on the beach before returning home. Full of the day and memories of what had been, she walked into her house and found her phone ringing. To her amazement, when she picked it up, she heard an all too familiar voice. "Hey, Ann. This is Dan. For some reason, I've been thinking of you all day and thought I'd just give a call to see how you were doing."

Now, this story sounds almost made up, the sort of thing that only happens in movies. First of all, the timing is too perfect: receiving a phone call from an ex-lover the very moment you walk into the house from a day trip to his town. But this is my point. The particular sort of coincidences which are the subject of this book, those meaningful coincidences which we will be calling synchronistic, always have, I've found, a rather distinctly dramatic or novelistic quality to them, because of the way in which an internal, emotional state—Ann's feelings for Dan—are reflected in a chance occurrence in the external world—Dan's phone call. I would venture to say that most of us do not usually think life is like that, with outer occurrences so neatly arranged to mirror, confirm, or transform our own inner lives, and yet such things do happen. Truth can be every bit as strange as fiction.

Second of all, because of the emotional impact of Dan's phone call, it is hard to believe that he happened to phone just by chance. If you are like most people, you are probably thinking about the various ways to explain it all away rationally—Dan saw Ann in his town that day but forgot about it, or only registered seeing her subliminally and then called her later. Or somehow he mystically picked up on her presence. Or she sent him "vibes" which "made" him call her. Nevertheless, the plain fact of the matter is that Dan's phone call on that day and at that time was a chance occurrence, but a chance occurrence with a crucial difference: it was significant to Ann, for having spent the day immersed in memories, she found her connection to Dan reestablished through no action of her own.

It is the meaningfulness of such chance events which makes a synchronistic coincidence different from other sorts of coincidences. Obviously, if Ann had walked in the door and her mother had called her at that moment, that would have been a coincidence as well. "Hi, Mom, funny you should call. I just walked in the door." But it is the story behind Dan's phone call, the history of their relationship, the setup of the day Ann had just spent which makes this coincidence different.

Now aren't all these elements the very things that form the basis of a good story? We expect an interesting and well-constructed plot, in which events occur according to a plan, a plan which we might not necessarily be able to perceive completely at the beginning but which, as the story then continues, becomes more and more clear to us, so that what seemed random and meaningless actually turns out to have been quite important. And the importance of the plot has mostly to do with the emotional impact such events have on the lives of the characters, the way such events change and transform them, sometimes for better, sometimes for worse, but always significantly.

Synchronistic events, such as Dan's phone call, bring to our attention the way that our lives *are* stories, the way that our lives have a structure: a plot which we may not always perceive at the moment but which at key points in our lives is brought to our attention through the sort of confluence of external event and inner state that we—mistakenly, I contend—imagine can only happen in fiction. And as in fiction, synchronistic events have a significant impact. They bring about a different way of seeing ourselves, a broader perspective on our lives, or a deeper understanding of others or the world.

Let me tell another story which illustrates what makes a coincidence synchronistic and why. Again, this story sounds as if I might have lifted it straight out of an O. Henry tale, but like all the stories in this book, it is true.

In stark contrast to her very Christian upbringing, one of my clients, whom I'll call Bobbie, began to have a series of dreams containing images that I recognized as images from the Tarot. Although she was completely unacquainted with the Tarot and strongly disapproved of what the church of her childhood would have called occultism, nevertheless there the images were: the Empress on her throne, the Emperor with his scepter, the Fool walking over the cliff. And as always with dreams when one ignores their message, her dreams became even more explicit, until she actually had a dream, right before her birthday, of an actual Tarot layout, thirteen cards arranged in a diamond shape. Despite her skepticism as to what insights the Tarot might have to offer her, this dream stayed with her. Yet the very idea of going into a New Age store, looking at Tarot decks, and then paying money for one was just too weird, in her opinion. She couldn't bring herself to do it. Having accompanied over the course of my professional life more than a few people through patches of resistance to what we might call elements of their story—elements which for the time being they do not want to recognize as important parts of the plot—I knew better than to push her.

Then, the session after her birthday, Bobbie came in, and to my surprise she was carrying a Tarot deck.

"I didn't buy it," she said to me in response to a question I hadn't asked.

"Oh. Then . . . ?"

She was smiling, as much, I think, at herself as at the situation. "My husband gave it to me for my birthday. And no, I haven't told him about any of the dreams you and I have been talking about. You know my attitude toward all this stuff; I'm hardly going to go around talking about it, especially to him." Like Bobbie herself, her husband was rather conservative and, according to her, even thought her being in psychotherapy was a little out there. "So on my birthday, I open the box, just dumbfounded. I immediately think, 'Has he been reading my journals? Has he been listening in on our sessions?' But no. I ask him, 'Whatever made you give me this?' And in this completely uncharacteristic way, he says, 'I saw them in the window of a bookstore and something said to me, I need to get these for Bobbie, they'll help her. Happy birthday, honey!'"

As in Ann's story of the phone call from Dan, Bobbie and her

Tarot deck is the tale of an unexpected coincidence of an inner situation and an outer event which seems, like all synchronistic events, almost too perfect in its timing and its significance. In Bobbie's case, the inner situation was her many dreams of Tarot imagery, imagery which for all sorts of reasons she persistently refused to acknowledge. The outer event, of course, was the rather surprising gift from her husband, and the synchronistic element of this coincidence was the effect of this particularly perfect birthday present on Bobbie's resistance. She finally began to work with the Tarot, after having a deck literally delivered into her hands, and her work with the imagery began a long period of spiritual and psychological growth that made her a far more creative and tolerant person than she had been.

Though Bobbie's dreams had been making clear for months where the plot of her particular story was going—namely, away from such an exclusive reliance on the religious imagery of her childhood to give her life meaning and toward a wider appreciation of the wisdom manifested in other forms of spirituality and religion—it took the random action of her husband's gift, giving her something she hadn't asked for, something she could not have even imagined getting from him, to dissolve her resistance. Like Dan's phone call, Bobbie's gift was not something she could have caused; it was an event that occurred by pure chance which nevertheless had a significant and life-changing impact. This significance is what makes this gift—as opposed to any other, a diamond ring, a book of poetry, say—synchronistic. We expect this sort of coincidence to happen to characters in novels, because in novels we expect the timing, the plot, and the events to lead to the development of the protagonists. My point, again, is that our lives have a narrative structure, like that of novels, and at those moments we call synchronistic this structure is brought to our awareness in a way that has a significant impact on our lives.

Notice in this example the way that, when faced with this synchronistic meeting between inside and outside, Bobbie herself began searching for ways to explain away the wonder of this chance event. If her husband had read her journals or had somehow been privy to our sessions, then his gift of a Tarot deck would have "made sense" in the manner that most of us usually think about our lives. In this way, Bobbie, I think, is a fairly typical person, and her need to feel in control of her life, what she'd call her "straight-forward attitude" toward life, is, in my experience, common to most of us.

Bobbie's gift from her husband challenged her; before she received it, she thought she knew what the plot of her story was. In fact, ours is a culture that encourages us to believe that we are—or should be—the author of our stories. But when external events so precisely mirror our own inner state that the impact of the coincidence cannot be ignored or its significance denied, while at the same time our lack of control over the events is indisputable, then we are faced with the question that Bobbie had to grapple with: if I am not the author of my story, who is?

Though the answer to this question is one which we will be exploring together in the chapters to come, my point here is to make clear just why synchronistic events are nearly always met with a tendency to deny, dismiss, or discount on the part of readers, and even on the part of the participants themselves. Synchronistic events confront us with the fact that sometimes the stories we make up about ourselves, the stories we would like to live, are not necessarily the stories we are actually living or, to go a step further, are meant to live. Our conscious sense of ourselves, our ego, is even inclined to be offended by the irrationality, the randomness of synchronistic events. But as you read the many stories of synchronicity which follow, I urge you to pay attention to your own resistance to believing that such events can happen.

• • •

Of course, being a writer, perhaps I more than anyone can be seduced into thinking that I am the author of my own story. So to illustrate just how many twists and turns of the plot it may take for the illusion of authorship to be defeated, let me tell the story of how I met one of my best friends, Phil. As a long-standing member of my local YMCA, I have seen staff people come and go with a fair bit of regularity. One day about five years ago, I noticed a new guy working there, altogether the kind of guy you expect to see at a fitness club: in his late thirties, Italian-looking, a bit on the sullen side, muscular. Now the YMCA here is definitely *not* one of those places where the big boys go to pump serious iron. Folks come to the Y to do aerobics, lift a weight or two, and go home, so the fitness staff generally does not have a lot to do. The friendly ones socialize with the members to pass the time, and the unfriendly ones sit at the desk and don't talk to anyone. This new guy mostly sat at the desk and looked bored, and for many months I would walk past him, do my thing, and leave, assuming that he was yet another one of the many jocks I had seen go through the place.

Then a close friend of mine died, and while his death was not unexpected, it was a blow for me, since I had already lost many friends to accidents and illnesses. The creeping loneliness I felt, as my social circle grew smaller and smaller, had been the subject of a fair bit of my emotional attention over the past years, and many of the attempts I had made to expand my circle of friends had not really yielded much, some short-term and superficial friendships but nothing deeper. I went about my interests pretty much by myself, going to the gym alone, going to the opera alone, out biking alone. When my friend died that April, I had gotten somewhat used to this situation and had learned more or less how to take care of myself. So on the morning of his memorial service, at which I had agreed to sing, I decided to get a massage at the Y from the masseur I had seen a number of times before.

I was keyed up about the service, anxious about performing, and feeling physically tense. As you might expect, the version of the story I thought I was living that morning was that I would soon be lying on the massage table, fully relaxed and loose. But, as it turned out, there was another plot afoot. As I sat in the lobby for my 9 A.M. appointment, the hour came and went. No masseur. 9:15. No masseur. Now, this was very uncharacteristic, since the masseur was one of the mainstays of their staff. No one could locate him. 9:30. No masseur. By then, I felt a mixture of anger, frustration, disappointment, and even greater physical tension, which the employee at the desk sensed. With profuse apologies, he set up an appointment with another masseur for the next day, with the cost of the massage on the house. Yet I was still livid, because this was not at all the way things were supposed to happen.

The memorial service that day was difficult, not helped by the incident that morning, and, behind my anger, my feelings of loneliness and abandonment were holding sway. The next day I showed up at the Y for the complimentary massage I had been offered only to experience a reprise of the previous day. The masseur was a different one this time, but after waiting half an hour we learned that his car had died and that he wouldn't be able to come after all. Now this was *definitely* not supposed to be part of my story, and the script I had in my head for this whole situation was very much at odds with what was happening. By this time I was in a state of fury. I made yet a third appointment for the next evening with the only masseur available, to my surprise, the sullen, bored-looking Italian guy, who looked no more like a masseur to me than Rocky Balboa. Despite my hesitancy about getting a massage from him, I went ahead and made the third appointment.

Like a fairy tale in which it always takes three tries to get things right, the next evening I showed up for my massage with Phil and became acquainted not with the dumb jock I had assumed he was but rather with a very intelligent, well-read man with whom I had much in common. It had been he who the week before had posted a list of Men's Center events, including a lecture of mine, on the Y bulletin board. As we talked, I discovered that he had plans to become a therapist and was an avid cyclist to boot. In short order, in the months following that first massage, he became first my cycling buddy, then my workout partner, and now, as the years have gone on, my best friend.

That it was a series of chance events which brought the two of us together as friends—repeated cancellations on the part of a usually quite conscientious massage staff—is the outer event in this synchronistic occurrence; yet this outer event gave birth to a friendship at a point in my life when my inner loneliness, grief, and anger were in great need of transformation. As we will be hearing in many of the stories that follow, some of the most memorable synchronistic events in people's lives have to do with meeting just the right person by pure chance at just the right moment, at a time of great need, or at a time of unusual openness.

But there is an additional synchronistic element to this story which has to do with the story I thought I was living versus the story I was actually living. Without the chance series of cancellations, I probably would not have ever really gotten to know Phil, for on the basis of mere appearance, I had already written his and my story: he was a dumb jock with whom I had nothing in common. The impact of our friendship, begun only after months of passing each other in the gym and then only "accidentally," had as much to do with what we did have in common as with the lesson it taught me about my own illusions of authorship—that I don't know as much as I think I do about who's who and what's best for me. It was the sort of lesson that, it seems, many of us can only learn by meaningful chance.

• • •

If one can tolerate a play on words, this book could be called a novel approach to synchronicity, based as I have said on the idea that each of our lives is a story and that synchronistic events call our attention to the structure of the story, the "novel," if you will, which we are living. Moreover, to examine synchronicity from this angle is, in yet another sense of the word, also a novel approach, as most of what has been written so far on synchronicity comes at the notion from either a purely psychological point of view or from a scientific perspective. The psychological, written mostly by followers of Jung, sees in this phenomenon an argument for the primacy of subjectivity, while the scientific makes an argument for the new physics via synchronicity.

My perspective here, novel therefore in many senses, is not to argue but rather, after a short introduction to some of the aspects of synchronicity, to simply tell stories and examine their meanings. Some will be love stories—amazing connections between people, lost loves found, fine friendships begun. Some will be the stories of our professions and vocations—opportunities lost and gained through chance encounters that no one could have caused or predicted. Along this line, there will be stories of inner transformation and growth, for dreams, as we have already mentioned, are often synchronistic events, as are forms of divination which rely on chance, such as the Tarot, the *I Ching,* and so on, which make use of synchronicity to help us see more clearly the story we are—or perhaps should be—living out. Then, because every story has a beginning and end, there will be stories of synchronicities around those two transition points which we all face, our birth and our death. All along, I will be including those stories of what we, with our delusions of authorship, call "accidents," unfortunate events which we have done our best to avoid but which some-

times, synchronistically, are neither unfortunate nor insignificant to the stories of our lives.

In each of these stories—some of which were personal experiences, some of which were told to me by the people involved, and some of which are examples drawn from the literature on synchronicity—the line between what sounds like fiction and what are, in fact, real-life events becomes blurry. You the reader might doubt the veracity of some of these experiences or find it hard to appreciate the meaning that these events had for the people involved. As I have already mentioned, nothing is easier than to dismiss someone else's synchronistic experience. But throughout this book and the many stories which are to come, I encourage you as often as you can to examine your own experience, particularly when you find yourself saying, "That's impossible, he made that up," or "So what?" At those times, remember when the truth of your own life, the significant but entirely chance occurrences which helped shape your own story, seemed indeed stranger than fiction. As the author of *The Unbearable Lightness of Being*, Milan Kundera, says, we are right to chide those who are blind to the coincidences of life, for as this book will show, those unique coincidences which we call synchronistic make us aware, again and again, of the beauty, order, and connectedness of the tales we are living.

Chapter One

When Are Coincidences Not Just Coincidences?

Defining Synchronicity

C. G. Jung, whose book *Synchronicity: An Acausal Connecting Principle* was published in 1952, coined the term "synchronicity" and launched it into psychological parlance, after which it was quickly taken up by popular culture. As with many ideas that catch fire in the public imagination, Jung's notion of the meaningful coincidence was neither new nor unique, but to Jung's credit, his approach to synchronistic events allows us to see them in a clear and useful way.

The son of an Evangelical minister and a mother with distinct psychic, if not psychotic, tendencies, Jung followed a life path not uncommon for a pastor's son. Deeply religious, Jung nevertheless repeatedly and explicitly rejected organized religion with its dogmatic theology and institutionalized spirituality, and his choice of a career as a psychiatrist, as described in his autobiography *Memories, Dreams, Reflections*, had much to do with his father's crisis of faith. Because of his background, Jung devoted himself throughout his long career to understanding what Heraclitus called the "boundaries of the soul," using the tools of modern psychology. He consistently applied scientific methods to examine so-called "irrational" phenomena and to elucidate the psychological meaning and function of such experiences in human life—paranormal experiences, extrasensory perception, UFOs, psychokinesis, and the like. His doctoral thesis, for example, entitled "On the Psychology of So-Called Occult Phenomena," attempted to provide a rational, psychological explanation for the mediumistic abilities of a woman whose trance states, automatic behavior, and psychokinetic abilities were notable.

Jung's application of scientific methods to make sense of occurrences which many dismissed as fantastic, meaningless, or worse, disturbed, was seen by the psychological establishment of his time as a sign of Jung's foolishness and eccentricity, since research in the field of academic psychology was (and still is) organized along strictly behavioral or cognitive lines. When Freud's psychoanalytic theories began to challenge such a mechanistic approach to psychology by positing such events as the result of unconscious processes and conflicts, Jung initially gravitated to this newer way of thinking. Eventually, though, after disagreeing with Freud over the role of sexuality and the nature of the unconscious, Jung once again found himself excluded and isolated, while Freudian psychoanalysis gained ground in Europe and the United States.

Even today, misunderstandings about Jung's interest in such phenomena as synchronicity lead many to hold a derogatory view of his work, devaluing it as mere mysticism in psychological garb or as the result of his own self-indulgent subjectivism. What is often not understood is that Jung always approached such phenomena as ghosts, astrology, and synchronicity not in a simplistic, credulous way but rather from as objective and rational a standpoint as possible. His intention in his studies of these events was always to ask, "What are the inner psychological conditions, both conscious and unconscious, such that our external experience is affected in such unforgettable and transformative ways?" Unlike many from both sides of the argument, Jung attempted to approach these events without either prejudging them as ridiculous or immediately assuming that the most literal way of understanding them was the whole truth.

In the course of my research for this book I found that many people are confused about what exactly a synchronicity is or is not. Perhaps it is best, then, to start with the simplest definition of the concept as Jung developed it, as a "meaningful coincidence." Yet the problem with such simplicity is that if you look up the dictionary definition of the word "coincidence," you will read something along the lines of "an accidental sequence of events occurring simultaneously or in the same period of time." Unfortunately, this bald definition leaves out the way in which we generally use the word, which makes all the difference in the world.

If I am typing this sentence and, say, a bird flies through my window, according to the dictionary, this is a coincidence—an accidental sequence of events occurring in close temporal proximity. Most people, however, would not call such an event a "coincidence." On the other hand, if I am typing this sentence and a friend calls and tells me that she, too, is currently attempting to write a definition of synchronicity for an article of her own, most people would call that a pretty interesting coincidence. Yet if you knew that my friend and I had agreed last night to spend an hour this afternoon attempting to write a definition of synchronicity, the fact that both of us were doing the same thing at the same time would suddenly not seem to be much of a coincidence, would it? In other words, the mere simultaneous occurrence of two or more events would not lead us to call something a "coincidence," even if the dictionary would. Instead, in the common use of the term, a coincidence is a sequence of events which occur in close proximity to each other and which *by chance are related to each other* through some kind of noticeable similarity.

However, even that does not quite cover the way in which we use the word "coincidence," for if my friend calls me at six o'clock in the evening to say she is cooking dinner only to have me reply that I happen to be doing the exact same thing at my house, most people probably wouldn't think it much of a coincidence, given that most people are probably fixing themselves dinner around that time of day. In other words, the dictionary definition of the word coincidence also leaves out the fact that a coincidence is an *unusual* sequence of simultaneous events which bear some sort of relationship to each other. Coincidences are, as we generally use the word, extraordinary occurrences.

Now, in defining synchronicity, Jung took yet another step. Coincidences—accidental but related sequences of unusual events—occur now and then to everybody, but such coincidences are not necessarily all that meaningful. If in fact this friend of mine who is writing her article on synchronicity is someone whose interest in such topics mirrors mine and is part of the reason we are friends, it might be quite interesting that she should coincidentally be involved in writing about the same topic as I am, but the coincidence would not necessarily have any significance beyond the mere fact that it happened. But if at the time of my writing I am feeling very isolated, thinking to myself that no one knows about or even cares about synchronicity, only to have a friend call to say that she, too, is writing about synchronicity this afternoon, well, then, the coincidence is considerably more meaningful to me and could well have a significant effect on the way that I see myself and my writing. This then would be what Jung came to call "synchronicity," or quite simply, a meaningful coincidence.

The examples I gave in the introduction are good illustrations of synchronistic events—*meaningful* sequences of unusual, accidental events. Throughout her long relationship with Dan, Ann had never visited his town. Her day trip there with her friend, therefore, was an unusual event. Likewise, since the time that Dan had ended the relationship, she had not heard from him. Thus, when he called the moment she walked in that day, not only was the call coincidental, it was full of significance for her as well, for she had spent the entire day silently trying to deal with her feelings about him and the relationship. If, as I have already mentioned, her mother had called the moment she had walked in, even if Ann had not heard from her in a long time, the event still would have been a coincidence—along the lines of "Funny you should call, I just walked in"—but it would not have had the emotional meaning that Dan's phone call had.

Likewise with Bobbie. If her husband had just happened to give her the diamond ring she had seen the day before in a jewelry store window, it would certainly have been a coincidence, but it would not have had the meaning that the gift of the Tarot deck had for her, given her months of dreams about Tarot imagery and her resistance to working with it. Similarly, my friendship with Phil, begun by pure chance after the unusual and accidental cancellation of a series of appointments, might not have been all that synchronistic had it happened during a time in my life when I had not been feeling so much grief and loneliness—but it did, and thus, the coincidence of our meeting held and still holds great significance for me.

So then the question arises, what exactly does "meaningful" mean? Far from useless philosophizing, this question is important to address right away not only because it is crucial to Jung's own definition of the concept of synchronicity but because, without appreciating that synchronicity is about the subjective meaning of the events for the individuals involved, many readers will find the stories that follow to be without any real significance. In telling the stories that appear in this book to a number of people, I have found that the same story that elicits excitement, interest, and wonder in some can garner a bored "Big deal!" or "Who cares?" from others. What accounts for the difference? Why, for instance, when we go to a movie with a friend, does she walk out moved to tears while I find the same film ridiculous and sentimental? What makes something meaningful to one person and meaningless to another?

When we say something is meaningful to us, generally we are indicating one of two things. Either we are saying that something has an importance to us because of certain values that we hold—in other words, it means something because it is valuable to us—or we are saying that something has had a significant impact on us—that is to say, it means something because it has affected our lives in a major way. Obviously, something can also be meaningful in both of these ways. To continue to use our examples from the introduction, Dan's phone call was important to Ann because she valued their relationship, and the fact that he still cared enough to call affected her emotionally. With Bobbie, the gift of the Tarot deck was meaningful mostly because of the impact it had on her, but also because it was given to her just when what she valued as important in her life, her spiritual life, was in the process of changing. For me, friendships are relationships that have always influenced me greatly—they mean a lot to me.

Thus, a synchronistic event is a coincidence that holds a subjective meaning for the person involved, and like all things subjective, what one person finds meaningful—that is to say, valuable and/or significant in its effect—another might very well find meaningless. A perfect example of such an aspect of synchronicity is an incident that occurred to my friend Jill. Dining in a crowded restaurant, she found herself seated next to a man who was animatedly telling his dinner partner the story of two friends of his who had been having extramarital affairs with each other's siblings. He didn't know, of course, that the stranger beside him, my friend Jill, also knew the people he was talking about. At the dramatic end of the story, he sat back in immense self-satisfaction and said to his companion, in a rhetorical flourish designed to end the gossipy tale, "And you'll never guess who he is seeing now!" to which Jill couldn't resist leaning over and ending the story for him by saying, "Mimi's cousin!"

The man was flabbergasted; for him, what an experience it must have been to have a complete stranger end his intimate tale seemingly out of nowhere in a public restaurant! But for Jill, who had none of the man's emotional investment in telling this juicy story of marriage and betrayal, it was simply a hilarious coincidence. Now both of them, factually speaking, experienced the same event, but what was for Jill just a funny anecdote could very well have been experienced as an incredible synchronicity by the man whose story she had finished, replete with a significant lesson about telling gossipy stories in a self-important way in public places. Of the many stories presented here, of the many more that I have heard, I am often reminded how the same incident, occurring to two people, might very well have yielded two completely different experiences, one synchronistic and meaningful, the other not.

Such subjectivity makes it easy to scoff at, dismiss, or make fun of other people's synchronistic occurrences. In fact, I predict that anyone reading this book will discover that certain stories hit you deeply while others leave you cold. Some stories will remind you of a time when almost the same thing happened to you, while others will seem trivial, uninteresting, or forced.

Moreover, we will see that the description "synchronistic" will apply to a wide range of meaningful coincidences. In some coincidences, as in our examples, the extreme improbability of the event or the uncanny parallel between internal state and external occurrence will be the most salient feature. These kinds of synchronistic events usually have an "Aha!" sense about them. In other meaningful coincidences, it may not be until much later that the significance of what occurred becomes clear, or you may find that the meaning of an event may develop slowly over time. These sorts of synchronicities have much more of an "Oh, *now* I see. . ." sense to them. In some cases the external event occurs first and the internal, subjective meaning follows. In others, the meaningful coincidence is between an internal image, such as a dream, and a subsequent, external event. In all of these various synchronistic events, however, the connecting principle between inner and outer is the meaningfulness of the event for the people involved.

Some people, usually analytically oriented individuals, can become absorbed in trying to decide whether something is or is not a synchronicity: Does it fit the definition? Does it meet all the criteria? I would like to emphasize here at the outset that the concept of synchronicity is best used as a tool rather than as an end in itself. As with ideas concerning what constitutes a true work of art, one can get easily engaged in idle questioning, over whether this or that is *really* synchronistic, particularly since in all synchronistic events, as in works of art, considerable subjectivity is involved.

A far better use of the concept is one that is exploratory and evocative. Does the idea that an event *might* be synchronistic give you a different perspective on the event, deepen your understanding of it, or intrigue you enough to look further at what has occurred? If so, then, the notion which Jung has proposed has served its highest purpose and the purpose for which this book was written—to help people see the meaning of the stories they are living each day.

Though synchronicity is an idea that has existed almost since the dawn of human culture, Jung's contribution was his observation that the special confluence of events, to which he applied the term "synchronicity," almost always had three distinct characteristics, to which my own experiences and research has led me to add one more. Thus, those events which we are calling synchronistic generally have four features.

First, such events are *acausally* connected, rather than connected through a chain of cause and effect that an individual can discern as intentional and deliberate on her or his own part. Second, such events always occur with an accompaniment of *deep emotional experience*, usually at the time of the event itself, but not always. Third, the content of the synchronistic experience, what the event actually is, is always *symbolic* in nature, and almost always, I have found, related specifically to the fourth aspect of the synchronistic event, namely, that such coincidences occur at points of *important transitions* in our life. A synchronistic event very often becomes a turning point in the stories of our lives.

If I Didn't Cause It, How Can It Be?
Acausality and Our Egos

To say that we are, as a culture, used to thinking in terms of cause and effect would be an understatement. Our very conception of the world, at least for those of us of a European-American intellectual heritage, is based on the idea that every action causes a reaction, every stimulus causes a response. Certainly, and not surprisingly, much of modern scientific thought since the so-called Age of Enlightenment and on through the amazing productivity of the Industrial Revolution has been founded directly upon this idea. We act, there follows a consequence, and we are said to have caused the effect produced by the action. We introduce a chemical into a solution, it reacts, and we have caused the reaction. Or we press the computer keys to spell a word, hit the Print button, and out pops a sentence on a piece of paper. We have caused the writing that appears on the page. Or perhaps we do not act, for example, we forget to eat lunch and consequently get dizzy. We have caused our dizziness by skipping lunch. This habit of thinking in cause-and-effect terms is such a fundamental part of the Western mindset that we are hardly aware of it. That is, until we are faced with a sequence of events that by their very nature illustrate a different way that events may be connected.

One sure-fire conversation-starter at any social event is to ask people if they have ever experienced a synchronistic event. Almost everyone has their favorite example, and my friend Cathy is no exception. Her story is a good illustration of how our habit of causal thinking is challenged by synchronicity.

During a certain period of her life, Cathy was, as they say, betwixt and between. She had graduated high school but was unsure what to do next. As is often the case, she gravitated into a relationship with a man around her own age and they dated for a year or two before finally, again as is often the case, separating and going their own ways. For Cathy that meant moving to California, getting married, and having two daughters. As the years passed, throughout her marriage, divorce, and second marriage, she occasionally thought of Richard, her first real boyfriend, but after three decades, the thought had more the nature of idle curiosity, as if remembering the plot of a movie she had once seen a long time ago. For all she knew, he was far away and, since she was fairly content in her own life, she didn't have a great deal of motivation to do more than just wonder about him now and then. The story of her life, now that she was in her fifties, seemed fairly well written, and all the previous plots and subplots she had lived felt insignificant.

What then led her to begin to think more and more about Richard at a certain point? Was she having dreams about him that she didn't remember? Was she meeting people that reminded her of him? Was she unhappy in her life or in her marriage? When I asked Cathy, she couldn't tell me why, but only that suddenly she had an insistent inner prodding to find out what had happened to him. Was it boredom? Was it psychic connection? Was it random chance? Who knows? But the fact is that she had begun to make a few phone calls to try to trace him, first by calling folks in her home town, then with her curiosity piqued, by following their leads. She learned that he worked for a certain insurance company back East, but the insurance company was enormous with branches all over the country and his name was a very common one: Richard Johnson. She spent about a year trying to find him, talking to many Richard Johnsons and to people who knew Richard Johnsons who had been in insurance, but none of them was her Richard Johnson. Since there was no compelling reason to locate him, and since the difficulties in finding him had begun to outweigh the curiosity she felt, she stopped her active efforts and put the whole thing on that side of the mental ledger we all carry that reads "Things We Will Never Find Out in Our Lifetime."

One day, though, at a dinner party, she found herself across the table from a woman who purported to have psychic abilities, and since all her best efforts at locating Richard had failed, Cathy thought that asking the woman to find Richard Johnson would be a good test of her supposed gifts. So Cathy told the woman her story and asked her how she could find Richard Johnson. The woman told her to write his name down on a piece of paper, draw a thick black box around it, the purpose of this being to hold the energy around him, and look at it every day. Hardly a believer in this sort of thing, Cathy laughed and decided to do just that, mostly to prove how ridiculous the suggestion was. If all her phone calls and inquiries and conversations had failed over a year, how could this absurd exercise work? So she did it. She wrote his name down, drew a thick black box around it, and put it on her mirror, where she looked at it every day.

We have heard enough of these stories by now to figure out the ending. After a week's time, Cathy went to her mailbox and in it found a letter from the long-lost Richard Johnson, who knew nothing at all of her previous year's search for him but had decided from his home in the Midwest to get in touch with some of the folks from his past. He had contacted Cathy's sister in her hometown, gotten her address with a single phone call, and decided to write.

As Cathy's experience demonstrates, synchronistic occurrences involve an *acausal* connection between physical events, between Cathy's actions and Richard's letter, events that cannot possibly be linked by cause and effect as we understand it but are connected instead through the subjective meaning of the events. While the significance of Cathy's connection to Richard is made plain by her actions—her search, her pursuit of advice from a psychic, her writing his name down and meditating upon it—it is also plain that none of her actions *caused* Richard to call her. One could, I suppose, argue that nonphysical factors came into play in this incident, that some form of secret, silent, or magical communication occurred between them such that it *caused* Richard to look for Cathy, but belief in nonphysical causes that cannot be proven or disproven is just that, a matter of personal belief rather than what is generally understood by the term "causality." In "causal" terms, the re-establishment of contact was pure coincidence, an unusual, but meaningful, event that occurred by pure chance to Cathy.

The reason, I think, that synchronicity, "the simultaneous occurrence of two meaningfully but not causally connected events,"[1] has remained controversial and difficult to accept since Jung's develop-

ment of the concept, is because synchronicity forces us to shake off
the unconscious tyranny of cause-and-effect thinking. Why, one might
ask, do we hold so tenaciously to this view of life as a chain of action
and reaction? What is the benefit we derive from believing that all
connections are and must be cause and effect?

In my opinion, causal thinking seduces us into an illusion of
complete power over our surroundings and enhances our sense that we
are in control of our destiny, a vision quite flattering to our own egos.
Cause-and-effect thinking enables us to feel in control, to split ourselves off from the world "outside" and operate upon it. In this causal
worldview, we are limited only by the consequences of our actions, but
if we accept the consequences of our actions, then act we may, and
freely.

To think differently, particularly in the way that synchronicity
invites us to, is to grapple with the idea that chance events may be
meaningful rather than simply meaningless. Generally speaking, this
idea can be quite a blow to our ego, challenging the vision of complete power and control we create for ourselves. The idea that random events may occur *to* us, events which we cannot control but
which may have a deep effect on us, is one, I daresay, that elicits
anxiety in most of us. As Jung's associate Marie-Louise von Franz
puts it in her lectures on synchronicity, "Chance is the enemy—
chance is what you have to eliminate . . . ,"[2] a succinct way of
describing most people's attitude toward the place of random occurrences in their lives.

Yet contact with individuals from non-European cultures reveals
that there can indeed be other ways of thinking and being in the world.
By seeing ourselves as simply one part of a greater whole in which all
of life is connected, Native Americans or people from a traditional
Asian culture such as China or Tibet perceive their own actions in a
very different way, not as a cause producing an effect, not as an indi-

vidual acting upon the world, which is separate and objective, but rather as one part of a web of subjective interconnections.

To act effectively in these cultures, therefore, requires discerning the appropriate time, scrutinizing one's own attitude, soliciting and using the support of the larger community to which one belongs, and attempting to determine the will of the Divine. In such cultures, it is still common to consult the stars or visit the village wise woman before taking an important step in one's life. To act, within this worldview, is a humble, careful process. This way of thinking, in which one's subjective experience of interconnection with the world is more important than individual mastery over the environment through cause and effect, is a mode of living which accommodates the reality of meaningful chance quite easily. And we do not even need to go outside of our own historical roots in the West to discover precedents to the idea of synchronicity. As I will be discussing in Chapter 5, such areas of interest as astrology, Tarot, and other methods of divination rely on the fact of synchronicity for their effect.

Besides challenging the sense of control which cause-and-effect thinking provides us, to allow for acausal connections between events would also mean acknowledging that the physical world is not separate from interior psychic events. Yet the division of the world into "inner" and "outer" is deeply ingrained into our thinking, so deeply, in fact, that most people are not even conscious of it. Cathy's feelings about Richard are "internal," Richard's phone call is an "outer" event. Her actions with his name on the index card are "external" behaviors. His impulse to find her is an "inner" phenomenon. To term their coincidental rediscovery of each other "synchronistic" is simply another way to say that, at that moment, "inner" and "outer" are connected.

Indeed, in another part of his work on synchronicity, Jung defines synchronicity as "the simultaneous occurrence of a certain psychic state with one or more external events which appear as meaningful parallels to the momentary subjective state."[3] Thus, by definition, synchronicity suggests that our radical division between "inner" and "outer" is in fact false. "Inner" phenomena, such as feelings, values, thoughts, dreams, intuitions, longings, and so forth can be and, in decisive ways, sometimes are very much connected to "outer" events, such as phone calls, gifts, social life, love affairs, and the like. Synchronistic events urge upon us a view of the world as a unified field in which one's own experiences and actions are fundamentally connected to the experiences and actions of others.

Besides challenging our illusions of control and the neat division between subjective and objective reality, synchronicity as an acausal connecting principle also challenges our notion of time, specifically, the way in which we rely upon a linear notion of time to organize our view of the world. Cause-and-effect thinking necessitates the concepts of "before" and "after": causes have to occur before the effects. But acknowledging an acausal connection between events makes *when* something happened less important than *what* happens and what it *means* to you or me. Not that the timing of an event is completely unimportant, but, to use our example of Cathy and Richard, the timing of his letter merely made the event a coincidence. It was the *meaning* of the letter which made it synchronistic for Cathy, after all the energy she had spent trying to contact him, after managing the frustration and disappointment of hitting a dead end, after taking private actions of her own to focus her attention on him by writing his name down as instructed by the psychic. Her actions and his letter were connected through the significance of the coincidence, not by the mere temporal proximity of the two events.

Synchronicity invites us to see our lives from a different angle, in which our subjective experience determines our place in a universe of random events that occur around us and to us and which are connected through what they mean to us. In our lives, it is these connections between ourselves and the world that create the stories we live.

This brings us to the second feature of synchronicity: emotion.

Think, Don't Feel: Synchronicity and the Modern Distrust of Emotional Reality

Elaborating further on what synchronicity is and how it works, Jung noted that the events we call synchronistic have a certain unmistakable emotional tone to them which he called "numinous," borrowing the term from theologian Rudolph Otto. Numinosity is that experience we have when we feel that we are undeniably, irresistibly, and unforgettably in the presence of the Divine, our experience of something which transcends our human limitations. This heightened quality of feeling which accompanies synchronistic events is perhaps the most striking characteristic of such events. If synchronicity is above all a connecting principle, then the quality of feeling produced by a synchronistic event, the numinosity and psychic energy which it evokes, is the medium by which such a connection is made. Simply put, synchronistic events are always deeply emotional in character.

When I first began to study Jung in graduate school, I felt quite alone and isolated. Of course, graduate students are by nature prone to this sort of feeling, and some are even fond of the pose of the misunderstood intellectual. I can't really say that I felt that way. I had come from a Lutheran seminary in which none of our studies included much psychology at all and even less someone like Jung, a lapsed Evangelical with mystical tendencies, and many of my fellow students thought me a little crazy for thinking so highly of him. As a way of containing some of the wild dreams and experiences I had been having since my acquaintance with Jung's writing, I decided to begin working with a Jungian analyst and thought that this would also be one way to overcome some of the intellectual isolation I was feeling. I simply picked up the yellow pages, looked under the listing for psychiatrists, and called the first one that advertised his Jungian training. I made an appointment for 3 P.M. on Saturday and thus began therapy.

Meanwhile, at the internship site where I had been working for a number of years, an incongruous program that provided long-term Freudian psychoanalytic treatment to University of California students, a new counselor joined the staff. Pleasant and fun, she and I hit it off, with many common interests, particularly in the arts. I was a writer; she was a storyteller. I had been involved in theater; so had she. She was from New York; I came from New Jersey. But it wasn't until many months into our friendship that I discovered not only that she shared my interest in Jung but that she was in fact seeing the same analyst as I. Moreover, when we began comparing notes, we discovered that the week before I had begun my work with him, she had changed her regular appointment time, 3 P.M. on Saturdays, to another time. In other words, synchronistically, I had met the person whose appointment time in my therapist's schedule I had taken.

What made this coincidence of appointment times significant to me, and thus what makes this synchronistic, had mostly to do with the feelings I had about having shared something, completely coincidentally, with this new friend at a time before I even knew her. The story that I had thought I had been living—the poor lonely graduate student with an interest in a crackpot that no one knew about—was, I discovered later, not the real story. The real story was that a place had been made for me in my analyst's office by a woman with whom I had a great deal in common, and the emotional effect was enormous. I felt considerably less isolated and crazy. I felt the presence of a community of like-minded people around me and, therefore, felt more supported and sure of myself. I felt the importance of my Jungian studies confirmed for me.

Unfortunately, our culture has about as much trouble with an acknowledgment of feeling as it does with leaving behind cause-and-effect thinking. As discussed earlier, we are used to dividing the world into "inner" and "outer," into "subjective" and "objective," and though this division in itself is not necessarily troublesome, as Westerners we are part of a tradition which values and exalts the "outer" and "objective" while devaluing the "inner" and "subjective." And nothing gets more "inner," more individual and subjective, than our feelings.

The great ideal of the Western world is to achieve objectivity. In science, this means eliminating the subjective bias of the experimenter and canceling out, through replication and statistical analysis, the effect of chance on a process. In intellectual thought, we ruthlessly support and document every conclusion with evidence, facts, and demonstrations. In industry, we prize productivity and profit, both of which can be measured and monitored, at the expense of other concerns, such as the welfare of workers or the quality of the product. In our tradition, feelings are an encumbrance, a contaminant, a possible source of skewing, falsification, and error.

The essentially subjective, emotional nature of a synchronistic event, the profound effect that this type of coincidence has on our feelings, throws down the gauntlet before us and leads us to question this Western ideal of objectivity: what if we valued feeling as much as thinking, as synchronistic events invite us to do? In all synchronicities, including our examples so far, what is important is not the "objective facts" of the coincidences but the emotional impact they had on the people involved, an emotional impact so strong that years later people like Ann or Cathy were able to tell me about the incidents in great detail. Synchronistic events call forth from us our capacity to feel deeply and to be conscious of our feelings, since the quality and intensity of our feelings are what make such coincidences meaningful.

But strong feelings are feared in this culture, for the same reason, I believe, that acausality presents such a problem to most of us. To allow yourself to feel means that you must loosen the grip of control upon yourself and open yourself to your experience. You must permit yourself to be who and what you are rather than who you think you are or who you have been told you should be. To feel means to be vulnerable, and vulnerability is a humbling experience.

The fear of losing control is not the only thing which makes our emotional lives so threatening to our rational minds. Like acausality, feelings challenge the assumption that we are separate from each other, that there is a strict division between outer/objective and inner/subjective. If we are open to feelings, we can feel not only our own feelings but *others'* feelings as well. The nature of feeling and the power of empathy demonstrates that we are all connected, or at least potentially so, through an experience of another's pain, happiness, grief, satisfaction, pride, or shame. While sharing feelings is for many of us an experience which can be profoundly gratifying and enormously healing, it is also an activity which transgresses some important cultural values, such as autonomy, individuality, and independence, so that open displays of feeling are allowed and seen as appropriate in a limited number of social situations, most of them private in nature and only very few of them public.

Because feeling is spontaneous, natural, free—like a current of water that we stand in and feel around us but which we cannot direct or control—in my experience it takes great courage in this culture for people to place themselves deliberately in such ever-moving water, especially when the feelings are deep and strong and the current is running fast and hard around us. And a synchronistic event lands us right smack in the middle of that current. Little wonder many of us back off from a synchronistic event, deriding it—and our feelings about it—as a fantasy: "It's just my imagination." Synchronicity means having to affirm one's feelings as a crucial mode of experiencing life, every bit as important as one's thoughts, and, in certain situations, even more so. Our feelings are the mainspring of our stories, and it is our feelings that drive the plot forward.

This brings us to the third feature of synchronicity: its symbolic nature.

If I Am Not Aware of It, How Can It Be? Synchronicity and Archetypal Symbols of the Collective Unconscious

A third aspect of synchronistic events can be found in the content of the event itself, which, as I have mentioned, is always symbolic. Unfortunately, in my experience, this fact often gets overlooked in the course of working with synchronicity, overwhelmed as we often are by the numinous feeling the event inspires or by the amazement that such unlikely events could have actually happened. And yet, whenever there is a meaningful coincidence, I have found, the events themselves always have a potent symbolic character.

One striking example of symbolism in a synchronistic event occurred to me during an impasse with a client when I was an intern. Having been dominated by his mother through most of his life, including his adulthood, my client, Frank, had a hard time believing that anyone might treat him differently. This was why he had started counseling, so it followed that his perception of other people's wish to control and dominate him figured largely in his experience of me, too.

In the midst of a series of difficult sessions over some time, I came in one Saturday morning for our regularly scheduled appointment. There was a huge rainstorm outside, but I didn't worry too much about whether or not Frank would show up, since he only lived down the street from the clinic. Just before our session was to begin, I was reviewing my notes when, boom, the lights went out. Now the office I was using had a small window and the dim light was enough to see by, so when Frank arrived, we went ahead. Our conversation that day was much like many of our previous discussions. Frank was convinced that I had become a therapist to control people, that I enjoyed having others dependent on me, that I took pleasure in making people pay for their neediness, and so on. As always, my responses, which tried to get him to connect his experience of his mother with these perceptions of me, did not seem to do much good.

Then, at one point, seeing that we weren't getting anywhere, I decided to take another approach, to challenge him more openly. I wondered aloud how he might account for the fact that I had showed up in the middle of the rainstorm, with no electricity in the building, so that he could continue to tell me how much he disliked me. Wasn't that evidence that I cared about him? Why else would I choose to do something like this, so inconvenient, so patently *un*enjoyable, unless I was really concerned for his welfare? Here Frank fell silent and I could feel an emotional shift taking place. After some moments of thought, Frank said, "I see your point. Maybe you do care, maybe it isn't all about power." And at that moment, the power went back on and the office was suddenly, synchronistically, brightly illuminated once again.

The symbolism in this story of the "power failure" is both obvious and important for understanding the nature of what occurred in my relationship with Frank. Beginning our session in the literal darkness of the power outage reflected the emotional state of the relationship in which neither of us was able to see our way through to the light of awareness. He could not clearly see me, metaphorically speaking, as caring about him, and the power outage made his inability to see literally true. Nor could I see that what I needed to do was to begin to be a real person in the room with him, assert how much I cared and demonstrate it, rather than interpret his mother dynamics. There was for him both an inner and outer "power failure," that is, until I finally succeeded in getting through to him on an emotional level. Then the lights went on—literally but also symbolically—as the office suddenly lit up with literal and emotional electricity. A connection was re-established between us, and he felt his power again.

This story is a good illustration of a point I made earlier about synchronistic events, specifically, how the same coincidence might very well be meaningful to one person and at the same time be ut-terly lost on the other: Frank, very much trapped in his perceptions of being dominated, had not noticed, as far as I could tell, whether or not the lights were on or off. It was I who noticed how perfectly the external event seemed to mirror our inner states, how potent the symbolism of this particular coincidence was. Indeed, how this syn-chronicity figures into my life story as a therapist has specifically to do with the symbols here and what they stand for, namely, power. I was struggling myself, as a relatively inexperienced intern, to figure out the most effective way to get across that I was not like his mother, so coming upon an intervention which seemed to work with Frank was, as the symbolism of the event itself indicates, quite an empowering experience for me. For Frank, however, it was just one of many experiences of direct communication which he needed from me until he began to believe that not everyone sought to dom-inate and control him.

Contemporary Jungian analyst Jean Shinoda Bolen, in her brief, engaging book on synchronicity, *The Tao of Psychology: Synchronicity and the Self*, uses an expression to describe the symbolic nature of synchronistic events, a phrase I have heard others use as well, that such a meaningful coincidence is "like a waking dream."[4] This expres-sion captures, I think, much of what makes a synchronistic event such a unique occurrence in the stories of our lives. Like dreams, which we do not cause and which are generally infused with feeling, synchronis-tic events also have a symbolic character. Such meaningful coinci-dences are memorable precisely because they have the kind of symbolic coherence that most people only experience in their dream life. Or through stories.

Tell the story of the power failure, or Dan's phone call, or Bobbie's Tarot deck, to someone unfamiliar with the concept of synchronicity, and you might very well hear, "Who are you kidding? That sort of thing only happens in the movies," or, from the less skeptical, "What a great story!" Indeed, the parallel between the symbolic coherence we expect from stories and the symbolic coherence we experience in such meaningful coincidences is undeniable. As in stories, the symbolic dimension of our lives is brought to the fore in a synchronistic event, and we are forced, so to speak, to examine the various aspects of what occurred. We find ourselves asking the same sorts of questions with regard to our lives as we do when reading a story or watching a movie. What was the point of this? And where is this going? What does it mean about who I am, who I have been, who I am becoming?

The difference between a sign and symbol is important to understand at this juncture. Briefly put, a sign is an object which points to something beyond itself which is definite, finite, and knowable; whereas symbols are objects, situations, or events which point to a reality beyond our awareness or full understanding. Hence, if we acknowledge the symbolic nature of synchronistic events and ask ourselves the question, "To what beyond myself does this event point?" we find that the answer, if we are faithful to the symbolic reality of what occurred, will always be a multiplicity of things.

A symbol is always and essentially a mystery; a sign is not. The red hexagon on the pole at the corner means "STOP." That is all it means, and that is all it will ever mean: when you approach in a moving vehicle, put your brakes on. It is a sign, not a symbol. However, if you go to a museum of modern art and see hanging on a wall a piece by some avant-garde political sculptor—pictures of concentration camps, bombs, guns, and slaughterhouses surrounding a red hexagon with the word "STOP" on it—you are no longer looking at a sign. The once straight-forward stop sign has been transformed by its artistic context into a symbol. On the wall in that museum, "STOP" means many things: that killing is wrong, that the murder of innocents is something you should take action to prevent, that eating meat causes violence, and so on.

Likewise, a synchronistic event, as a symbolic occurrence, may mean many things and indeed the symbolic meaning of an event, like that of any story, may in fact change over time. In the many synchronistic events which we will be discussing in the following chapters, the multiplicity of symbolic meanings a single event has for us can at times be a bit overwhelming. Yet, as with the many layers of meanings in a story, one can, with time, patience, practice, and familiarity, tease them out, with a thoughtful and open attitude.

Synchronistic events function, as all symbols do, to make the unconscious conscious. Jung's unique contribution to psychology lay in his contention that the unconscious does not merely consist of personal leftovers, so to speak—things that happened to us which we no longer remember or even actively keep forgotten and repressed—but that the unconscious is also the psychic storehouse of the human race. Jung called this storehouse the "collective unconscious," and it contains a shared collection of symbols which we are for the most part unaware of, except in special circumstances or states of mind. The contents of this level of our existence, those patterns, situations, and symbols which constitute this collective unconscious, are what Jung termed "archetypes."

I have always found the notion that we share with all other human beings certain common ways of thinking, feeling, and imagining something rather easy to understand and accept. Indeed, how could it be otherwise? Do we not all have mothers and fathers? Do we not all have an experience of birth, childhood, aging, and ultimately death? Are there not certain constants that go beyond individual experience and culture, beyond time and place, which make us human and which we, therefore, share with all other humans? These patterns make up the archetypes of the collective unconscious, some of which are experienced in personal form, in figures such as the wise old man, the trickster, the maiden, the eternal child, as well as the gods, goddesses, demons, and angels of mythology and theology. But many archetypes of the collective unconscious are not figures at all but are instead typical situations and experiences—growing up, experiencing wholeness, being caught in an unresolvable conflict, losing our innocence, achieving ecstatic union with God—and it may be these "situational" archetypes which synchronistic occurrences bring to our awareness as well.

The stories that we live, the stories that the symbolic nature of synchronistic events brings to our awareness, are thus in one manner of speaking mythic. Yet how many of us think of ourselves as characters in a story, no less as figures living out a myth? The unusual occurrence of a synchronicity serves to heighten our sensitivity to this sacred and symbolic dimension of our everyday lives. But why do so many of us resist such a way of thinking? Why would we want to dismiss or ignore the story we are living?

One answer, I believe, is that direct contact with the collective unconscious is an experience of such enormous power that through it we are often in danger of losing ourselves and our own standpoint. An archetype is like a natural force, a pattern of perception so ingrained that few individuals are able to maintain their own personal perceptions when an archetype holds sway. So while we must guard against allowing our egos to stand in the way of a full experience of archetypal events by our being close-minded and attempting to control our inner lives, our egos may conversely be the very thing that enables us to withstand the onslaught of archetypal symbolism with all its wealth, wonder, and power. Here again our ability to reflect symbolically upon experience is what is most important in helping us understand the archetypal basis for the story of our lives. With this ability to reflect upon experience and discern that which is particular to us as individuals and that which we have in common with others, such experiences as synchronistic events, dreams, and stories can enrich and deepen our humanity.

To say this more simply, the symbolism of a synchronicity shows us on some level the specific part of the story of our lives where a connection with all other human beings might be found. Through the synchronicity of receiving a set of symbols through her dreams and then a gift which paralleled the dreams, Bobbie was brought into a living relationship with all the wisdom contained in the symbols of the Tarot. Dan's phone call, Richard's letter, and the synchronistic beginnings of some of my friendships helped Ann, Cathy, and me, respectively, to participate in that universal experience which human beings usually call love. My initiation, as a counseling intern, into the mysterious power of attending to another person's welfare is, thanks to the synchronistic experience of being "led into the light," one which I have shared with many other apprentices throughout all time and all cultures.

Quo Vadis: Synchronicity and Life Transitions

There are periods in our lives which feel settled, when things, for the most part, have reached a point of relative stability. Our relationships are satisfying, our work life and personal activities seem to be going well. If not rapturously happy, we are content enough, and if there are certain concerns or anxieties out there on the horizon of our awareness, they are far enough away not to disturb the ordinary course of human events.

But, as all of us well know, there are other times in our lives when the stability is no longer internally satisfying and we feel we must make a change in a life that has become boring and benumbing, or when events outside of our control intervene to disrupt a life we feel contented with. Sometimes such periods of transition may even be motivated by both at once—an internal need to move forward and a set of external events propelling us out of a rut we might not have even known we were in.

In times of such transition, people often seek out help from others. At times those others are professionals—therapists, ministers, doctors, or counselors. At times those others are friends or family members who have gone through similar transitions or just friends in general. During such transitions, in seeking help from experienced others, we often feel that we are being led from a way of being which no longer fits and guided into another fuller and more satisfying way of life.

However, many people receive a form of help in making transitions which isn't simply external or social in nature but is internal and psychological. Without willing it or seeking it out, help often arrives in the form of an accidental sequence of events which occur at precisely the right time to aid us in moving on in our lives, very often when we feel there is little else we might do.

One of the principal ways in which Jung's ideas about the psyche differs from those of many other thinkers lies in his contention that the psyche is a natural phenomenon and that all aspects of the psyche, even those which seem to us pathological or destructive, actually serve the function of furthering our psychological development. A simple example of this way of thinking has to do with what most people call defenses. A person who has had a traumatic experience of falling from a great height may for the rest of his life experience great anxiety in high places. Consequently he would actively, even unnecessarily, avoid such places. Depending on how severely this person's avoidance behavior restricts his life, one might see it as an interesting quirk or a full-fledged dysfunction, but the fact remains that this defensiveness serves to protect the person against a recurrence of the overwhelming trauma and functions, as Jung would see it, to preserve his mental balance. You and I might make a judgment about whether this is healthy or not, good or bad, and so forth, but from the point of view of the psyche and its natural process, even phobic responses make sense and function to further an individual's ability to move forward and grow in a balanced way.

Jung's view of the purposive nature of psychological phenomena undergirds his concept of synchronicity. In chance events both emotionally and symbolically meaningful, our psychological experience of a synchronicity always occurs to enable us to move forward in some way. This is why synchronicities happen at those all-important points of transition in our lives. Much like the external, social help we often seek out during such periods, the psyche sometimes provides, in the form of meaningful coincidences, a form of internal and psychological help.

At times that help may merely consist of a kind of wake-up call, with a coincidence that might simply bring to our awareness the fact that a transition we have been attempting to avoid or deny is indeed happening, whether we like it or not. Bobbie's experience with the Tarot deck was of this ilk. At other times, the significance of the synchronicity has to do with teaching us a lesson about our need to develop a different attitude or perspective—as with me and my client Frank, when I stopped dwelling on his past and began to focus on my relationship with him in the present. But in all cases, if a person experiences the sort of meaningful coincidence we are calling synchronistic, some sort of important life transition is occurring.

A young woman I know named Ellen had moved to California

to start college only to find herself in rather severe conflict with her father, who had agreed to pay for her education but who also held certain ideas about how his daughter should live. He wanted her on campus; she wanted to live off campus with friends. She wanted a car; he didn't feel that a car was a good idea. She felt her social activities were an important part of her education; her father felt she should not be spending money and time on anything but her studies. As the feelings grew more and more heated between them, through a series of transcontinental phone calls, her father finally said that unless she behaved as he wished, he would discontinue his financial support. In anger, she responded, "Fine. Go ahead," and hung up the phone.

Stewing furiously about a situation which had finally grown untenable, she walked around campus the following day in a funk, not knowing what she was going to do. She had no skills, and her father's controlling attitude had virtually assured her dependence on him, so making good on her threat seemed a bit beyond her. She continued to walk through campus until she bumped into a friend and, sitting under a eucalyptus tree, she told her friend the story. Not feeling that her quandary was all that amusing, she almost got offended when he laughed—that is, until he told her why he was laughing. He had just come from his job as a word processor in a nearby engineering firm and that day his supervisor had asked him if he knew of anyone who wanted a job. They were paying well enough to enable Ellen to support herself, the schedule was completely flexible, and they were willing to pay her while she was being trained. In this way, synchronistically, Ellen found a job that allowed her to resolve the uncomfortable reliance on her father and strike out, quite appropriately, on her own. Moreover, the word-processing skills she learned from that job led her into a career in publishing that she had hardly expected when she had gone to school to study biochemistry.

* * *

Every movement forward in our lives, every degree of growth, involves three parts. First, we become aware that our current situation no longer fits us or works. Sometimes outer events make this clear—our father threatens to withdraw financial support—while sometimes it is our inner feelings which point this out to us—we are unhappy with the constraints upon our freedom to live as we want to. Then we enter a state of confusion and transition. We begin to imagine how things might be different and we might even leave our current situation without fully knowing what is to come or how we are to proceed. We hang up the phone, shouting "Fine. Go ahead," but then are left in a state of betwixt and between. We can't go back, but we don't really know yet what to do, and this transitional state may last a day, a month, or years, until finally, something happens—we get some help, our feelings become clearer, an opportunity presents itself, we take a certain action—and we move into a different and more satisfying way of being.

In Ellen's story, her need to make a break with her father had been amply clear before the job she needed synchronistically landed in her lap, so to speak. But sometimes synchronistic events occur that draw our attention to the fact that we are making a transition we didn't even know we were making. This was the case with a friend of mine named Sam who had been transferred from the East Coast to his accounting firm's San Francisco branch and found the new job considerably more grueling and a lot less satisfying than he expected.

Despite being a talented musician, Sam plugged away at the accounting job. Then a synchronistic pair of events occurred: the church Sam attended received money to inaugurate a music program at the same time that decisions from up top in his firm led to his being laid off. Of course, the experience of immediate and unexpected un-employment led him to feel more than a little bewildered. But I encouraged him to acknowledge the synchronicity of the events and to pursue the opportunities that presented themselves in music, which he did. Sam makes less money now, but is far more fulfilled in his career, doing something in a field he had long loved but had been too frightened to try. The synchronistic events in this story, the shutting door of his lay-off and the opening window of his new career, made him begin to live the story of his life that some of us around him, knowing his love of music and his talent, always felt was the story he should be living.

For me, stories like Ellen's and Sam's have reinforced my conviction, grounded in Jung's way of thinking, that people move in their own time and in their own way toward a meaningful consolidation of who they most deeply are, even when others may think, looking from the outside in, that their process is crazy, destructive, or evil. If our life is a story, then it is a story which, like all stories, has various chapters. At times, only the profound, symbolic meeting of inner and outer in the form of a meaningful coincidence can provide the sort of psychological boost we may need to turn the page and move on to a new episode in the story we are meant to live.

Now the idea that people move in their own way toward who they are most deeply does not mean that "things are getting better every day in every way." After all, some stories are tragedies. But in the chapters which follow, you will be hearing from people for whom the worst event of their life—the death of a loved one, the failure of a business, a near-suicide—turned out to be a synchronistic event, an important and transformative moment of their existence. Synchronistic events—meaningful coincidences—make us acknowledge that there may well be more to our story than we think, and that everything, even things which may seem to us frightening or bad, like losing a job or being cut off by our parents, is a part of the narrative structure of our lives.

As we have seen in our previous discussions about the acausal, emotional, and symbolic aspects of synchronicities, the fact that synchronicites always occur within a transitional context, when we are standing on the threshold of a new way of being, once again makes a case for seeing ourselves as one part of a greater wholeness in which we participate. If we are characters in a story, the ending may not be a happy one, but the life we are living is at least one that is whole and coherent. It is the function of synchronicity to help us see this wholeness—if not goodness—behind the ups and downs of each chapter of the life we live.

Why Now? Accounting for the Interest in Synchronicity

As I have mentioned in this introduction, synchronicity is a relatively new term to describe an idea and a set of experiences that are as old as the human race and common to all cultures. Why now do we suddenly see such interest in the concept of the meaningful coincidence? Why have Jung's writings on synchronicity sparked an entire literature in the past twenty years?

I think the four characteristics of synchronicity which I have described above are what account for the attention, for each of these four characteristics presents modern people with a fuller way of thinking, feeling, and being in the world. Used to thinking in cause-and-effect terms, we are called by synchronistic events to acknowledge that the line between objective reality and subjective experience is not as neat as we have been given to think. If this realization is sometimes befuddling and scary, it also enriches our experience of the world and restores to us a sense of wholeness and belonging. Likewise, synchronistic events, with their emotional and symbolic levels of meaning, serve to remind modern people of two very valuable and uniquely human qualities: our ability to feel and our ability to imagine, fundamental aspects of our humanity which have unfortunately been misplaced in a world increasingly obsessed with rationality.

With the breakdown of coherent communities and the increase of individualism and isolation in our society, important life transitions have become for many of us more and more difficult to manage, and as our culture has played down the once-central role of spiritual advisor, shaman, medicine woman, or community elder, we too often find ourselves at a loss for help in how to proceed. Meaningful coincidences, which always occur at points of change and transformation, are thus symbolic of our profound connection with others and reassure us that indeed we are never really alone in the midst of such transitions.

Yet the most essential and distinctive aspect of synchronicity is the experience of meaning upon which such coincidences are based. Through our ability to uncover and live out the individual meaning of what befalls us, we receive in a synchronistic event a reminder of an important truth: that our lives are organized, consciously and unconsciously, the way a story is, that our lives have a coherence, a direction, a reason for being, and a beauty as well. Synchronicity reminds us how much a work of art the stories of our lives can be.

Chapter Two

Like the
Lightning

Synchronicity and
Our Love Stories

> It is too rash, too unadvised, too sudden,
> Too like the lightning, which doth cease to be
> Ere one can say, "It lightens." Sweet, good night!
> This bud of love, by summer's ripening breath,
> May prove a beauteous flower when next we
>   meet.
>
> WILLIAM SHAKESPEARE, *Romeo and Juliet*

Love and friendship in their various forms—
passionate or affectionate, slow-blossoming or lightning-quick—are at
the center of most of our stories. Whom we meet and how we meet
them, whom we fall in love with or who falls in love with us, who our
friends are and how those relationships came to be, how those relationships deepen or, sometimes, fail, all these twists and turns of love
and friendship serve to give each of our lives the particular shape that
it has. Love between two people is, of course, fundamentally a coincidence, two lives crossing by chance; and so, naturally enough, synchronistic occurrences often lay the foundation for our stories of love and
friendship.

One of the hallmarks of a synchronistic event is that it is always unique and unrepeatable, a once-in-a-lifetime experience. When we think about how rare true love is, about how unlikely it is that, among the many millions of people we encounter in the course of a lifetime, we manage to meet those few people who fit us so well, it becomes obvious how much chance figures into whom we choose as partners, lovers, and friends.

Have you ever noticed that in the novels and stories we read about love there is always a certain feeling of inevitability about the plot? We know inside ourselves when two people are destined for one another. We witness the rivalry between the families in *Romeo and Juliet,* and yet we feel what will happen, what *must* happen, when the young lovers come together. And yet, always, at the same time, there is that unmistakable sense of wonder, a delight that something so precious has come to be, purely by chance.

While talking to people about the loves of their lives, I was struck by the parallels between our lives and the stories we read. The fragile thread of chance upon which so many of these relationships hung was astounding—but for a minute or two delay or just plain acccident, many of these people would never have met the person who, through love, permanently and irrevocably changed their entire history. The feeling of inevitability we sense in the love stories we read is not simply because we, like the omniscient narrator, are apart from the plot. As the true stories that follow show us, this feeling is part of the meaning of our chance encounter, a stroke of fortune that never ceases to amaze throughout our lives.

Many of the synchronicities in love and friendship have to do with meeting the right person at the right time and in the right circumstances, but for sheer unlikelihood the way Pete and Mary began their relationship should win a prize. They first met one another at a large open house, a hot tub party for which Marin County, California, in the late 1970s had become known. Despite obvious mutual interest at the time, perhaps not too uncommon an occurrence among twenty-somethings, they parted ways that night without exchanging anything more than first names, as each of them was involved with someone else. The week after the party, Mary left California entirely, to follow her boyfriend to another part of the country, but before she left, she quizzed the host of the party about Pete, managing to get his address and phone number. Initially intending to call or write, she never got around to it, as the hubbub of the move and then the normal routine of life intervened. However, for reasons obscure even to her, each year she recopied Pete's address and phone number into a new address book, never calling or writing but holding on to the information for nearly a decade.

On Pete's side of the story, Mary came to mind about two or three times a year, when he would happen to chance upon the friend who had thrown the party. Given his own history of dating frequently without making any lasting commitments, Pete never failed to ask his friend what he heard from the "hot tub girl" and always facetiously asked his friend to let him know when she was available. As far as his friend knew, Mary was happily living with her boyfriend in Texas, but going along with the jest, he promised again and again that he'd let Pete know.

One winter years later, Pete got word that his aunt had died in Las Vegas. More from duty than affection, he booked a flight from San Francisco for the next day, thinking that perhaps when family duties were concluded, he might stay on a bit and enjoy the city. When he arrived at the airport, however, he found that no flights were leaving because of fog, and there was no guarantee of when they would start up again. Thus, on the spur of the moment, he decided to rent a car and drive to Las Vegas; it would take a while, but at least he'd be assured of getting there, and the prospect of a road trip appealed to him. In fact, once on the road, he thought he might stop overnight in the town of Mojave to visit a friend and get some rest before pushing on to Vegas early the next day. As he puts it, he never realized that this accidental road trip would change his life.

Approaching Mojave late that day, the rental car began to act up and it appeared that there was a slow leak in one of the tires. So Pete pulled over at a service station, filled up the tire, and went to call his friend, who it turned out was not home. Pete remembers thinking that nothing about this trip to Vegas seemed destined to go right, drawing from this a lesson about doing things halfheartedly, out of duty, rather than out of true commitment. This habit, he told himself, was responsible for most of what was wrong with his life.

He was checking into a small roadside motel as darkness fell when his mood suddenly changed: turning to get his bags, he bumped smack into Mary, who at that moment walked into the motel offfice. Unable to believe that of all the places in the world they would actually, after eight years, chance upon one another here, in this most unlikely of spots, they were further amazed when they learned the circumstances. Mary was returning to San Francisco to scout out a place to live. The week before, she and her long-term boyfriend had broken up for precisely the reason that Pete, only moments before, had reproached himself. Her boyfriend, after many years, was still unable to make a commitment to her and rather than spend her life waiting, she'd decided to take charge and go back to where she once felt more herself. The rest, as they say, is history.

In this story of how they met, what comes across as meaningful to Pete and Mary is not just the amazing external coincidence—imagine meeting someone you have been attracted to for almost a decade in the middle of the California desert—but much more the psychological timing of their meeting. Pete, having just concluded that his own half-heartedness was at the root of his problem, was seemingly presented with an opportunity to make a change by meeting Mary after so many years. At the same time, Mary, on her way back to the one place she felt she belonged, met the very man whose address and phone number she had inexplicably kept and whom she fully planned to call the next day when she arrived in town. The chance that such a meeting in such a place would happen without any action on their own part to have caused it is, indeed, extraordinary. But what makes this a synchronistic event is that it occurred at such a significant time for each of them emotionally, in the midst of a psychological and, for Mary at least, a geographical transition from an old life to a new chapter in her story.

This element of timing, the coincidence between external events and internal state, is of course one of the more inherently wonderful parts of a synchronistic experience. It shows us that we are indeed part of a story, that there is, like in the tales we read, a meaning and purpose to all the seemingly random events that happen to us. Pete and Mary concluded from the synchronistic timing of their own meeting that indeed they were meant to be together, just as the delicately timed sequence of events in the next story concerning my friends Gery and Rosanne made the beginning of their relationship a synchronistic experience for them. Married now for years, with three kids, Rosanne tells the story of how they met.

"I was in Detroit working a part-time job, living with my parents and saving up to move to Colorado, after having just come back from an extended visit to Europe. I had about a six-week window of time when I would be home, and in the middle of this, I went out with a friend of mine, and he said, 'Oh, you know, I just want to go over and say goodbye to my friend Paulie, who's going to be leaving for the West Coast soon.' So I went over to Paul's house with my friend, and Paul was talking about how when he got to San Francisco, he was going to meet this friend of his, Gery, whom he knew from Detroit and who was living out there.

"At that moment one of the guys turned to me and said, 'Hey, in two weeks we have our annual party. Why don't you come, too?' And I agreed, not really knowing why I was interested, but I was, and so I went.

"So there I am, at this party, standing in line for the bathroom, when this voice says in my ear—this is so prophetic—'Do you know where the beer is?' So much for enchanted glances from across the room. It turns out that this voice was Paul's friend Gery from California. Well, for an hour and a half, we talked and talked and talked—I didn't even go to the bathroom—until finally we tore ourselves apart, deciding we'd better go mingle. And Gery was still thirsty, he hadn't gotten his beer yet. We exchanged phone numbers at that point, first and last names.

"Now my parents had moved away from the home I had grown up in, and I was staying with them, so I gave him their phone number—at least I thought I had—and throughout the rest of the night, we kept bumping into each other at the party. We ended up hanging out until five in the morning, and by this time I knew I was really interested in him. As we went our separate ways in the morning, I thought to myself, I'll give him two days and then I'll call him.

"It's three days later when I go to call him and that's when I realize that I hadn't given him my parents' phone number—I had given him the phone number of Chatham Supermarket. I thought to myself, Chatham Supermarket? Why would I do that? and eventually, I pieced it together.

"I had worked four years before that for Chatham Supermarket as a payroll clerk, and when Gery and I exchanged phone numbers, and I saw his last name, I recognized it as the name of one of the guys who had worked with me at Chatham Supermarket. I had given him the number of this place we had both worked, instead of my own phone number.

"Anyway, time was growing short, because I was leaving in three days for Colorado. When I called Gery, I found out that he had actually tried to call me but had gotten this woman answering the phone, of course, saying, 'Chatham Supermarket,' and thought that I was giving him the brushoff, because he hadn't remembered working with me there.

"The thing is, though, that, given the window of time, it was pretty amazing that we had met at all. He was only in Detroit for Christmas, since he lived in California, and the next day he was going up north to visit friends for two days. Before he'd be back, I would have gone to Colorado. So the window was really short. But the mix-up with the phone numbers, both of us having worked at the same place in our past, is what made the whole thing just too coincidental."

From that first phone call came even more phone calls to California, followed by a visit, followed by a decision to move to California, followed by marriage, home, and kids. The timing of the meeting, in a window of only a day, is what amazes Gery and Rosanne, a window made even smaller by the accidental mix-up in phone numbers which delayed their talking to each other but also underlined for each of them the common history they shared. When Gery and Rosanne tell the story, what comes across more than the extraordinary timing is the emotional meaning of these accidental connections and disconnections, the feeling that what seemed like a mistake—giving out the wrong phone number—actually turned out to mean a great deal to them.

In our earlier discussion of the acausal nature of synchronistic events, we acknowledged our very human tendency to try to exert and establish control over our lives, as if somehow our consciously deciding what story we are going to be living and doing whatever necessary, come hell or high water, to make it turn out that way, is the best or the only way to achieve happiness and fulfillment. Certainly part of the wonder of synchronistic events is the way that such an attitude gets turned on its head. By pure accident, without our willing them, certain events sometimes occur to us which show us that our lives may well be on another narrative track altogether, that the story we have made up for ourselves may not be our story at all, and only our own openness to reconsidering the plot will allow us to use this meaningful coincidence to our own benefit.

For this reason, I think, meaningful coincidences seem to thrive in circumstances where love is resisted. Rena tells the story of how she met her husband, Bob, whom she had purposefully avoided meeting, having had his praises sung to her over many months by a pair of married friends who were very interested in fixing her up. He was perfect, he was artistic, he was handsome, he was thoughtful, but, for Rena, he was not in the cards. She was in the midst of carrying out a very deliberate life-change for herself, planning to spend the next year traveling around the world. There was no way that romance, even with Mr. Right, was going to stop her from fulfilling her long-time dream.

Now, her friends saw that a bit of cleverness was required if they were ever to get Rena to meet Bob. So one day, having bumped into Rena on her bike, her friends invited her out for a drink, and the completely fortuitous character of their meeting led Rena to drop her guard. In fact, her friends knew that Bob was going to meet them at the restaurant, and through this bit of well-meaning manipulation, Bob and Rena at last met.

As Rena tells the story, the attraction between the two of them was instant and strong, and it wasn't long before the idea of traveling around the world by herself began to look less and less attractive. Thus, she and Bob decided, on the basis of an admittedly short, though thoroughly intense, acquaintance, to spend the next year traveling through Europe together, going wherever they felt like going, staying wherever they wanted for as long as they wanted.

Now Rena's dad had died the previous year, and her mother had had a heart attack shortly afterwards but seemed to have made a complete recovery, so Rena wasn't too worried that she could give her sister only one phone number where they could be reached in an emergency, the number of a friend of Bob's in Germany. Given the looseness of their plans (which, of course, lent this trip most of its romantic allure), Rena and Bob had no idea when they might end up staying with this friend. Thus, it was really up to them to check in regularly, which they did as they wandered about Europe.

As the trip wore on, the romance of it all, as romance so often does, began to grow thin. Bob, who was an architect, approached traveling with an orderliness that soon began to annoy Rena, planning intineraries around famous buildings and monuments, while Rena, self-described as a "people person," found such things of considerable less interest. With a laugh, she describes her experience as "him looking up all the time at the towers and cathedrals, with me looking down all the time at people." It was, as traveling so often is, an experience of finding out more than you often wanted to know about the other person, and in Rena's case, what she was finding were serious doubts as to whether or not this man was the one for her.

Which is when synchronicity presented itself. Rena and Bob eventually made their way to Bob's friend in Germany, where they planned to stay for three days. On the first day there, fortuitously, they received a phone call from Rena's sister in the States, informing them that Rena's mother was extremely ill and would in all likelihood die shortly. The chance that they were staying at the only place in Europe over the course of a year for which her sister had the phone number was significant enough, but the timing of the crisis held even more meaning for Rena.

As her doubts about Bob had grown over the course of their traveling, she suddenly found this rational, organized man quite insistent upon accompanying her home. "He stayed in the room with me as my mother died that whole week, day and night," Rena told me, with a great deal of feeling, "and, you know, that changed everything. Every question I had had about him was answered by how loving he was while I was going through this. If my sister hadn't been able to get hold of us, in fact, if my mother's death hadn't occurred when it had in the course of my relationship with Bob, I don't know if I'd be with him now. I had even resisted meeting him in the first place."

Rena's story is a good illustration of how the story we have decided to write for ourselves very well might make someone seem to be the "wrong person at the wrong time." It shows us how we might need a random set of events, occurrences over which we have no control, to demonstrate how he or she is really "the right person at the right time." A strong and decisive woman, Rena had had her life planned, but when word came to her in the one place in the world she could be found, it became a meaningful coincidence that revealed the true nature of the man she had been planning to write out of the storyline of her life. By appointing ourselves sole author of our life, what else but the inherent chaos of life's randomness could show us the foolishness of our grandiosity?

The question is often asked of me, "How do you work with synchronicity?" to which I reply most frequently, "Be open to the meaning in what you did not want to happen." Only such an attitude of openness, an ability to set aside our own agendas and consider that ours might be a story we did not, could not, anticipate will allow the meaning of what seems initially like mere bad luck to flower into what it is destined to be.

Rena and the others in the stories above point to the amazing timing of the events which brought them together, but their openness to considering a different narrative slant on their lives made the coincidence a meaningful one to them. Had Pete not been feeling rueful about his inability to commit and the misfortune it seemed to bring on him; had Rosanne accidentally given Gery the correct phone number, as she intended; had Rena forged on with her diffidence about Bob, all of their stories would have been quite different. It was their willingness to look at and live out the significance of what should *not* have happened, that is, according to the scripts they thought they were writing for themselves, which made all the difference.

Meeting Mr. Wrong: Synchronistic Lessons in Love

Every relationship, obviously, does not get transformed in such romantically story-book ways as Rena and Bob's. At least as many love stories end unhappily (*Romeo and Juliet* is, after all, a tragedy), and yet, even in unhappy stories, there is an important sense of meaning. Thus, in examining some of the synchronistic occurrences that transform our love lives, we can find growth which comes not only from meeting Mr. Right but rather from the "bad luck" of meeting Mr. Wrong.

Kathryn's story presents a slightly different twist on the way that synchronicity intervenes when we resist opening ourselves to love. Of the many stories I have heard, hers is among the most incredible and amusing of this "wrong person at the wrong time" type synchronicity: in her words, it is the story of her "blind date from hell."

A lawyer by profession, Kathryn had gone to school in New York City and had begun working for a firm there after graduation. She had dated a few guys in college but had found that her strong personality— no-nonsense, careful to a fault—and her fairly ambitious approach to life were not appreciated by the men she had been with. Having had these bad experiences, therefore, she decided that hers would be the story of the career woman: success in her field would be paramount, and relationships would always take second place. Indeed, when various friends attempted to arrange meetings for her with this, that, or the other "perfect guy," Kathryn politely and very firmly refused to cooperate and went about running her life as she saw fit. One friend in particular, whom Kathryn describes as "about as hard-headed as I am," determined that a male friend of hers was someone Kathryn needed in her life, and by slowly wearing Kathryn's resistance down over the course of nearly a year, this friend finally managed to get her to agree to a blind date with Charlie, who was described by the friend as someone who might be able to match Kathryn's "intensity."

With much reluctance, Kathryn met the guy in a nice restaurant downtown. Though admittedly handsome, he was, Kathryn found to her dismay, every bit as intense as described, so "intense" that he managed to have a minor argument with the maître d' before they even sat down, another argument with their waiter about the correct pronunciation of a dish on the menu, and yet another argument with the woman at the coat room on the way out. In between, he monopolized the conversation with his great plans for his career as an actor—at the time he was employed as a banquet waiter—and he regaled her for the entire course of the dinner with stories about the rich and famous people he knew, many of which, Kathryn knew from her own connections, were nothing but pure fantasy. In short, the minutes flew by like hours, and at the end of the evening, Kathryn vowed never again to listen to her friends, no matter how well meaning. It was, she decided, her first and last blind date.

Unhappy with her law firm in New York after a time, she sent out feelers for another position and managed to land a job in the legal department of a film studio in Los Angeles, where there seemed to be a lot more possibility for advancement. She moved across the country, and in California started a new and more satisfying life for herself, continuing to stick to her conviction that her job came first and relationships later. Meddlesome friends evidently know no geographical boundary, for in California, too, her refusal to entertain the possibility of a relationship just seemed to incite those around her to try to change her mind, with all the various eligible brothers, cousins, colleagues, and friends with whom they were sure she would get along. Using her now legendary "blind date from hell" story as a social shield, Kathryn successfully fended off all attempts to be fixed up.

More than a year went by before one of her work colleagues, by using a bit of reverse psychology, succeeded in making a dent in her resolution, occasionally talking about this loner of a friend of his, a quirky, unusual guy, a native Californian who was "just like her, not interested in relationships." Never really pressuring Kathryn, he'd tease her now and then with a little information here, a funny comment there, about his friend, until one day off-handedly at a lunch, when doubting out loud whether the two of them would hit it off, Kathryn had to admit she found herself intrigued. "Maybe it was the sun, maybe the Chardonnay, maybe," she said to me, "it was growing up a little bit." In any case, she asked her colleague to see if his friend might be interested in meeting her, the second and only other blind date in her life.

Meet they did, at a very casual place by the ocean at sunset, but since you know this is a book on synchronicity, you can probably imagine what transpired. To her complete amazement, she walked in to find Charlie waiting for her at the table. Having turned him into a near-mythic figure, though, she had found that time had mellowed him some, and besides, the incredible coincidence of going on two blind dates in her whole life with the same man on opposite sides of the country was too humorous to get upset over. Indeed, the coincidence was hilarious. They shared a cocktail in a far more relaxed atmosphere than years before, and she learned that he had moved back to California a few years earlier and changed his name, managing to get enough work to keep him afloat without really hitting it big.

The date that night was very pleasant, though Kathryn still didn't find his personality attractive enough to reconsider her decision to avoid relationships. But within a month or two, she did stumble across a man with whom she really did have a lot in common and with whom she is currently very happy.

"Funny, isn't it, that it took two unsuccessful blind dates with the same man to finally convince me to open up a bit," she said with self-deprecating wisdom. "Or maybe it was just the fear that, if I didn't get busy, I might be condemned to date him a third time!" Kathryn's story illustrates the way that synchronicity and romance do not always lead to the unmitigatedly happy ending we might expect from fairy tales and movies, but it can help us see that bringing an attitude of openness toward what the coincidence means in our lives might actually help us live a fuller and richer story, however unexpected the ending.

In deciding to script our stories on the basis of what we know about ourselves, deciding as authors do what the beginning, middle, and the end of our tales will be, we forget that what we consciously know about ourselves is only part of the story. The significance of Kathryn's synchronistic blind date with the same man had to do with a transition in her life that she was making slowly outside of her awareness, an unconscious transformation from resisting relationships to accepting her own ability to love and be loved for the woman she was. That unconscious story, the subtext, so to speak, of her life at that point was what rendered the coincidence meaningful. Only her openness to seeing how Charlie had changed let her in on the fact that she, too, had changed. A page had been turned in her life, and a new, more mature chapter synchronistically, and significantly, had begun.

• • •

Alex tells a similar "wrong person at the wrong time" story. During his last year in college, he developed an infatuation with a young woman who sat next to him in class. Tall, dark, mysterious, and exotic, Beija was a year or two behind him, and he found her enormously, even overwhelmingly, physically attractive. At the time, however, it was well known at the small liberal arts school they were attending that her interest lay not in men but in women. Rather than make a fool of himself, he kept his acquaintance with her on a friendly level and allowed his fantasies about her to flourish in the safe privacy of his own psyche. Following graduation, he relocated for graduate school and subsequently met a woman in the same field, fell in love, and got married.

Yet the memory of Beija stayed with him for years, during which time he would often have dreams of her, sometimes explicitly erotic dreams, sometimes merely romantic dreams of the two of them in a relationship. As his marriage began to suffer from difficulties of various sorts, some situational, some emotional, his dreams of the "love that never was" began to keep him more and more company. He and his wife went together to see a counselor to try to improve their relationship, and during a session alone with the counselor, Alex told the therapist that he had long nurtured a very complex set of fantasies about Beija, who had come over the years to represent everything he had ever wanted in a relationship. She was beautiful, she was giving, she was intelligent, he was going to be the only man she ever let herself open up to, and on and on. His counselor listened, trying to extract from the fantasy some sense of what Alex thought a good relationship was in order to use this information in the couple's counseling. But what the counselor did not know was that this was the first time Alex had ever told anyone about this secret crush from his college days.

The week after his confession, Alex went out with a few of his male friends to a sports bar downtown, and on the way out the door at the end of the evening, he encountered, to his complete astonishment, Beija, the woman of his dreams. She was happy to see him but didn't seem especially bowled over by the coincidence, whereas Alex could barely contain his amazement. Not only was Beija here in this unlikeliest of spots, a sports bar, but as they talked further, it turned out that she, too, had gone into the same professional field as he and indeed had just moved to an apartment around the corner from where he was working. Moreover, after a polite but pointed inquiry concerning her love life, he discovered that her lesbian relationship, so notorious on campus years ago, was in fact a one-of-a-kind event for her and that she had decided in the intervening years that she was heterosexual after all, though at the moment she was unattached. Attempting to remain calm and collected, Alex parted amicably after deciding to meet for lunch in a day or two to catch up.

For Alex, this meeting was momentous. No longer a mere fantasy, this "love that never was" now lived only a block away from where he worked, was in the same field as he was, and she was both available and heterosexual. Unhappily married himself, for reasons that both he and his wife were pessimistic about resolving, Alex interpreted this chance encounter as a sign that he and Beija were destined to be together, an interpretation reinforced by his just having articulated for the first time to another person his long-cherished fantasy of her. The timing of his confession, now that she had come back into his life, seemed full of significance.

Keeping his date a secret from his wife, Alex proceeded to have lunch with Beija, and indeed, in the course of what became a weekly lunch date with her, he decided that he would wait until she indicated an interest in deepening their relationship, and then leave his wife to be with her, the only woman, he was sure, he was meant to love.

As Alex tells the story, this fit of romantic idealism took some time to wear off, but wear off it did. It gradually became clear that Beija was not interested in him romantically but considered him a confidant with whom she felt safe enough to tell endless stories of her own sexual adventures, as she, new in town, hopped from bed to bed to bed with a lack of care Alex began to find distasteful. As the reality of who Beija actually was came into focus for him, Alex found himself understandably more and more appreciative of what he and his wife shared with each other.

In this way, the ending of the story is that Alex's failure to have an affair with the "love that never was" led him, ironically, to a renewal of his marriage. Despite occasional struggles, his relationship to his wife is now, Alex says, a satisfying one on the whole. In an epilogue to this story, so to speak, it just so happened that Beija abruptly pulled up stakes and moved out of the area six months after arriving there, as if staying just long enough to help Alex get his fantasy of her out of his system once and for all.

Now what is the moral of this real-life fable? It is hard to refrain from drawing out of significant coincidences a bit of wisdom for ourselves, and this, indeed, is yet another way to work with the meaning of such events. Alex certainly could tell you what the moral of this story was for him: when I asked him, he said to me that what sometimes looks like the right person at the wrong time might actually be the wrong person at the right time, which, to my mind, is about as succinct a lesson as any Aesop ever wrote.

Synchronicity and Forbidden Love: When Fate Steps In

There are stories of love welcomed and stories of love resisted, but perhaps none exert quite so much fascination on us as stories of love forbidden. Literature is full of such tales, in which the external bonds of family, culture, or religion place a barrier between people which only serves to enflame the connection. These are often stories of the right person in the wrong time and place—Tony and Maria from *West Side Story*, like Romeo and Juliet before them—or conversely, the wrong person in an unfortunately propitious time and place—the faithless Count Vronsky and Anna Karenina, from Tolstoy's novel, or in another way, Emma Bovary and her lover, in a relationship that destroys both of them. In either case, the archetypal quality of forbidden love almost virtually assures a tragic outcome in the tales we read. Happily for us, the synchronicities that occur in real life when our passions run up against the strictures of our social lives often lead to transformation rather than tragedy.

I especially love the story, told to me in very strict confidence, by a former co-worker of mine whom I'll call Camilla, of how she and a man she met over the Internet conducted a year-long computer sex-chat affair that centered mostly on vivid descriptions of a particular sexual fantasy they both shared. The details of what they found themselves both interested in are less important than the amazing coincidence they each felt upon finding someone else who shared this rather peculiar turn-on. Because each of them was already in a relationship and because Camilla was somewhat cautious about revealing her own sexual tastes, it took a few conversations before they discovered their unusual and yet mutually exciting interest, which neither of their respective partners shared.

Now, as we can well imagine, the names they gave each other over the Internet were false (an interesting coincidence here, too, eventually came to light, when they found out that each had used a parent's name), and since the pleasure of forbidden love always lies in the act of transgression, after many months of torrid computer chat, during which each of them began to feel more and more comfortable, Camilla and her computer-sex partner got up the courage to go beyond the bounds and make a date. They resolved to meet, not with any explicitly sexual agenda at first but merely to extend their acquaintance from the realm of the verbal to real life and to see what happened.

What followed was a synchronicity that had none of the charm or satisfaction of the others we have heard but was significant nonetheless. When each of them showed up at the café wearing what they had agreed to wear to identify each other, Camilla and her sex-chat partner discovered that they already knew each other from a particularly nasty interaction they had had with each other in professional circles some years earlier. In fact, as Camilla approached the coffee shop, she saw her old nemesis walking down the street and immediately knew that this man, who in her own mind had been identified for many years with all that was wrong with her own profession, would be the person she had come to meet.

When I asked Camilla what she thought the meaning of this coincidence was, to find an ideal sex partner in someone whom she had grown to loathe in other areas of life, she laughed a little uncomfortably and, interestingly, enunciated what again sounded a great deal like the "moral of the story."

"First," she said to me, but also to herself, I sensed, "fantasy is fantasy, and reality is reality, and never the twain should meet. Fantasy's fun because it has no baggage, but this weird coincidence showed me that behind all the disguises and flights of imagination we threw up to hide our real selves, each of us was a real person. Not a lesson I wanted to learn—it's a drag, really—but frankly I feel a lot more grounded since this happened."

Other lessons? I asked. She thought a bit and then, with a hint of a smile, said, "I don't know, maybe this is a contradiction, but don't judge a book by the cover. You never know what kind of relationship you might be able to have with someone you hate! I thought I knew this guy—knew him and disliked him—but completely by chance I discovered what I could not have discovered any other way, that he and I actually shared something quite unusual."

By being open to having her story rewritten for her, Camilla's tale of forbidden love taught her that who's "right" for us and who is "wrong" might not always be who we, in our authorial wisdom, think it is and wish it would be. To use von Franz's phrase again, "chance is the enemy"; random events scramble our plans and work sometimes quite dramatically to confound us into a new level of what is "right" and what is "wrong," not on the basis of conventional morality but on the basis of our own subjective experience. The significance of sharing a unique point of contact with a man she had previously disliked reorganized her way of thinking about herself in a way that could only have happened by chance. It takes a bit of courage to turn around and ask ourselves some of the hard questions about our assumptions which a synchronistic event sometimes confronts us with about ourselves. But, if our life is a story, it serves us to be aware of what an English teacher of mine used to say: writing is rewriting, vision is revision.

My friend Ann, whom I consider a specialist in forbidden loves, tells of how she met a man named Richard Rosenstein and his girlfriend at a party in New York City. The next week, for reasons mostly professional in nature, Ann went about trying to find this Richard Rosenstein. She knew he lived on the Upper East Side and got his phone number from directory assistance. Calling the number, she discovered she had indeed contacted Richard Rosenstein but not the Richard Rosenstein she had been looking for. However, she found herself in a conversation with this second Richard Rosenstein, and they spoke to each other every night for the following week. They finally felt comfortable enough to meet. Though both were involved with someone else at the time (indeed, Ann was married but was making quite a hobby of extramarital affairs during this period of her life), they became involved with each other in a relationship that lasted for years.

Part of the appeal of this story lies in the irony that seems almost writerly in style: Ann's wrong number turns out actually to be the right number, metaphorically speaking, leading her by chance to a man she ended up knowing and loving for a long time. Through this sychronistic event, together with the synchronistic phone call she received from Dan, her married lover already presented in the introduction, a portrait of Ann is given shape through these synchronistic events, is it not?

Now to meet Ann, you would soon discover that unlike many of my friends she is not a particularly psychologically-minded person. At first glance, she seems a very conventional, down-to-earth woman, certainly not someone given much to philosophizing about her life or drawing profound lessons from her experiences. Yet the striking quality of these synchronistic experiences, in the course of her many "forbidden loves," so to speak, brings forward quite a different part of her personality, the rather unconventional and frankly romantic side. The external circumstances of her life—married, young and briefly, then divorced and never remarried—only superficially describe her life story, for the synchronicities show us a woman who makes deep and lasting connections with men, however much social convention mitigates against those connections.

Is Ann conscious, despite the apparent settledness of her life, of how unconventional she is on another level? Knowing her as I do for many years, I would have to say, only to some extent. For all her normality, she does enjoy the role of the rebel and has tended to think of herself more often as a person wary of commitment, but these reflections about herself definitely do not occupy center stage. Do I think it would help her to do as I am doing now, namely, to take seriously the ways in which significant relationships in her life are punctuated by meaningful coincidences, coincidences that show her to be a person with an aptitude for love, a person with a special talent for connection? I think it would: loyal to a fault as a friend, she sees herself, I sense, as someone ambivalent about love. But the synchronistic stories she tells only help me appreciate how truly loving a person she can be. The synchronicities reveal Ann's deeper character the way random clues in the course of a mystery tells us not to believe everything we see about this "specialist in forbidden loves."

Because synchronicity is in essence about connections, it is no surprise that telephones and wrong numbers crop up in many stories. (I wonder sometimes how some of these sorts of coincidences used to occur in the days before it was easy to mix up a number or two and, in this way, stumble across destiny.) To complete this trilogy of forbidden loves on the telephone is the story of Yvonne and Gert.

In the last days of her marriage, Yvonne, a colleague of mine from graduate school, began to develop a friendship with strong romantic and erotic overtones with a fellow teacher at her school named Gert. Though the two of them were manifestly interested in each other, physically and emotionally, each of them was technically still in a committed relationship with someone else. Gert, being German and quite intent on respecting social forms and moral propriety, therefore kept his arrangement with Yvonne strictly but reluctantly platonic. However, it is in the dramatic nature of our love stories to have such high-minded resolutions erode away, despite the best intentions of the protagonists, and Yvonne and Gert, in this way, were no different from Abelard and Heloise or Tristan and Isolde. By degrees, they found themselves spending more and more time together, much of it usually in Gert's office which, unlike Yvonne's, was private and thus the only place to be conducting an affair-in-waiting.

That is, until a series of synchronistic wrong numbers began to occur, wrong numbers of a specificity and frequency that were startling: every time Yvonne's husband James would call her at school, over a period of months, the switchboard, oblivious to where she was, would by sheer chance erroneously put James's call through to Gert's office. In this way, through a series of more than a dozen or so such "wrong numbers," these two men, both involved in different ways with the same woman, synchronistically ended up developing an acquaintance with each other long before the previous relationship had ended or the new one began.

The eerie quality of having her husband constantly put through, by accident, to the man who was becoming her lover was, according to Yvonne, one of many things that confirmed for her the direction she had been taking to make the transition out of her marriage and into a different life with Gert, with whom she shared many more interests and much deeper passions. The wrong numbers created a bridge between what had been and what was still in the process of becoming, both literally as well as symbolically, an external set of crossed wires which stood for the crossroads in which Yvonne at that time found herself. This forbidden love, this tale of the right person at the wrong time, finally came to a head synchronistically as well, as I heard when I went out to dinner with Gert and Yvonne in the San Francisco restaurant which had been the setting of this last meaningful coincidence.

Having progressed, despite the best of intentions, from desirously platonic to pleasurably enacted, Yvonne and Gert thought one evening that they might sneak out for a dinner at a place far from where they both worked, in an area of town noted for its tourism, where it would be extremely unlikely to come across anyone they knew. They discovered the following day a coincidence of which French farces are made: Yvonne's husband's department at work had decided on a lark to hold their Christmas dinner at this very same small and quite out-of-the-way restaurant. Only by sheer luck, literally a matter of minutes, had Yvonne and Gert missed being found out.

Feeling quite certain that the message in all these synchronicities between her husband and Gert was that sooner or later she and Gert were to be discovered, the two of them began to take action to end their previous relationships so as to pursue their own with freedom and without moral qualms. With the help of nearly relentless synchronicities, Yvonne and Gert made the transition into recognizing their relationship as important and public.

A Common Tale: Coincidental Confirmations

As these stories demonstrate, when synchronistic events happen to us in our love lives, they can function in two different directions to raise our consciousness: they sometimes contradict the direction we have chosen, showing us something new about ourselves and our relationship; or conversely, a synchronistic event may confirm and consolidate a relationship we have had doubts about. When a deep and abiding connection between people exists, the sometimes abundant coincidences between them and their life experiences takes on the second, more confirmatory meaning, by synchronistically supporting the relationship and helping the people involved to acknowledge their feelings of connection.

Such was the case for Greg, who wrote about an extraordinary set of coincidences between him and his girlfriend. "The number 11 began to surface after I began dating my ex-girlfriend in late 1992. It was then that she said to me, 'I always look at the clock at 11:11.' Teasing her, thinking she was weird or something, we laughed about it and didn't really give it any more thought. It wasn't until we broke up that I came to realize the unusual 'bond' that we shared with this number. We were together 11 months. We broke up on November 11. I lent her my favorite hockey jersey with the number 11 on it. I pretty much thought that all of this was some silly, mushy relationship thing.

"I immediately noticed, however, that this number didn't go away

with our breakup. There were just too many strange and random encounters with 11 for me to simply label them coincidence.

"I once came home in the evening and sat down in front of the
TV, only to glance at the VCR which was recording a program, and
noticed that it displayed 11:11 P.M. on channel 11 with the recording
time being 11:11:11.

"Curiosity has gotten the best of me and I have unsuccessfully
tried to find a meaning behind all of this. With encounters occurring
frequently, randomly, and at times when I have no physical or emotional ties with my ex, I now see her association with the number 11 as
that of a 'trigger.' She claims not to have had any personal contact with
number 11 at all since breaking up."

Haunted by the number 11, Greg seems at a loss about what to
make of the repeated appearance of this number in connection with
his relationship. The way he writes about the experience—as if a
meaning is to be found outside somewhere, "behind" it all, rather than
in his own experience, in the feelings and associations that this number evokes in him—provides an example of a not very fruitful way to
work with synchronicities.

Since there is no single objective meaning to the symbol 11, for
like all symbols it points to something that cannot be fully known,
there is no end to the meanings the number 11 could have. $1 + 1 = 2$
might be an allusion to the way that he + his girlfriend = a new,
integral unit together. The repetition of the number 1 might indicate
the repetitive singleness of his life without her. Undoubtedly, anyone
reading this book could add their own associations and interpretations
to this number with regard to Greg's relationship. While amazing as a
coincidence, the continual appearance of this number in connection
with his girlfriend is synchronistic because Greg is able to experience
in another way what it means *for him* from the inside: specifically, how
his emotional connection with his girlfriend may not yet be finished.

Like an arcane image in a spooky story, his experience of knowing this woman is manifested in the external world by the completely random appearance of a number. Greg, like many people, is straddling the boundary between his subjective emotional experience of what she means to him versus what the number 11—or any symbol of their relationship—means in itself.

By contrast, I turn to a client of mine who entered into a relationship with a much older man. When she first met him, she thought, "He's attractive but, gosh, he's old enough to be my father," only to find out quite soon that she was right: he was in fact born on the same day in the same year as her father. Though her experience was not like Greg's of being haunted, certainly, the uncanny coincidence of the dates confirmed for her the importance of the relationship and couldn't fail to bring to her attention her need to consider carefully the age difference between them. She approached this interesting coincidence from the "inside out," in a manner of speaking. The date itself did not objectively stand for anything; it was not a sign. Rather, it was a symbol and was important because of what it meant *to her*: succinctly put, she experienced it as a warning to be careful about transferring onto this man feelings that had more to do with her father than with him.

A colleague of mine at work, Ralph, had gone through a long and very rocky relationship with his lover, a relationship begun synchronistically ten years earlier in a bar when, locking eyes across the proverbial crowded room, the man with whom he would become involved finger-spelled "I WANT YOU" behind his back at Ralph while engaged in a conversation with someone else. It was only by chance that Ralph happened to know sign language, having grown up with a deaf niece. The relationship that ensued, as Ralph tells the story, was wonderful and difficult, ending sadly with his partner's death from AIDS.

After that, again by accident, he became reacquainted with a man whom he had known years before, on whom he had always had a slight crush. This man, named Jack, who had himself just broken up with a long-standing boyfriend the week before, never took the subway into San Francisco, but that day had decided to on a whim. Thus thrown together synchronistically, the right person at the right time and the right place, Jack and Ralph subsequently began to discover all sorts of connections. Their aunts were best friends in a small town in upstate New York. Similarly, when Ralph mentioned the name of the woman he had been asked to pick up from the national office of the organization for which he worked, he found out from Jack that this woman's sister had been Jack's best elementary school friend some thirty years before in a small midwestern town.

Such confirmatory synchronicities, as I have come to call them, serve to assure us that we are meant to be with the person we are with and often form an integral part of the love story we live. Undoubtedly though, the people we love are people with whom we probably should, if not must, have a great deal in common. The question then arises: do we invest such commonalities with significance *because* we love someone? When we are in love, do we not go about finding areas of agreement that we can then experience as meaningful?

The answer is, of course, we do. But the point about synchronicities of the sort illustrated here is, first, that these commonalities present themselves to us *without* our causing them or seeking them out. For example, if Ralph had had his sign-language experience while attending a conference for deaf gay men, rather than in an ordinary gay bar, we would not think of it as much of a coincidence, no less a synchronicity. The extraordinary experience of a man whom Ralph had never met communicating in a language he just happened to understand in a public place drew him to his lover. He indeed invested the coincidence with significance, but he did not create the external circumstance. It occurred *to* him.

One could also say, I suppose, that, this being the case, then people make up synchronicities to suit their psychological purposes by reading meaning into anything that happens to them. We have probably all met such credulous folks, ever on the lookout for signs, usually in quite a literal way, and drawing sometimes quite ridiculous conclusions from the omens they perceive.

Those coincidences we are calling synchronistic are different on the level of the individual's *experience* of them: they are experienced as *extraordinary*, *random* events that occur first, the meaning of which *then* becomes clear. If you go out intentionally looking for a man who is much older than you and you find him, it's hardly a coincidence, however meaningful his age might be. There are lots of older men in the world, and you have already invested his age with meaning for yourself before you began your search. If, however, in the course of living your life, you discover that a man you find attractive shares with your father the exact same birthday, the coincidence is an unusual external event which indeed you *then*, like my client, might very well invest with meaning.

Of course, the meaning of any event varies from person to person, and in that sense, perhaps we do "make up" our synchronicities. Women, for example, who have always been attracted to men their father's age might very well not experience discovering a man with their father's birthday all that unusual or significant. But for my client, it was quite extraordinary and felt much like Jung's definition, the "occurrence of a certain psychic state with one or more external events which appear as meaningful parallels to the momentary subjective state." By paying attention to the external events of our lives in which an extraordinary, random occurrence has immediate significance to us psychologically, emotionally, and symbolically, we do what we always do with stories: we allow them to mean something to us, to have an impact, to change us.

Is that "making something up"? From one perspective, it could be called that. But if one's subjective experience is valued as real and as important as objective, external events, then the dismissive, cynical tone of such a phrase does not fit, because all people make up meaning from the events of their lives, using symbols to organize and deepen their lives and their connections with each other. It is an activity at the heart of story-telling, the essence of creativity.

Moreover, as the stories of Alex and Beija or Kathryn and Charlie illustrate, synchronistic events are as likely to underline the fact that something is *not* meant to be between two people as they are to foster that sense of fate or destiny which couples often feel when first meeting. For an example of how second-guessing fate on the basis of signs and symbols is a risky business, Sharon's story serves well.

Sharon told me that she comes from a long line of strong and psychically gifted women, and something she and her grandmother once did together just at the moment in her life when she began to be interested in boys always stuck in her mind. Her grandmother was baking an apple pie with Sharon, at twelve years old, helping, when Granny told her to take an apple and be careful to peel it so that the whole peel was one long strip. Knowing her grandmother's ability to "see things" and the wealth of traditional lore she possessed from her Appalachian background, Sharon did as she was told. Granny then told Sharon to take the peel, hold it in her hand, think hard of the man she would have in her life as her one true love, and then toss the peel over her left shoulder. "Whatever letter the peel makes on the floor is the initial of your true love's first name." That letter, both she and Granny agreed, could only be P, given the shape of the peel on the floor, but Sharon, herself heir to this tradition of female gifts, decided to improve upon tradition and threw the peel once more, so as to obtain the initial of her true love's last name as well. This, too, ended up being a P, which both she and Granny laughed about at the time, joking that she was fated to marry Peter Piper and pick a peck of pickled peppers. Nevertheless, in a family in which predictive dreams were common and the psychic connection between the women were taken as every-day occurrences, Sharon never forgot the incident, though she never spoke of it to anyone, and secretly, as she began to go out with boys, she stayed on the lookout for Mr. P. P.

Of course, none of the guys she dated ever had those two initials, and after college, she met David, and fell madly in love really for the first time in her life, ignoring the prediction from years before. She and David got engaged and married within a year, and a number of years went by. Then, one Christmas, she and David were home at his fa-ther's house, the year after her mother-in-law had died. Her father-in-law was planning to sell the family home and she and David were helping him go through all the things in the attic, deciding what to pitch and what to keep. David came across some toys that his late mother had stored away in a box for sentimental reasons, and with a laugh he held up an old black songflute, the kind handed out in school to help kids get used to playing an instrument and reading music. His father shook his head affectionately and asked David if he remem-bered how he had played incessantly for a year, driving the whole family almost mad.

Not knowing the significance of his words, David turned to Sharon and offhandedly said, "Yeah, they started calling me Peter Piper, and it got so that my brother even had the kids in school calling me that. Didn't really help my musical self-confidence much!"

To this day, Sharon told me, she has never quite gotten up the courage to tell her husband that an apple peel had "predicted" their relationship, but with the proviso that I change their names, she said she'd let me use this story of how sometimes, even when you think you know what your story is, there's a plot twist that only a synchronistic event can bring your attention to.

At first glance, Sharon is exactly the sort of person that our cynical side might expect to find synchronicities in everything; from a long line of psychic women, she held on to an image of an apple peel as predictive. And yet, the coincidence of her husband's childhood nickname with the nursery rhyme character she and her grandmother had joked about years before is hardly something that one could accuse Sharon of "making up." The external coincidence simply *had* a meaning for her, in this case a confirmatory one about the rightness of her being with her husband. Did she need this message in some way? Obviously not, since, according to her, she was quite happy with her husband, despite the fact he didn't have the "right" initials. But the coincidence nevertheless made her feel that the story of her life was in fact coherent, that her childhood and her clairvoyant heritage were connected with her present life and her future with the man she had married. As if in a story, the symbol of the nickname and its initials tied up a loose thread and made Sharon feel as if a circle had been completed.

For this reason, the question people sometimes ask me, "How do I make synchronicities happen to me?" is, of course, off-base, for synchronicities are acausal, or as Jung might put it, naturally occurring psychological phenomena. In simpler terms, they just happen, and when they do, the meaning of the story of our lives and our loves becomes clearer. Perhaps that is why synchroncities seem so common when the story is a love story, for isn't the experience of love one of the most profound coincidences anyone can ever have?

Why We Meet Who We Meet When We Meet Them: Reflections on Synchronicity in Love

Having heard stories of how people, often without lifting a finger and indeed in spite of their best efforts, end up getting together, readers might be able to confirm what I discovered when I assembled all the stories I heard from friends, acquaintances, and strangers for this book. Mention that you are interested in meaningful coincidences and it is quite likely that you will hear a story about the love of someone's life. Love stories have endured as one of the most popular forms of entertainment because our own love stories represent an important way we go about understanding our lives.

Why is it that some people's relationships begin and end under such dramatic auspices? Is it just that I live a boring, humdrum life, you might be thinking to yourself, while others more psychically in tune or fortunate than I get to live out what I can only read about in books like this one? The answer to these questions, I think, lies in the purpose that our love relationships seem to serve for us and our growth.

If we assume there are no accidents, in the sense that all things that happen to us are potentially meaningful, many of the synchronistic stories of love seem to suggest two truths about the role of our relationships. First, the person who can most help us to grow is not always the person we are initially attracted to. Both from my personal and professional experience, I have come to see that often what we are immediately attracted to in another person becomes what drives us crazy over the long run while, on the other hand, things we initially experience as major differences often, when appreciated and worked with, provide us with far more emotional growth.

Second, a transformative relationship with another person may not be about *who*, in some absolute sense, but instead about *when*. I would be surprised if there are many readers who cannot find the truth of this statement in their own experience. Is there any one who has not been carried away emotionally by an irresistible attraction—physical, emotional, or spiritual—to someone who did not treat them well? This is certainly the lesson Alex learned when he bumped into his old flame Beija from college. Is there anyone who cannot think of someone who would be good for them and their development but for whom they feel little attraction? This is certainly what came home to Rena in the midst of her ambivalence about the man who eventually became her husband after he showed such care for her when her mother died.

In marriage counseling, we often talk about the unconscious bargain in a relationship, the tacit agreement between two people which is the real reason they are together as opposed to the reason they each think they are. Sometimes these bargains are malevolent and are not helpful, for example the one often seen in traditional marriages: "You provide for my material comfort and let me stay a child, and I will do all your emotional work for you and let you stay a child, too." Sometimes, though, as these synchronicity stories seem to indicate, the wonder of relationships is that an unconscious bargain is struck, despite our own conscious sense of what we want in a partner, which does provide for our growth. Rena and Bob's story is heartwarming for that reason: what she needed in a partner was not what she thought she wanted as she traveled Europe immersing herself in the people and their culture, but what she was given in Bob, someone stable and present in a crisis, who was reliable and caring, was precisely what fit. Alex's story of infatuation with Beija, who most certainly would have driven him mad as a partner, is an example of the converse situation, an unconscious bargain that would have been awful for everyone involved. Fortunately for Alex, a synchronistic event made this obvious to him before any disastrous consequences ensued.

This second truth—that much of the wonder of relationships lies not so much in the fixed and unchanging characteristics of our partners but rather in the mystery of the timing—is frequently brought home by synchronistic events in our love lives, happening at a particular moment in our lives when we are able to see *who* a person is and not just *what* they might provide to us, emotionally or materially. The tendency to think about people as objects and about relationships as a commodity to be acquired or exchanged is one that has a long history. Nowadays we can advertise for a person in the newspaper in the same way one advertises for a car or an apartment, just as parents used to evaluate potential marriage partners for their children on the basis of wealth and status (and in many places in the world still do).

This objectifying approach to people and relationships—believing that finding the person with just the right combination of features will guarantee our happiness in love—loses sight of what these synchronistic events in love remind us: that no laundry list of characteristics can provide for a satisfying relationship unless the timing is right. Pete and Mary, who are quite happy together and had always sensed they might be, had to wait many years until, synchronistically, the time was ripe. It was the timing of Kathryn's second blind date with Charlie which had its effect on her resistance to relationships, occurring at a moment in her life when she had, in her own words, grown up and was able to see the amazing coincidence of meeting him again as a lesson and not just a curse. Even Rena and Bob's relationship, "arranged" in a manner of speaking by their friends, only blossomed when circumstances beyond everyone's control intervened.

Love is not a matter of "right" people versus "wrong" people, but rather, it seems from these love stories, more a matter of our own inner attitude and how that attitude creates a special moment in our lives when we can encounter another person on their own terms. This meeting between inner and outer, this synchronistic moment, is at the heart of so many of the love stories we read and is the very essence of so many of the love stories we live.

A Good Plot, Good Friends, and Full of Expectation: The Meaningful Coincidence of Friendships

From love stories where synchronicity intervened to transform the shape of a person's life, we move to that other realm of human attachment which for most of us is at least as important as romantic passion and for some people more so: friendship. If the flames of romantic and erotic love burn hot and quick, depending upon our attitude toward love, they all too frequently burn short and fast, whereas the less intense but deeper glow of our enduring friendships is very frequently a much more satisfying part of our lives. In some ways, friendship, because of the absence of erotic passion, presents a more mysterious sort of relationship that psychologists, writers, poets, and philosophers have struggled over the centuries to define and describe.

The fever of love can be traced to the chemistry of hormones or to that obscure bundle of primitive needs and desires born of our primary relationships, but the cause of our friendships and the nature of this unique form of relationship is not quite as easily discerned. In friendship, there is chemistry, naturally, but not an urgent, overwhelming passion. With our friends, there is commonality, to be sure, but without the urge to consume, to merge, to lose oneself. Friendship is one of the rare places, in a culture that idealizes male-female love, where we know the love of another man or another woman, an indispensable part of a full and well-rounded life.

Because our friendships hold out to us the possibility of connectedness without the intensity of our love relationships, many wise people have considered a true friend more valuable than a hundred lovers, an insight which is the core of thousands of stories throughout the ages. Some of these friendships have become legendary: the warrior love between Achilles and Patroclus, or the tender fidelity of Ruth and Naomi come to mind. The classics of literature as well as contemporary film have given us the tales of some memorable friendships, from the adventures of Huck Finn and Tom Sawyer to the mad exhilaration of a more recent pair, Thelma and Louise. Our own friendships, if not always quite as exalted or daring, have inarguably changed our life stories.

During the time in my own life when for various reasons I found myself bereft of friends, I spent much time thinking about what friendship was and why it was so important. My analyst, who has long been an invaluable mentor, provided me with one idea of what the basic conditions of friendship are, an idea that has always stuck in my mind. According to him, friendship consists of "propinquity and common interests," that is to say, a good friendship requires both physical closeness and shared activities. Lacking one or the other, our friendship, too, soon goes lacking. Many a rich friendship has foundered when, for reasons internal or external, geography gets in the way or when life changes bring about a shift in our interests and attention.

Expectably, therefore, through either propinquity or common interests, synchronistic events occur in our friendships, since friendship, as in romantic love, is itself always a coincidence—two people encounter each other and their lives become intertwined. Such was the case when I made efforts to expand my social circle, ending up with no fewer than seven different men named Steve in my life, the symbolism of which to this day I have not yet quite fathomed. It made for distinctly difficult communications, requiring an elaborate and confusing code of initials. And yet, awash in a sea of Steves for a while, I found the synchronicity reassuring, reminding me by the sheer repetition of the name that I was not alone.

In the same vein is Becky's story of the Deborahs in her life:

• • •

"I met the first Deborah sixteen years ago. We have the same birthday, the same height, build, hair color, eye color, complexion and look enough alike to be sisters. We were both swimmers in college and both quit before graduating. We both married at age twenty, had our first children at the same age, and both stayed home to raise our kids. We both moved to South Dakota at the same age and live less than three miles apart. Her second daughter and our first dog were both named Missy (both named before we met). Deb's husband and my favorite horse were both named Skip. Deb's daughter's name and my husband's name are Dawn and Don, respectively.

"The second Deborah (also a horse and dog person) came into my life about four years ago, 'by chance' when we both dropped in unannounced at the same time at the home of a mutual friend. This Deb turned out to be into some alternative massage therapies and at the time I was having serious back problems from a riding accident. Needless to say, she started my back on the road to recovery.

"The third Debra entered my life within six months of the second Deborah. The house next door to us had been vacant for about a year, and I had been fervently praying that someone would move in who loved horses and would be happy to live next to our barn. The day Deb moved in next door and we spoke for the first time, we instantly became fast friends.

"Now the similarities between Deborah Two and Debra Three are amazing. They were born within six months of each other and each is nine years younger than I. They are both the same height, weight, build, hair color, and complexion. Both were married twice, both experienced marital problems at the same time, which resulted in each of them moving out of the same city at the same time. Deb Two moved sixty miles east, Deb Three sixty miles south.

"Deb Three and I have so many unusual things in common that I am truly amazed. Her husband once remarked in exasperation that we both must have been hatched from the same egg. Our husbands are both physics and computer nuts and both have hearing aids. Her husband and my oldest brother are both named Michael. Her brother and my son are both named David. Her brother David and my brother Michael both named their firstborn sons Brian. Debra and I both had abusive mothers. We both grew up with Holstein cattle. Both of us are going back to school in the sciences, and both of us are sculptors.

"When Deb and her husband Mike moved away last fall, they rented their house to a very nice young couple. His name is also Mike and he is the third consecutive Mike to live next door in that same house.

"But the following coincidence is the strangest of all. When Debra was sixteen years old, another girl, also sixteen and not a relative, moved into her home and died that same year of leukemia. When I was sixteen, I lived as a companion in the home of a sixteen-year-old girlfriend who died that year of leukemia!"

Of course, any one of these commonalities by itself might not be too remarkable or could be dismissed as Becky searching for signs in the outer world to confirm her own need to belong. As an ensemble, however, like my own plethora of Steves, the common elements between her and her friends are so numerous and exist on so many levels—family, geography, interests, names, and experiences—that the synchronistic nature of these coincidences, their significance for Becky, is undeniable. As with the synchronistic commonalities between lovers, synchronistic commonalities between friends serve to confirm and support one's sense of the significance of these relationships. The obvious delight Becky takes in telling her story of the web of sharing she has with her friends reveals the meaning that she experiences through those coincidences: that she is connected to others in ways that are profound and abiding. Without everything she shares so synchronistically with the various Deborahs, of course, her friendships might well continue to be meaningful, but they might not be as strong a reminder of her good fortune and of the extraordinary interconnectedness she is living with her friends.

Lauren's story of how she found her friend Danielle at a point in her life when a friend was what she most needed provides an example of a life-changing synchronicity that comes in the form of a friendship.

"I don't really know where to start the story," she said to me one day in her office, "except maybe by saying that my whole life has been shot through with difficulties around food and weight. I grew up in a household where being big was both encouraged and ridiculed, and though for long periods of my life I have been at normal weight, sometimes through less than normal means, such as radical diets and obsessive exercise, there have been at least as many periods in my life when I have been out of control around food, weight, and my relationship to my body. As a musician, singer, songwriter, and pianist, this has been a problem, since it has made me self-conscious as a performer and has often gotten in my way, leading me to choose small-time gigs, so to speak, where the pressure was lower, rather than challenge myself to get into the big time.

"When I turned thirty, it was like a day of reckoning. I had gained fifty pounds in three months, following a period of near-anorexia, and having been through every diet and exercise program there was, I was really at the end of my rope. A co-worker of mine, at my day job, had been talking a great deal at that time about her decision to go to Overeaters Anonymous. It was an idea that had never appealed to me, as I was turned off by the spirituality of the program. Nonetheless, that year, as my birthday rolled around and there didn't seem to be any relief in sight from my bingeing and weight gain, I decided that I would go to a meeting and see what was what.

"Now, about ten years before, my best friend at the time asked me if I would sing at the wedding of one of his friends. The marriage was going to be in this very out-of-the-way little church way up high in the Sierras, and my friend was asked to be the organist. He didn't want to travel all by himself and thought that I might want to go with him, you know, just knock off a couple of standards for the ceremony and keep him company. At the time, I thought, what the hell. So I went and I sang, and everyone was grateful, particularly the bride and groom, Danielle and Hank, and as it turned out, that was in fact the last wedding I have ever sung at, this little gig up in the mountains.

"But back to the present. Being my ornery self, I decided that I wouldn't risk going to an OA meeting in my own city, positive that I would run into someone I knew and wanting to be as anonymous as possible. So what do I do? I get a meeting schedule for the next big city, about an hour south of where I live, and plan to go to the meeting which, in my mind, I have decided is going to be the largest, where no one will notice me.

"I go there, that day, feeling awkward, of course. I quickly sit down, not really looking at anyone, and then suddenly I feel a hand on my arm from the woman next to me, who smiles and winks. It was of all people Danielle, whose wedding was the last one I had ever sung at.

"We managed to get through the meeting without talking—no cross-talk is allowed at OA meetings, like AA—and then spent hours afterwards simply amazed over coffee. This wedding, for all its loveliness and romance, I found out, ended in a marriage not so happy, and Danielle had taken refuge in an eating disorder until about three years before when she got to OA and got into recovery, at which time she and her husband separated and divorced. I told her some of my story: how I had resisted coming; how I actually lived more than an hour away; and even how her wedding had affected me.

"Truly the coincidence was too much for even a hard-headed

person like myself to ignore. I asked her if she'd sponsor me, she agreed, and thanks to that synchronicity, I managed for the first time in my life to get into come recovery around food. She and I are still the best of friends."

While Lauren's isolation was internal and emotional, synchronistically relieved by meeting Danielle at a singularly unlikely place and time, my college friend John's story of meeting a friend just at the right time and place is hands-down the most geographically exotic. My own friendship with John, my roommate during our junior year abroad in Italy, became strained after graduation. He had chosen to go into the Peace Corps for two years, during which time, stationed on a remote island in the Philippines, he somewhat consciously refrained from communicating with any of his old friends, including myself. I subsequently found out that he had been going through what he calls a period of spiritual discernment, trying to figure out what direction to take in his life.

When his Peace Corps commitment ended, he decided to travel the world, and en route to India, he found himself island-hopping in the South Pacific. Because of the progressive smallness of the islands and the unreliability of planes and boats, he unintentionally and unwillingly ended up having to spend a night on what he describes as a "postage stamp in the Pacific," the minuscule island of Truk, where there was a Jesuit guesthouse. As he sat on the porch of the guesthouse that evening, the potentially long period of real isolation and loneliness on this forgotten bit of land in the middle of nowhere weighed heavily on his mind.

At that moment, he heard his name called from behind him, and stunned, he turned around to find a friend of his from college. She had gone to nursing school with us at Georgetown, and, since graduation, had traveled the world as he had. Only now she was actually living on Truk and working at the small hospital the missionaries had set up.

Over an after-lunch espresso at my house, I asked him what effect bumping into this friend at one of the more remote outposts of the world had on him. He responded, "It's funny, you know. Here I was, feeling really quite alone in the world, but as you know, I had chosen to wander and not settle down. Bumping into someone I knew from Georgetown on the island of Truk made me realize, made me feel, that really no matter where I went in the world, I was connected, I wasn't really alone. I would be taken care of, no matter where I went. When I left Truk the next day, setting out for India and who knows where else, I really felt more settled about what I had decided to do. Seeing her on Truk changed things for me."

Lauren's and John's stories show us that sometimes our synchronistic connections with friends occur at a point of loneliness and need, when we are isolated either psychologically or physically and could use a reminder that, despite how we feel, our relationships abide. It is as if the friends that came to them synchronistically were themselves symbols of a sort, people whose propinquity and common interests pointed beyond the loneliness of the present to a connection that had always been there.

The ending of Sandra's story has still not been written, according to her, but her tale illustrates how synchronicity sometimes comes to us in order to re-establish a connection which we do not want or are still too ashamed to acknowledge. I know Sandra from a class we were in during graduate school, and when I told her about the book I was working on, she volunteered the following story for the price of tea and cookies.

"I grew up in a small town on the East Coast, and being one of the brighter kids in my classes, I naturally hit it off with the other class brain, whose name was Adam. Now Adam and his family lived near us, my parents and his were active in the PTA, and so on. Because we were both writers, we were often paired together in our elementary school classes to do special projects and assignments while the other students would be still learning things which he and I had already grasped.

"It was one spring day, I remember, and he and I were about nine or ten, that age when you first start to kind of like boys but still need to pretend you don't. Anyway, we were walking home, and I had just found a best friend in this little girl, and as little kids do, I was very concerned with impressing her, doing everything like her, saying the same things, dressing the same way, you know how it is. So the three of us are walking home together, when suddenly she starts to make fun of Adam, makes fun of his glasses, his hair, his clothes, and I start to join in on it, not really knowing why, because after all he and I had always been friends. Naturally, he gets angry, but is mostly hurt, I think, which is when I start to feel bad about what I am doing. And then, perversely, I step up my attacks on him, maybe to impress my friend, maybe to push him away because I secretly liked him. To this day, I don't know.

"But suddenly, out of my mouth comes pouring all this anti-Semitic stuff—Adam was Jewish—and I start saying that everyone says that the blacks are ruining the country but it's really you dirty Jews, and too bad the Nazis didn't get you all so we wouldn't have to deal with you anymore, and even more than that. It was crazy, and I still don't know why I said it all, or where I got it from. Half our town was either Jewish or Italian, being East Coast and all, and I had never heard this sort of stuff in my family ever, not even racist comments about blacks, nothing.

"Of course, Adam starts crying, and my friend and I go in for the kill, throwing stones at him and chasing him home, and thus ended my childhood friendship, in a moment of completely irrational cruelty. We went to school together for the next ten years, never speaking to each other again, despite everything we had in common. He turned out to be quite introverted and unpopular, whereas I was in the in-group in high school. Growing up the whole time what had happened between us hung on my conscience, but I have never really known how to address it or make amends. I don't even know why I did it.

"So I move away from town to go to college and grad school, ending up in California. In the course of my job at a community counseling agency, we have an in-service training one day on prejudice and cultural differences. During one of the small group exercises, I actually get up the courage to tell this story of me and Adam and of my unconscious anti-Semitism to the group, framing it as a moral problem I have not yet been able to resolve, or even admit to. This was the first time I talked about it with anyone in years, twenty years to be exact.

"The next week, I am having coffee in a café near my house, thinking about nothing in particular, when Adam, looking almost identical to the last time I saw him, walks into the café. Now, I look very different from when I was in high school—different hair color, much heavier, different glasses. A lot of people don't recognize me when they see me, and Adam didn't either. I just sat there, paralyzed, mortified, as if it was just yesterday when I had said what I had said to him. I watched him get his coffee and leave. Having just dug it all up the week before, it felt incredibly synchronistic to have him walk into my neighborhood café right past me, both of us having found our way out to the same town in California.

"Well, the story has not yet ended. I continue to see Adam all around town, in the most unlikely of places, probably the most unusual of which was when after they remodeled my gym I bungled my way into the men's room just as he was leaving. I had never seen him at the gym before and have never seen him since. I'm not sure if he recognizes me or not, and having told this story to all my friends, they keep saying that the universe isn't going to let me off the hook until I make amends to him for what happened. But so far, I haven't been able to."

Sandra's framing of the synchronicity here as a kind of haunting by her conscience to repair a friendship permanently damaged in a moment of childish immaturity and hatred recalls Kathryn's story of her blind date from hell. Is the lesson to be learned from such a series of synchronistic appearances that any attempt to refuse awareness of our connectedness with others will be met with a compensation, with an insistent reminder to us that love—romantic or friendly—is an ever-present reality, whether we accept it or not? This, indeed, seems the point of the story in Sandra's experience, almost as if she is living out her own psychological version of *Crime and Punishment* or *Les Misérables* where an offense from her past continues to dog her throughout her life.

Every relationship is a sort of synchronicity: a unique occurrence in which an external meeting of people takes on emotional, symbolic, and transformative significance. What many of the synchronistic events recounted in this chapter illustrate is that we are far more connected with one another than we often appreciate, and each of the meaningful coincidences I have recounted gives credence to Jung's idea of the collective unconscious, the notion that all human beings share on a psychological and spiritual level a connection with all other humans on the planet.

As if we were characters in a plot, we often meet the person or persons we need to meet. In times of crisis or at times of great openness, a character is introduced, by chance, who becomes for us one of the major figures in the story of our life—a spouse, a best friend, the love of our life. At other times, when we are content with ourselves and our life, connections occur with others that feel like a force of nature, like something that was meant to be. At still other times in our lives, when we close ourselves off from the world out of egotism or fear, synchronistic events bring us relationships that serve as haunting and insistent reminders that our connections with others cannot so easily be ignored. When such events occur, we feel the story we are living more deeply, the story that says: you are not alone.

Love is a central human desire, or, in Jung's terms, an archetypal reality. Because we are drawn to stories in order to give structure and meaning to events, we find within our own stories of love and friendship, such as those in this chapter, a significance that is unique. The synchronicity of whom we love, therefore, lies not just in the amazing circumstances that make up our love stories but in the inner meaning we see and live in these stories of our lives.

Chapter Three

Getting and Spending

*Synchronicity
and the Work
of Our Lives*

The world is too much with us; late and soon,
Getting and spending, we lay waste our powers:
Little we see in nature that is ours.

WILLIAM WORDSWORTH

Better the rudest work that tells a story or
records a fact, than the richest without meaning.

JOHN RUSKIN, *The Lamp of Memory*

That synchronistic events should occur in our relationships seems quite natural, since the relationships we have with our partners, spouses, and friends are among the more meaningful experiences in our life stories; after all, both relationships and synchronicity are essentially about connections between our inner selves and the world around us. However, love alone is not enough to answer all our needs, hopes, and dreams, even if popular songs and romance novels might encourage us to think so.

In my experience, the real narratives that people live are far more like those classics of nineteenth-century literature, where a richly woven tapestry encompassing many characters and situations is the norm. The minute attention authors like Dickens, Tolstoy, Zola, and Melville paid to the social conditions of their characters, the realistic quality of their descriptions of the activities by which people organized, fulfilled, or wasted their lives, reflects how the work that we do and its significance is always a central part of our stories. Freud's well-known comment about the purpose of psychoanalysis has not yet, in my opinion, been surpassed in simplicity or accuracy: when asked what psychoanalysis would help people to do, he responded, "To love and to work." I know very few people who would disagree with the essential importance of each of these human experiences.

There was a time, before the rampant development of industry and technology, when the significance of the work we did was undisputed, when even the humblest job held a meaning. Because of their time-consuming nature, many activities necessary for survival are frequently repetitive and mind-dulling, mere grunt labor; but at one time growing and preparing food, creating and repairing clothing, building and maintaining shelter were understood as activities central to the community. Around such humble activities rituals were created, guilds or social circles were formed, and the public life of a civilization developed. Such activities were *assumed* to be meaningful.

In this older worldview, occupations that departed from the core survival needs of a community, that had as their aim the greater welfare of the society or goals essentially non-material in nature, were called either "professions" or "vocations," indicating, once again, their significance to the society. To profess something is to make a statement of belief or of value, and so, to be in a profession once had a fuller, almost spiritual meaning, indicating that one had organized and dedicated one's life to activities consonant with a sworn oath or stated set of values; one's work was a statement of what one believed, a profession, as in the phrase "a profession of faith." Similarly, a vocation, from the Latin word *vox,* or voice, was an activity to which one felt called, usually by a Something or a Someone far greater than one's own personal interests or tastes. To have a vocation was to have work one was *meant* to do for reasons that went beyond earning a living.

Some might lament the loss of such an assumption of meaning in the day-to-day work that we do, now that the major distinction people make in their work lives seems to be between a "job," something we do merely to earn survival money, and a "career," which denotes the longer-term perspective with which we view our jobs but which may or may not indicate that we find our work significant. It is no surprise, in such a cultural context, that Joseph Campbell's advice to "follow your bliss" during the series of his interviews with Bill Moyers on public television became a catchphrase in popular culture, just as did the title of Marsha Sinetar's book, *Do What You Love, and the Money Will Follow*: people sorely miss the deeper sense of satisfaction that comes from feeling that our livelihoods fit into the larger story of our lives.

The veneer of busyness with which we fool ourselves in our "jobs" and "careers" cannot hide the fact that success, measured in purely material or social terms in the form of money or reputation, is not enough nourishment for our souls and is not much of a foundation for a truly satisfying or interesting narrative. One should not be surprised, therefore, if meaningful coincidences abound in our work lives, perhaps more now than ever before, as we seek to find meaning and purpose in a post-industrial society. Work has a central place in our lives, and as always, synchronicity turns up wherever there is—or needs to be—greater understanding of the story we are living day to day.

Do We Find Work, or Does Work Find Us?

We have already heard many stories concerning people whose heads were at odds with their hearts, who had decided that their future lay in one direction only to have a synchronistic meeting quite thoroughly change their life through the power of love. In many of the stories concerning synchronicity and work that I have been privileged to hear, I found a very similar phenomenon. Many of the people I talked to had fully intended to proceed in one direction professionally when a synchronistic event derailed them, leading them mysteriously and sometimes surprisingly to another, more satisfying job, or into an entirely different line of work altogether. The earlier example of my friend Sam, who was laid off from his job in accounting only to be offered a far more satisfying job in music, his real love, is this sort of a synchronicity. In response, then, to the recurrent question, "How do I work with synchronicity?" I extend the apparently paradoxical advice to "expect the unexpected."

A singer, who spoke to me on the condition of confidentiality and whom I'll call Elise, told me the story of what she considers her big break, which came to her completely unintentionally and indeed almost in spite of her best efforts. Like most professional singers, Elise had spent much of her life in voice, acting, and movement classes, all at her own expense and with the full knowledge that the possibility of earning a decent living from performing was a gamble against poor odds. Like artists in any field, though, she did what she did because she loved it, despite the difficulties, frustrations, and uncertainties.

Because she was classically trained as an opera singer, her interest in appearing in musical comedy productions was not especially strong, though her coach and colleagues had often urged her to try out for such roles, given her sparkling, naturally comic personality and the remarkable versatility of her voice. But, in spite of such advice, Elise resisted their encouragement and continued trying to break into the very small and highly competitive world of opera, going to audition after audition with middling success, landing a small part here and there in local companies, while working her day job to pay the rent.

For a small but well-regarded opera company's production of a popular opera, Elise spent a good month polishing her audition aria, and when scheduling the try-out, had specifically requested one of the last audition appointments, knowing she sounded better later in the day. When she arrived at the community center where the auditions were being held, however, it was immediately clear from the deserted air that a mistake had been made. Anxiously approaching a woman who seemed to be an assistant and who was in the process of packing up her papers into a folder at the end of the hall where "Auditions" were indicated, Elise said with as much self-control as possible, "Don't tell me auditions are over. I had a five o'clock appointment."

The woman seemed taken aback. "Actually, they are," the woman said, "but the committee hasn't left. Let me see if they'll hear you."

After a brief consultation behind closed doors, the woman returned and led Elise into the room. Elise told me that she did remember the pianist giving her an odd glance when she gave him her music, but at the time, she said, it didn't really register and she put his expression down to what she assumed was her own mistake about the appointment time. Two men and a woman sat behind the desk, looking, as always, impassive but attentive, and after centering herself, she launched into her audition piece, a coloratura aria in Italian. She felt it went very well, and at the end she thanked the committee a little more graciously than usual, given their indulgence of her lateness. As she was preparing to leave, one of the committee thanked her, then asked her, strangely, whether she had prepared anything in English.

Not understanding, she answered that she hadn't thought the show was being performed in translation.

"*Candide?*" the man responded with raised eyebrows, referring to Leonard Bernstein's quasi-operatic musical comedy, which has become a repertoire staple.

That was the moment Elise realized that she had stumbled into, of all things, the wrong audition entirely. "Oh. I really don't know what to say. I thought I was auditioning for another company and another show."

The woman at the door laughed. "That's tomorrow. Their auditions are tomorrow, Sunday."

But the director of the show motioned to the pianist and asked Elise if she was willing to sight-read a bit. Somewhere between mortified and game for a challenge, Elise went forward with the unfamiliar music, and at the end realized that they were interested in her for the difficult role of Cunegonde, Candide's wife, which she indeed got, finding out only later that she was only one of three sopranos they had heard that day who had been capable of actually singing the role. Most of the others either hadn't had the sort of musical background Elise had or couldn't adequately sing the music Bernstein had written.

From her performance in this musical, Elise received a great deal of attention in the press, from which came other offers for performances locally and then regionally, in musical theater rather than opera. But when Elise told me this story of her lucky break, she said, "I'm not complaining. It took going to the wrong audition to make me wake up and do what I guess I should have been doing all along. I'm working regularly, I'm happy. That's what counts, no? Though I don't think I want the world to know I was ditzy enough to stumble into the wrong place with the wrong music. Bad for the image, you know." Once a diva, always a diva, even in musical comedy, I suppose.

• • •

Synchronicities frequently happen, as one did for Elise, when we have our minds made up that a particular ending, and only that ending, for our story will do, a characteristic so common in the stories I have heard of such coincidences that it almost makes me want to answer the question, "How do I make synchronicities happen to me?" by responding, not altogether flippantly, "Get obstinate about what you will and won't accept from life, and see what happens then." But synchronicities also occur when our minds are not made up, when we are betwixt and between, and when, in openness, we stumble upon a significant person, place, or thing. Such was the story of my friend John who, in the midst of his own vocational transition, encountered a mentor in one of the unlikeliest places on earth.

Feeling vaguely called to the priesthood throughout college, John graduated and decided that some time in the Peace Corps would help him seek out his real vocation. However, as his two-year assignment in the Philippines drew to a close, the question of whether or not to become a priest remained as open as ever, and feeling the need for further time, John decided to spend the year afterward randomly traveling the world.

We have already heard of his reassuring synchronistic encounter with his college friend on the island of Truk. But before that incident occurred, this transitional period of John's life began with a first stop, chosen without any overarching plan, in India, where he thought to visit a particular ashram and immerse himself in the native culture.

Arriving at the ashram, though, his expectation of being the only Westerner was confounded when he discovered that another foreigner had arrived before him—a Jesuit from John's own home province. The coincidence, to John's mind, was striking: he had landed haphazardly in a remote ashram in India during a period specifically set aside for a discernment process concerning the priesthood only to find a Jesuit from his home province as the only fellow Westerner there. Their conversations, as we might expect, were significant, for John took the opportunity synchronistically presented to him to talk with this priest about his own uncertain vocation, about what life in the Society of Jesus was like, about what to expect and what not to expect. From this chance encounter emerged John's greater certainty that entering the Society was the right next step for him, which is what he did when he eventually made his way back to the United States.

Contrary to my (admittedly tongue-in-cheek) advice to be stubborn about the future as an invitation to synchronistic events, John's story inspires another bit of semiwhimsical advice to those who wish to cause acausal events. If you want a meaningful coincidence to change the story of your life, wander the world randomly and be willing to listen to whatever life presents. This last part, "be willing to listen to whatever life presents," is, I think, quite a good piece of advice when confronted with the random event that confounds our plans or shows us something other than what we expected. The unanticipated turn of events we are faced with might well be a turning point of a story we had not yet realized we were a character in.

But such an attitude of openness requires straddling a fine line between being realistically self-directed and pig-headedly tenacious. Being both determined and willing to let go is a challenge for anyone, and yet, it is a requisite skill if we are to draw meaning from the "accidents" that befall us. For example, Gail, a colleague of mine, had spent her whole life in pursuit of a goal as professor of comparative religion. Beginning in high school, she planned her academic career with great forethought, choosing undergraduate and graduate schools carefully, cultivating contacts, serving on committees, traveling to places on vacations where research potential existed for theses, papers, or dissertations.

Despite such assiduous planning and well on her way to her doctorate, Gail found herself stymied in ways she could not have anticipated. Her advisor and she were at loggerheads about the direction of her dissertation for reasons which superficially had to do with content, but which Gail thought had much more to do with personality conflicts and sexism. Lacking his support, she found herself unable to procure key fellowships and take advantage of other opportunities, as she had in the past, thus forcing her to grind away at jobs to meet living expenses and leaving her with little time and energy to do the writing and research she needed to advance. Moreover, the university she had chosen, one of the best in her field, was also one of the more expensive, and with the distinct probability that her degree might take her years longer than she intended, Gail began to ponder, with ever-increasing anxiety, the quantity of debt she was accruing.

As she tells the story, one morning she woke up and admitted to herself that she was in a career crisis. That day, she was sitting with a heavy heart at the café where she had her morning coffee, when from behind her, she heard a cheerful "Hello." Nancy, a woman Gail had known from her master's program but whom she had always had mixed feelings about, sat herself down uninvited.

Nancy told Gail that she, too, had been where Gail was but had reconsidered academia, deciding instead to pursue a career as a therapist. Initially hearing Nancy out simply to be polite, Gail couldn't help but begin to listen more closely, eventually asking Nancy a few questions about how she was going about her new career, what the regulations were, and so forth. At the time, the regulations for the license Nancy had decided to pursue were minimal, no more than taking a certain number of specified courses, gaining a number of hours of experience, and then passing a written and oral exam, all of which were made to sound quite easy and might be even easier, given the possibility that some of the courses Gail had already taken could be counted toward licensure.

From that day and that synchronistic meeting came Gail's eventual resolution to cut her losses concerning her teaching career and obtain her psychotherapy license, which she did and with a minimum of fuss. Licensed for years now, Gail told me that she is, ironically, doing more teaching—in the form of supervision, workshops, and adjunct faculty classes at local schools—than she even wants to be doing.

"I would have been miserable in an academic career, I see now," she said to me. "I was driven by an idea that didn't really fit me, an idea from childhood that I hadn't really ever looked at as an adult. If I had to teach the same three or four courses again and again for years, I'd be nuts in the space of five years. So, it all worked out—despite my best efforts, I'm embarrassed to say."

Though this last formulation is Gail's own, I found myself thinking that in fact Gail's ability to tolerate the betwixt and between and consider the possibility that her accidental meeting with her intrusive friend might yield some good was much of what made the coincidence synchronistic. Without the ability to straddle the line between determination and prudence, Nancy's appearance would have been simply a meaningless annoyance rather than a meaningful turning point.

These stories of people coming upon a wholly unanticipated or actively resisted direction in their lives make clear how synchronicity is indeed an acausal phenomenon. Nothing Gail, John, or Elise did intentionally helped them along as much as what occurred to them unintentionally. Thus, while one could quibble with the title of this book, stating from a literal perspective that of course there are accidents—chance occurrences without intention or meaning—stories such as those above make one wonder whether there really *are* any accidents, whether any of the smallest details are not important to the overall purpose of the tale we call our life. The truths of certain truisms, such as "It'll come to you when you least expect it," or "Let go, let God," are reflections of how, when we are our most ego-invested in our own limited plans or, conversely, most open, we create for ourselves a moment in the plot of our lives pregnant with possibility.

Do We Get Jobs, or Do Jobs Get Us?

Synchronistic events don't always lay the foundation for an entire career, as with John, Gail, and Elise, but they certainly have played a part in many a job. Recall Ellen from Chapter 1 who hung up on her controlling father without an idea as to how she would support herself without him and was offered a job the very next day through an accidental encounter: as with friends and lovers, synchronistic opportunities often appear when we need them most.

Tony D'Aguanno, a San Francisco Bay Area teacher and therapist who specializes in issues around work and money, tells the story of a friend of his whose own experience in finding work was significant not just for her but for Tony as well, confirming his sense that our work lives can be every bit as soulfully engaged as any other part of our lives. Tony's friend had been trained as a nurse-assistant in the highly specialized field of neurosurgery but had been unsuccessful in finding work. Walking through Westwood one day, she had the sudden urge to go through the UCLA campus instead of taking her usual route. Rather than shrugging off the feeling, as many of us would, she followed her instinct, and followed her instinct again when it told her to enter a particular building on campus, and walk down a flight of stairs. There she found a bulletin board covered with layers of notices, advertisements, and announcements. Impelled further by an obscure feeling, she began peeling through the flyers tacked up on this board she had never seen before, going through them all until she came across a small announcement for a job in her field of expertise at a hospital located some six hours north, in the town of Santa Cruz. She called the neurosurgery department of the hospital that day, applied for the job the following day, was interviewed the following week, and got the job.

Another story from D'Aguanno illustrates how synchronistic improvements in our material lives can come to us through the vehicle of our friendships. Tony's best friend was a therapist who, due to his commitment to community mental health, found himself in a series of somewhat satisfying but almost always low-paying jobs. While the non-material satisfaction of doing good more or less balanced the stress that came from never having enough money, Tony found himself more often than not commiserating with his friend over the difficulties of his financial situation.

As his friend's birthday approached, Tony quite creatively thought that what he would really like to give his friend would be a better paying job, but since that was out of the question, he decided instead to choose one of the bills from his own large collection of rare coins and paper money, have it framed, and give it to his friend as a good-luck token. The bill he chose was from Weimar, Germany, during that famous period of wild inflation when money was being printed in a haphazard way by individual towns in denominations of ever-more astronomical figures. However, the symbolism of giving this unbelievably large denomination bill to his extremely underpaid friend was less on his mind at the time, Tony says, than the beautiful scene depicted on the bill which, when mounted, looked like a miniature painting.

Tony's friend received the bill, offered with the story that it symbolized the gift that Tony really wanted to give: a better paying job. Immediately afterwards, from sources wholly unexpected, his friend was offered two part-time jobs, which increased his income fourfold, giving him spare time in his schedule to boot.

Since Tony has had quite a number of synchronistic experiences

in his life, he took this coincidence in stride, glad that his good intentions toward his friend had been realized, even if he had nothing to do
with it. Soon on the heels of his friend's stroke of luck, though, Tony's
own job situation began to sour, and thinking that perhaps he was
more in need of the "lucky bill" than his friend, who was now making
money hand over fist, Tony asked for and got the framed note back, "on
loan," as he put it.

The following week, incredibly, was full of good fortune. Tony's
boss announced, with no prior warning, that he was giving Tony a
raise. While standing aimlessly on a street corner, Tony met the
woman who was to become a partner in a venture that both he and she
are still running, which has brought both professional and material
satisfaction; and as a last stroke of luck, he received a message at work
asking him if he would be willing to teach a course at a local adult-
education school. Although many people had applied to teach this
course, the administrator of the program unaccountably offered it to
Tony on the basis of a friend's recommendation, even though Tony
hadn't even applied for the job. Seven years later, he is still teaching
this same course.

Of all the objects we encounter every day, there is none more
symbolic than money. What is after all nothing but wood pulp and dye,
made of the same substance as a Kleenex or a candy wrapper, money
holds more power, influences more lives, inspires more anxiety, pleasure, grief, joy, and ambivalence than almost anything one could name.
Tony's story of the "magic bill," in my opinion, is a good illustration of
the symbolism that money carries, for as a collector, Tony's interest
was in the literal aspect of money—money as art, money as collectible,
money as object—and not really in its more symbolic aspect—money
as power, money as choice, money as freedom, money as status. Indeed, wasn't this the problem with his friend, who had ignored the
immaterial, symbolic aspect of money in favor of other values—helping

people and self-sacrifice—and thereby found himself without enough literal money? As a beautiful object in its own right and therefore something to cherish, the bill had a potent symbolic value as well, both as a stand-in for the real gift Tony had wanted to give, but at the same time as an artifact from a time and place when money was being devalued in an extraordinary way, thus symbolically reflecting his friend's devaluation of his own material life. All symbols can have multiple meanings, and the synchronicity of this Weimar bill is no exception. That its possession had significance to both Tony and his friend—it had synchronistically appeared alongside opportunities that were both materially rewarding as well as emotionally satisfying—is therefore at the crux of this turning point in the plot of their lives.

A causal perspective on these coincidences would ascribe to the bill magic properties, in the way we are familiar with from fairy tales and campfire stories: the stories of lucky charms, amulets, or other objects to which people, modern and pre-moden alike, impute some sort of objective capacity to effect events in our lives. Possessing them "causes" our good fortune, and losing them "causes" bad luck.

The rational/scientific response to such magical beliefs, however, equally misses the mark in my opinion, in denying the objective power of such objects but without appreciating the *subjective* power they hold, the *symbolic* effect they produce in people's self-understanding. Tony was not credulous about the bill's occult properties, but neither did he discount the bill's all-important meaning as a symbol of a turning point in both his life and in the life of his friend—which is what made the coincidental events around the bill synchronistic for him, rather than magic.

The word "accident" is used in two different ways in common speech. If you are sitting at home reading the newspaper and your spouse walks in, announcing, "Honey, I had an accident today," in all likelihood you would run to look out the window at the car. This meaning of the word "accident," a physical mishap, is probably the most frequent we encounter—I had an accident on my bike, I broke my arm when I fell from a tree, my niece had an accident and wet her pants. But so far in this book, we have been using the word "accident" in its more abstract sense: an occurrence that seems random, unplanned, or without specific personal causation. However, sometimes the nature of a synchronistic event brings together these two senses of the word, as when literal physical mishaps, accidents in everyday parlance, bring about important changes accidentally, by pure chance. The accidents in Stephen's story of how his job got him, rather than the other way around, are both literal and figurative.

"In my teen years, my ambition was to be a filmmaker. After high school, I went to film school and got my first degree. Armed with my sheepskin and much youthful confidence, I set out to be a great filmmaker. I applied everywhere. No one was hiring filmmakers, and a year later, I was taking baby pictures for seventy cents a crack. One day in February, my car caught fire and blew up, almost killing me.

"As I needed a car to be a baby photographer, I decided to sell my Bolex [a type of movie camera]. I had given up on the notion of ever getting a job in the film business. Every TV station and production house in town only hired those with experience, and I had none: the old Catch-22. Admitting defeat, self-condemned to be a baby photographer forever, I put an ad in the newspaper to sell my film camera.

"At about nine-thirty in the morning, a fellow from a big TV network called in response to the ad. He was a cameraman who was looking for a second camera to keep in the trunk of his car as a backup, and he asked if he could come by after supper to check out the Bolex I had for sale. I said yes, of course.

"That afternoon, one of their cameramen was shot [but not

killed]. When the fellow from the network came by that evening, he asked, 'Can you shoot news?' I said, 'Yes, you bet.' He said they needed someone to fill in for a month or two and asked if I could start right away. Eagerly, I said yes, and the next day I started shooting news. Although it was only temporary while their fellow was recovering from the gunshot, I was able to get enough experience to get hired by another station several months later, and I never shot another baby picture.

"Despite will and intent, it was a series of negative and undesirable events that made possible that which could not be attained in other ways: no job; car blows up; sell camera; network guy gets shot; I get job.

"If the car had blown up on any other day, nothing.

"If the network guy didn't get shot, nothing.

"If I didn't put the ad in the paper, nothing.

"Life unfolds, despite will."

This series of synchronistic events, in which the accidents are literal and led to a significant career break for Stephen, shows, I think, quite clearly how the meaning of an accident lies not outside of us, out there, but in the events themselves which, after all, are accidents, random occurrences. The meaning has to do with how we, like Stephen in his succinct synopsis at the end, put together a story of what has happened to us in these accidents, of what they meant and how they changed our lives.

In our stories, these accidents either take on a meaning—or don't. Accidents occur every day. We mix up an appointment time like Elise, or get assigned a sexist, uncooperative academic advisor like Gail, or our car blows up and a colleague is unlucky enough to take a bullet, like Stephen. It is not the event itself but its place in the narrative of our lives which determines whether or not an accident is synchronistic.

What is interesting, though, in so many of these stories about the meaningful coincidences that occur in people's work lives is the admission of defeat that seems almost required before they are able to move forward, an admission forced upon them by apparent misfortune. Having to sacrifice his Bolex following the explosion led Stephen to the man who eventually got him a job. Elise's blunder led her to have to admit her own mistake in keeping her eye so narrowly on a single sort of musical career. Gail's bad luck, once accepted, helped her broaden her sights and find a profession in which she remains quite fulfilled. The expression "accidentally on purpose" comes to mind when thinking about accidents of these sorts, for in the arc of the professional lives of these people, the accidents they suffered and the sacrifice of previous attitudes that such mishaps forced on them actually were the hinge upon which the plot of their work lives turned.

From Out of Nowhere: Stories of Synchronistic Help on the Job

Synchronistic events, such as the ones in the previous stories, can indeed overcome our typically human hard-headedness about what sort of career we should have or what sort of job we should get. But meaningful coincidences, I have found, can also play an important part in helping us to succeed and take greater pleasure in doing the jobs or pursuing the professions we are in. Sometimes these coincidences will be confirmatory, sometimes confrontational, sometimes just accidental in that purposeful way we only understand much later.

When my friend Mark decided to leave his job as a social worker for a large New York hospital and come across the country, it was a decision fraught with all sorts of uncertainties. Although he was drawn to human services, a series of disappointing administrative decisions on the part of the hospital led him to see that in all likelihood there was going to be little chance for any sort of professional advancement for him in the near future. His relationship had just ended, and a visit to his sister on the West Coast made him hopeful enough to just chuck it all in New York and move to San Francisco. But the stress and uncertainty of this relocation, even after he got a job in a social service agency near his new apartment, lingered on.

That is, until he began talking to a colleague, John, from another of the agency's programs and, as with the three Debbies of Chapter 2, discovered an uncanny list of things he had in common with his new colleague. He and John had applied for the same job in the agency, which neither of them got, but then were subsequently hired for different jobs and had their offices next to each other. They lived across the street from one another in San Francisco and discovered that they had both lived in New York at the same time and that Mark had lived across the street from John's office there. During a rough period in his own life, John confessed that he had in fact sought help from the very clinic in which Mark had been working before his move to California, and going back even further, each of them had grown up in neighboring towns in the heartland of Iowa and had gone to the two high schools which, among a plethora of enormous high schools in central Iowa, were arch rivals in athletics.

This series of coincidences, in the midst of doubts and anxieties about whether or not he had done the right thing by moving to California, felt significant to Mark, as if his being given a comrade at work, with whom he shared so much, was a sign that perhaps he had, after all, been right to relocate. In John, Mark had chanced upon someone who knew "where he had been," in both the literal and figurative senses of the phrase. Put simply, finding John helped Mark feel he belonged at the agency where he worked.

In a different way, synchronicity played a role in what an acquaintance of mine named Patty told me was a serious miscalculation on her part when she took on the job of managing a newly created department within her computer software company. Well liked and industrious, she had long sought to increase her responsibilities and take on a managerial post. So when she got the nod to begin developing a small project with another man from the company with whom she had previously worked and gotten along, she was elated.

However, as she tells the story, Patty didn't see precisely how the newness of being a manager and her own insecurities could play a part in affecting her judgment. She took up the reins with her colleague, now her subordinate, with an enthusiasm and overcompensatory confidence that by the end of the first week had led to quite a number of hard feelings between the two of them. Without consulting anyone, she had decided to change various things about the project, about the organization of the work, about the direction of this new department, supported in her authoritarian attitude by her own experiences of her bosses and by her own inflated sense of being totally in charge. The result of her arrogance was quickly evident when the following Monday morning, the man she was supervising quite politely asked her if she would like to go to lunch at a Chinese restaurant nearby. Once there, over lunch, he let her have it, mincing no words in saying how he felt about how she had treated him and telling Patty very plainly that he would not be interested in working with her if a more cooperative style of working couldn't be found.

In another situation and with another person, she could easily have put his reaction down to difficulties he had in working under a woman boss, but the fact was Patty knew inside that she had been over the top, letting her own insecurities and joy about becoming a manager go to her head. She tried to apologize to her co-worker, who was clearly more interested in working *with* her—and not just *under* her or *for* her—in developing the new project, but the damage had been done, and she sensed it was going to take more than just an apology to mend the breach. So what did her fortune cookie say that day? "The great leader rules by the force of heart, not hand."

Telling me the story, Patty produced the slip of paper upon which, she said, she had been given "words to live by." A seemingly minor incident for Patty became a new attitude. She pasted the fortune over her desk, where it still remains, reminding her that being a figure of authority goes beyond a mere exercise of power. She was eventually able to repair her relationship with her colleague, and she says that the wisdom of the fortune cookie has stood her in good stead throughout her career.

In the artistic professions, as opposed to the service professions or the world of commerce, how best to do one's job is a subjective issue. Competence in managing the development of software products or in administering the social services of a hospital can usually be judged by objective standards. If the point of one's work is to create something of beauty, though, one must rely almost wholly on one's own instinct and experience. Therefore, the fact that synchronistic experiences—subjectively meaningful, random occurrences—are often an integral part of the creative process should not come as a shock.

As Matthew told me his story, he prefaced his tale with an observation about what he says is a long-standing tradition in vocal training of tyrannical teachers who are convinced their way is *the* way and will brook no opposition from their students. During the start of his career, therefore, Matthew found himself in a not uncommon situation in this field—in full-scale conflict with his vocal coach about which material to use for an upcoming audition. His coach insisted that Matthew sing a particular aria for the audition and, intimidated by his coach's reputation and forceful personality, Matthew slaved away at this difficult piece of music until he could perform it perfectly. To his coach's credit, Matthew could see that the aria would in fact show his voice off to best advantage in the shortest amount of time, but as it was still somewhat new to him and hadn't really been thoroughly "worked into his voice," as singers say, he felt ambivalent about using it. A relative newcomer to professional music, Matthew at that time had gone on only a few auditions and thought, despite his own mixed feelings, that maybe his teacher did know best.

One day, turning over the problem in his head, Matthew found himself singing an old Italian song, one of the standards of vocal pedagogy which all singers train on but which generally are seen as "practice pieces" rather than full-fledged music. With the rebellious fantasy of using this little ditty as his audition piece, he left his house and, still humming the tune, he got into his car, turned on the radio, and heard on the radio none other than Pavarotti pouring forth his own rendition of the very song Matthew had been singing. The odds of such an unusual recording existing at all, no less being broadcast on a classical music station not known for vocal music, no less Matthew's tuning in at the very moment it had been running through his mind seemed a significant enough coincidence to grab his attention. Pavarotti's version of this song, ornamented tastefully and sung with simplicity, made Matthew decide that he would follow through on his own intuition and use the song for the audition, without telling his teacher of the switch.

By understanding this random appearance of the song as encouragement to trust his own instincts, Matthew was surprised to find that events bore out his synchronistic interpretation of the coincidence, for at the audition, the singer before him sang the piece Matthew's teacher had wanted him to use with a voice so perfect that Matthew could only have suffered by comparison. Furthermore, Matthew later discovered, when he was offered a small but important role in the show, that the musical director had an absolute passion for the old Italian songbook. Matthew's daring decision was, he later learned, a source of great delight to the director, who admired Matthew's unconventionality, and had served to clinch his acceptance into the show.

What did this synchronistic experience teach Matthew? For all the help and advice Matthew received from his eminent coach, much of which was invaluable, Matthew's own subjective experience of his artistry—what felt right to him, what material meant the most to him—was far more important than objective considerations. Indeed, his coach's choice of an audition piece was "correct" for his vocal type, which was why, in fact, the singer before him at the audition had sung it. But it was not a piece that Matthew at that time felt good, relaxed, and comfortable about. In the story of his singing career, Matthew uses this synchronistic event as an example of how, after you have mastered the technical, more objective skills of your craft, you must always then listen to yourself and your own feelings: if you don't, he says, life might just gently remind you.

The synchronistic encouragement Matthew received to use a simple song for his audition is one example among many I have heard of how the very resources someone needed to complete a job appear to them out of the blue. Such real-life stories of our being given what is most useful to us in our work can have all the charm and dramatic impact that such fairy tales as Rumplestiltskin have. Appearing just in time to help the unhappy, imprisoned princess spin the bags of wool into skeins of gold, Rumplestiltskin comes out of nowhere and moves the story along to its happy conclusion. But that's just a fairy tale, right?

Not to Danielle, who as the head of a small, nonprofit corporation that she and two friends had founded, was dedicated to providing political activism and material help to the homeless of her mid-sized

Southern city. Her vocation was not an easy one, for the general attitude toward those who lived on the streets ranged from genteel disgust and indifference to outright hostility. Through hard work, social connections, and organizational creativity, Danielle and her partners had managed in the space of a few years to build an agency with enough credibility and effectiveness to apply successfully for grants from various government and private foundations.

The problem was, as is often the case, that success was harder to handle than failure. Their grants had become so numerous they found it difficult to keep track of them, and their part-time financial advisor was really not up to the task and knew it. Danielle and her two partners sat stymied one afternoon during their weekly managerial staff meeting, trying to figure out where they were going to get a financial manager familiar enough with nonprofits to do the job well on the modest salary they had for the position. The situation looked rather hopeless.

Just then, the phone rang in the small conference room where they were talking, even though the receptionist knew quite well they didn't take calls during such meetings. Slightly annoyed at the interruption, Danielle picked up the phone and, to her surprise, ended up speaking to an older woman who had been the financial manager for Goodwill Industries but who was now retired and recently widowed. The woman wanted to know, did they need anyone with her skills? Not much of a believer in synchronicities, Danielle found her skepticism punctured a bit when she met with the fortuitous volunteer and discovered that this woman was precisely the sort of person they needed. She arranged for a six-month trial period during which time she would attempt to find funding to make the job a permanent position, which is what eventually happened.

In Danielle's story, as in Matthew's, what was needed was given at the time when it was most useful, which leads me to think that perhaps fairy tales like Rumplestiltskin continue to delight us not because they provide us with a comforting fantasy of what life might be like but rather because they describe the stories of some of our lives as they actually are. So many of us, in one way or another, big and small, have actually had the Rumplestiltskin experience, so to speak. If we acknowledge the reality of synchronicity, that things come out of the blue and bring to our attention the story we are living, then the famous distinction between truth and fiction seems blurrier and even unfounded. Given the dramatic quality of synchronistic events such as Danielle's and Matthew's, it may well be that our fiction imitates our lives, and not vice versa.

Going, Going, Gone: Synchronicity and Leaving a Job

Getting a job can be a synchronistic event. Getting help to do the job well can also come through a meaningful coincidence. Likewise, stories of how jobs have ended center upon coincidences which either confirmed transitions people were unsure of, or in some cases even forced individuals into the transition out of the work they were doing.

My own experience of leaving three different jobs just before major reorganizations in the various companies remains for me, in my life story, a significant synchronistic pattern not simply because of the unusual repeated experience of getting out just in time but because of who I am. With a tendency to be loyal to a fault, I make a commitment and stick with it, sometimes to a point far beyond what is good for me or for those around me. Have three synchonistic experiences of the same sort taught me my lesson yet?

I was very happy at the first job, word processing at a consulting firm part-time while in graduate school, thanks to the flexibility of the hours, the stupendous pay for that time in my life, and the good friends I had made in my department. It was a place that I imagined I might be able to stay at and continue to earn good money full-time after graduation, as I accrued my internship hours toward eventual licensure as a therapist. I had been given every assurance that such a plan would be possible by both the head of the word processing department and by the overall head of the editorial staff. My performance reviews were consistently excellent, since I was more than a little overqualified for the work, and as I finished writing my thesis, I went ahead with plans to switch to a full-time schedule come summer.

Then, one day, I was called into the head editor's office and was rather abruptly told that there would be no way for me to work at forty hours a week in the near future. Other employees had asked for increased hours, and their requests would be given preference over mine. I was angry and disappointed, of course, mostly because I had imagined that my job at the firm would be long-term, a fantasy about this position that said more about me and my tendency to make long-term commitments than, obviously, the realities of the firm and its needs. Should I have been surprised that they decided to give other employees preference over me, who after all had made no secret about my real career objectives? Looking back, perhaps not, but still I was. Tired of not having enough money, tired of being a student working part-time, I reluctantly informed my boss that I would be leaving at the end of the semester. There was the requisite party in which I said goodbye to all the friends I had made, though the sadness was tempered a bit by my having by that time gotten a full-time position at another firm.

Two months later, I received a call from one of my former colleagues who told me that an audit at the consulting firm had uncovered all kinds of irregularities in the books. People were being let go left and right, and I had only narrowly missed participating in what was truly a horrendous situation. Indeed, some of the word processors were even being subpoenaed by the Justice Department for depositions concerning possible illegal activities on the premises! I don't know if there is anyone who would not feel a sense of relief at such news, narrowly missing having to participate in what certainly would have been quite a mess on the job, and so I counted myself lucky. But the luck of this incident didn't really begin to mean anything until the same situation happened again.

My new job, the second job, was for a small financial investment firm, where the full-time work during the day, at higher pay and with better benefits, complemented my nighttime and weekend work as an intern therapist. I spent six years with them. There was a feeling of family among the employees, and by the time I got my license and began my practice, I found myself once again very reluctant to leave the job. In fact, many of my friends expressed disbelief that as a licensed therapist, I was still working as a word processor, but again, my feelings of connection and loyalty to the people I worked with made it hard for me to quit. For a while, I reached a compromise of sorts, staving off the goodbye by arranging to reduce my hours to half-time, which gave me time to expand my practice but didn't force me to sever all connections.

Then, after hearing through a friend that an important mental-health clinic in the city was looking for an administrator for one of their programs, I applied for the position, without telling my bosses. To my surprise, despite my limited administrative experience in nonprofit agencies, I got the job. My leaving the firm was as sad as I anticipated. Still, I looked forward to working in the field I was trained for, rather than continuing to be clerical help.

Six months later, crisis struck this firm as well. Overextended in real-estate investments and credit during the boom of the 1980s, the company had to carry out a radical downsizing to save itself financially in the more austere economic climate of the 1990s. The resignation of two of the founding partners amidst all sorts of accusations and lawsuits took its toll and, forced to economize, the company moved clear out of town to a less expensive, inconvenient suburb. Once again, there was that feeling of being lucky, but this time it was beginning to sink in that my good fortune was just that—pure luck—for I had delayed leaving the firm for about as long as possible.

The coincidence of leaving two places of employment just in time to miss a crisis had slowly begun to make me re-evaluate the sentimental attachments I felt to the places I worked. Retrospectively, it had been a good thing to leave, but at the time my departures were difficult and were only undertaken because I felt I had no choice. All my feelings went in the opposite direction, urging me to stay put. The third time this happened drove home to me how problematic my tendency to put off terminations could potentially be.

After another six years of running what started as a small AIDS prevention program and which, through my efforts and those of like-minded colleagues, expanded over years in funding, services, and training, I was not quite as sentimentally attached to this agency as I was to my former places of employment, but again, it was a feeling of loyalty and commitment that kept me there at least for a year longer than I should have stayed. I told myself many things—that the work was important, that there were more things to do and to learn—but the truth was that my time at the agency had come to an end. This time the organizational issues which were to come to a head after I left were already in the air. In fact, much of my final year had been spent in discussions concerning a merger with another community agency. So at the end of a few projects I naturally felt beholden to see to completion, I gave my notice, enjoyed my going-away dinner, and took my leave. This time, though, it didn't take months for the crisis to hit. The very next week, I learned that the director of the agency had resigned, the newly designated director of the merged agency had whisked himself off for medical treatment never to return, and the place had been plunged into utter, organizational chaos.

So, three times I had narrowly avoided having to participate in ugly organizational wrangles, and for my good fortune I feel grateful. But the synchronistic element of this series of what, perhaps for someone else, would just be good timing lies in the way that these three experiences constitute the story of my working life, and specifically the way in which the coincidences brought to my attention how important it is sometimes to leave a job. This is not a lesson that I could have learned in any other way, being who I am, dedicated and committed, with a tendency toward too much attachment and a fondness for stability. In the coincidences of missing a crisis three times in a row, I perceive the story of a man who needs to stay open to the meaning inherent in ending something at the right time and for the right reasons, no matter how sad the process is, no matter how important the work and the relationships have been. These synchronicities revealed to me not the structure of reality but who I am more fully, to myself and to those who hear the story.

For another, more dramatic story of a synchronistic signal to leave a job, a colleague of mine named Val remembered a time when as a single mother she felt caught in her job, slaving away for a tyrannical boss at a considerable distance from her home because she so desperately needed the money and had so few marketable skills. Day after day, she dragged herself into the office, did what she was told, got her pay check, and kept her mouth shut. However, annoyance, then anger, then rage slowly built within her, making it harder and harder to get her body to the station, take the commuter train, then take orders from her obnoxious boss. The idea of leaving altogether, of course, crossed her mind about a thousand times a day, but given her circumstances, her lack of education, her financial needs, and her own hopelessness, it was not an idea that she felt was practical or even possible.

Then one day, standing on the train platform, in her usual funk about the coming day, Val felt an intense mixture of feelings—fury at her situation and an acute longing for just one day off, one day when she wouldn't have to face it all. "But it'd have to be something catastrophic for my boss to let me do something like that," she told me. "He wasn't the sort of person that calling in sick meant much to, he'd just make life that much more difficult for you when you came back, and it wasn't worth it. No, to get out of there would take something really unusual."

At which point, Val said, she heard a huge explosion, and far down the track she saw gigantic flames shooting up amidst a cloud of black smoke. Word came immediately to the platform. The engine of the train that she was just about to board, the train she took every day to work, had just blown up. Mesmerized by the sight, Val stood in awe as the emergency services overran the platform, firetrucks, helicopters, and ambulances arrived to handle an extraordinary and previously unheard-of disaster. For Val, though, the explosion was a symbol which told her: get out of her job or explode. She left the job immediately afterwards and did not look back, and she is now employed in a field where she is much happier. The symbolic aspects of a synchronistic event do not always hit us over the head so forcefully, but in Val's case, she was glad the message was unmistakable.

The Myth of Success and Failure: When a Door Closes, a Window Opens

If the timing involved in leaving a job voluntarily can be surrounded by synchronistic phenomena, either, as in my case, retrospectively understood, or as in Val's case, indicated by a powerful symbol, then leaving a job involuntarily—in other words, being fired—might well be one of those sorts of synchronistic events whose significance is only appreciated in hindsight. More than any other, this aspect of synchronicity, where apparent bad luck turns out to have a significance, brings to our awareness how much our life is like a story. Little did Bob Crachitt know, in Dickens's *A Christmas Carol*, what sort of transformation was in store for his relationship with his boss Ebenezer Scrooge on that dismal Christmas Eve when he had almost been fired. Thus, when understanding our lives as stories through the significance that random events may ultimately hold for us, we are enjoined to reconsider the whole question of what constitutes "success" and "failure." Conventional definitions of these terms get turned a bit on their head when we begin to see that it may be that there are no accidents.

Early in my career as a therapist, for example, I learned this lesson when, repeatedly, I would have a client "fire" me, so to speak, that is, abruptly break off treatment with me, often expressing dissatisfaction with the course of our work or with my abilities, only to get a call soon after from someone wanting to begin treatment and having only one time to come and meet with me: the hour just vacated by the client who left. The frequency with which this sort of coincidence has happened to me in the course of my practice is so great that, I confess, it is hard not to begin to think causally about such coincidences, as if some beneficent force in the universe was personally looking out for me and my client's schedules, as well as reassuring me as to the rightness of my own professional abilities. But without such a belief in some objective external agent who is causing such coincidences (an issue we will discuss in some length in Chapter 6), the plan I sense in these intricate scheduling maneuvers is the subjective story of my life as a therapist, my own sense of changing from thinking egotistically and concretely about success and failure to recognizing how "success" and "failure" are relative, not absolute. As with my experience of leaving my jobs, it is my own growth I am perceiving when the same situation occurs again and again, not some objective force teaching me a lesson for my own good.

This question of the relativity of failure and success is a very compelling one, I think, for the same reason that synchronicity's acausality is compelling, for both have to do with the role of our ego in our lives. It is not hard to perceive the insecure professional ego of a beginner at work in the definitions of "success" and "failure" I used to use—my ego's need to be reassured that I knew what I was doing, that I was competent, knowledgeable, and in control. Synchronistic events, meaningful coincidences, confronted my ego with its limited vision, for in the long run, things which initially looked bad eventually took on an entirely other significance.

Depending on how much people use their egos to organize their lives, synchronistic events will be transformative or, on the contrary, missed opportunities for greater insight. So, here again, we come upon yet another answer to the question, "How do I work with a synchronistic event?" which is: "Don't assume you know all the answers right now, once and for all. Today's setback may look quite different when the whole story unfolds."

Take the example of a former boss of mine, Marco, who had his heart set on buying what he considered a jewel of a restaurant in a very tony New Jersey suburb with the dream of expanding his Italian restaurant business. The negotiations went on and on, for a variety of reasons, some of which had to do with the bizarre character of the man who was selling the restaurant and some which were sheer, random unavoidable delays. Anxious to remodel, redecorate, hire and train a staff, publicize, and all the other hundreds of things necessary to launch a new restaurant successfully, Marco's frustration grew in proportion to the time wasted in the seemingly endless wrangling. One point would be resolved, and another would emerge; they would resolve the next point, and then something else would come up.

Marco's own typically Italian personality suited him perfectly as an entrepreneur. He was by nature an extroverted person with lots of energy, very invested in his own power to make things happen, and completely comfortable with his ego being squarely in the driver's seat. So when his wife suggested to him, along the way, that perhaps he should reconsider the whole business—in her words, "this new place is jinxed"— nearly a year of unremitting difficulties had to go by before he began to seriously wonder if she might not be right. But then finally, a closing date was set for the sale, a turn of events which had thus far eluded them, and Marco was thrilled that his dream, costly as it was in time, energy, and mental health, would finally be realized.

His happiness lasted until the following week when he was informed abruptly that the previous owner was going to keep the restaurant after all, having gotten the sense from Marco's eagerness to acquire it that it might well be a gold mine. As Marco tells the story, at this point he experienced a state of rage beyond words. A year of battles had ended up in nothing, a prime restaurant had slipped through his fingers, and, worse, for his male ego, his wife had been right.

The closing date came and went, a day Marco spent gnashing his teeth, furious over what should have been. Then, one day soon after, he got a call from his real-estate agent. It seemed that the owner of the restaurant had just been informed by the state office of environmental protection that his license to own and operate a restaurant was under review. They had received reports that the restaurant was the site of a former dry-cleaning establishment, and they would need to close the business for a considerable period of time, well over a year, to ensure that toxic waste had been handled properly, a process that might actually entail razing the building itself. Only then did Marco realize what a stroke of luck his "failure" had been. If he had "succeeded" in buying the restaurant, it would have meant his financial ruin.

As one might imagine, Marco is not an overly psychological sort of person, so when I asked him what he thought the meaning of this synchronistic event was, he merely laughed, I think to distract me from the humble attitude he had had to take, an attitude that did not come easily. "The game's not over till the fat lady sings," he said, which is a more colorful way of saying that all is not necessarily what it seems at first blush and that the significance of what occurs to us may only be obvious later on.

Though I held my tongue at the time I was talking to him, I could not help but think to myself about the symbolism of this synchronistic event, wishing that Marco might be able to see and learn from how his own dreams, and his furious desire to build an empire with himself at the top, might well be hiding a toxic dump beneath, literally, certainly, but metaphorically and emotionally as well. Knowing his own background, as a second-generation Italian-American from a tough working-class environment, I wondered if lingering feelings of inferiority, anger at a lack of family support, and frustration at never seeming to have enough might not be the toxic waste upon which his ambitions rested.

What turned an apparent failure into a bit of good fortune, as it always is in an effective and satisfying story, was the timing. Something that "should" have taken less time was inordinately delayed, but it was the very delay that led to the fortunate outcomes. Like in the stories on love and romance in Chapter 2, these stories concerning work demonstrate how when things do not conform to our plans or schedule, the result can be fortuitous rather than disastrous—a point to remember when we are next faced with a situation, a problem, or an opportunity that seems to be going poorly.

The phrase that Jung often used to describe the effect of such synchronistic events on us is that they serve to "relativize the ego," that is, they tame our own desires to be master of all and lead us to see things from a larger perspective. The illustration of our being caught on a mountain during a storm, only to climb a bit higher and out of the storm so that we might look down on it rather than be caught in it, is a perfect analogy to describe how it is when we are able to acknowledge the relativity of our egos. It is not that the unfortunate event itself changes—the storm still rages on, Marco's acquisition still fell through, Sam still lost his job, Gail had to leave her doctoral program—but its meaning changes due to the change in our own perspective over time. We look back on our stories and finally see the ultimate importance of what occurred, rather than what at the time seemed, to our egos, simply a crushing blow or another defeat.

If synchronistic events demonstrate to some of us that a failure might be good luck in disguise, they also sometimes demonstrate that the converse is equally true: what we celebrate today as success might well turn out synchronistically to have an entirely other significance.

A sad story told to me by Larry, who has spent his professional career working in group homes for developmentally disabled and emotionally disturbed young adults, recalled a particular resident in one of his homes who evinced a strong fear of escalators. Even though such a phobia did not to any degree interfere with this young woman's life, since escalators could easily be avoided, the counselors in the home took on the challenge of desensitizing the resident with all the gusto of professional helpers, slowly working with her to overcome her fear to the point where, after some time, they managed to take her to the local mall and have her get on an escalator alone.

By tragic coincidence, at this very moment, a young child leaning over the railing on the floor above lost his footing and fell directly upon the phobic young woman. The good news was her presence beneath him broke his fall and undoubtedly saved the young child's life; the bad news was the young woman left the experience far more trauma-tized than before.

Now Larry, who told me this story, had drawn a number of conclusions about what this meant, to him at least, though, like Marco, the conclusions seemed to be more implicit than explicit. "You never know," was his final statement on the event, which of course is a very simple way to say something quite profound about the limited nature of our ego-consciousness. You never know when helping some-one may be doing the exact opposite, Larry seemed to be saying, and you never know when what you thought you were doing may have consequences far beyond what you intended. A helper by profession, Larry had a touch of rueful humility in his voice as Marco did when he reflected on his own unexpected reversal of fortune.

"You never know" is another answer to the question, "What sort of attitude should I use to look at synchronistic events?" An attitude of "you never know" certainly seems indicated by these stories drawn from people's experiences in their work lives and professions, areas of our lives where unfortunately our egos can be especially active, and where notions of success and failure, rather than the relativity of all our actions, determine much of what we do.

Why Do We Work? The Meaningful Coincidence of Our Livelihood

I invite the readers of this book to carry out an experiment of your own with regard to people's work lives. Ask ten people the question, "Why do you work?" as I did in the course of my work on this chapter and see if you get the same answers I did.

When I asked that question, I got variations on two basic re-sponses. The most common answer people gave me was put most imaginatively by a friend who immediately said, "Because I like to eat," his wry way of saying, in a word: money. However, a minority of people responded just as quickly but quite differently with, "I love what I do."

If we examine these two motivations for work more closely, keeping in mind the many stories we have heard about synchronicities in people's work lives, we realize that in the best of circumstances, the work we do is most satisfying when these two responses coincide, when we do something that we love which is also able to provide for our material well-being. Here the difference between a job and a vocation is germane. A job may well take care of our material needs but does not necessarily entail our doing something we love. On the other hand, a vocation is an activity we pursue for reasons that may or may not take care of our material needs but which most certainly attend to the nonmaterial aspirations we have as human beings: our need to feel useful and make a contribution, perhaps, or to embody and promote a set of core values or beliefs.

Can people be content to work at a job simply to earn money? Indeed, they can. But I happen to know that many of the people who answered my question by saying, "I work for the money," do their work because they like what they do. Or alternately, even if they are not all that thrilled with the content of their job, they are nevertheless happy in those jobs, because the money they earn helps them fulfill nonmaterial needs they have. The man who runs the cappuccino stand around the corner from my office is happy making coffee because he is providing for his family. The security guard at the place I used to work does her job because, according to her, she needs to; but the economic security the job provides gives her a social status that she did not have before, which is why she is content to answer the phones and receive visitors. My ex-boss Marco would say that he runs his restaurant because "it's a living," but it is very clear to me from the way he goes about his job that it is far more than just a job.

If you are happy in your job, in all probability it's a coincidence, in the sense that your need for a material livelihood coincides with a nonmaterial value you hold dearly. But what of those people involved in a vocation which does not reliably provide for their material needs? Can they be happy? Of course they can. But when you examine their lives more closely, you will find that many of these people also work to earn a living. While Elise and Matthew auditioned in search of a lucky break to fulfill their artistic aspirations, they waited tables and did telephone marketing. During the years I pursued my own professional training, I typed reports, took messages, and cleaned out the office refrigerator on Friday afternoons. So behind the happiness of even high-minded souls is the same coincidence: a material livelihood of some sort which supports their dedication to nonmaterial aspirations.

When we are unhappy in our work lives, therefore, I believe it is probably because one side of this coincidence is being ignored in favor of the other. Can we do something consciously about this situation, when we, like Val, hate our job because it provides nothing for our soul or when, like Stephen, we find ourselves at odds with our vocation because of pressing material needs? Of course we can. We can see vocational counselors, network with friends, put ads in the paper, respond to ads in the paper, and in general mobilize our resources to either increase our income or become clearer about what sort of job would be more emotionally or symbolically rewarding.

But, as these stories show us, sometimes it is a random event which puts the material and nonmaterial aspects of our work lives together for us, in the sort of event we are calling synchronistic. Sometimes the coincidence creates an internal shift. Patty, for example, did not need to leave her software firm; reinforced by the wisdom of a fortune cookie, she changed her attitude about being a manager. Elise's mistake in appointment times resulted in a synchronistic shift in her perspective about herself and her talents. I myself needed to take a look at my emotional attachments to the various places of employment, and yet it took the freak repetition of the same situation three times in a row for me over the course of fifteen years to become more inwardly discriminating about what I committed myself to and why.

Frequently, though, in our work lives, the transition a synchronistic event helps us to make is external in nature. Tony's friend from Los Angeles needed to find another job, even if on the basis of a hunch she had to search for it through a pile of papers on a bulletin board. Danielle needed to hire a financial director for her nonprofit organization, and a telephone call put through to her at the wrong time provided the director she needed. Val needed to give notice, a fact that became amply clear when the situation literally and symbolically exploded before her.

In all these stories of synchronicities, what is characteristic is that the synchronistic event brought together the material and immaterial aspects of people's work lives and created a coincidence between their jobs and their vocations, between the material need to earn money and the immaterial aspirations they had for themselves as human beings. Not that this union of objective needs and subjective meaning does not happen consciously for many people, for it does. But these stories demonstrate that our ego may need not *always* be the sole source of growth in our lives.

As we live out the stories of our work lives, we may be tempted to rely almost exclusively on our own ability to control and manage events, people, and objects. This is the story that those who responded "Money" to my question think they are living. Moreover, in a capitalist society such as ours, we are encouraged to think of ourselves in materialistic terms. In a manner of speaking, we are given a script in which we are agents of productivity.

That synchronistic events do in fact occur is a message that can relieve, hearten, and inspire us. We have now heard from people how the potentially creative aspect of their work emerged only when they managed to lay aside their own agendas and permitted randomness to have a place in the story of their livelihood. We have also heard that changing the external circumstances of our lives may well involve following the subjective movements of our hearts and minds—our intuitions, hunches, feelings, and ideals. If any attitude is going to "create" a synchronistic event and provide for a happy ending in the story of our careers, it will be one which balances the material and the nonmaterial aspects of why we work, making what we do in our lives a conscious profession of who we are and what is important.

Chapter Four

An Inner Tale

Synchronicity and
Our Dream Lives

The poet and the dreamer are distinct,
Diverse, sheer opposite, antipodes,
One pours out a balm upon the world,
The other vexes it.

JOHN KEATS, "The Fall of Hyperion"

Those who have likened our life to a dream were
more right, by chance, than they realized.
We are awake sleeping,
and sleep awake.

MONTAIGNE, *Essays*

Dreams, to use Keats's words, vex and dis-
turb our daylight world. Even the most obstinately rational people will
at some point in their lives remember a dream, be awakened by a
nightmare, or spend the day bedeviled by an image, feeling, or situation which came to them in their sleep. In the synchronicities recounted thus far, in the love stories and work histories of people's
lives, the meaningful coincidence took place when an external occurrence—a meeting, an unusual series of similarities between people or
events, a fortuitous phone call, an unexpected job offer, an accident

like an explosion or a shooting—coincided significantly with the inner state of an individual in the immediate moment or in the course of an individual's story. The direction, so to speak, of these synchronicities so far has been from "outside in": an extraordinary outer event had or came to have an emotional and symbolic significance inwardly.

With this chapter we move to synchronicities that go in the opposite direction, from the inside out, when an inner event occurs that, by sheer happenstance, coincides with an outer circumstance in a way that is important and transformative. Now of course the whole point of synchronicity is that the distinction between "inner" and "outer" may not be quite as rigid as we generally assume, so perhaps it is important to be as clear as possible on this point: that the difference we are generally denoting by using the words "inner" and "outer" has to do with the participation of others in our experiences.

In what we are calling "outer" events, people and objects other than ourselves are involved in ways that others can observe. When a train explodes in front of me or when I bump into someone in a hotel in the middle of a desert, it is an experience that is shared between me and other people. In the stories we read, this level of what occurs to the characters constitutes what is generally called the plot line: this happened and this happened and then this other thing happened. "Inner" events, on the other hand, occur only to one person, and in the stories we read, as well as the stories we live, this level of experience is what most people would call "character": who the protagonist is as a person, what they feel and think, what their personal hopes, dreams, and conflicts consist of.

The wonder of the synchronicities in this chapter lies in the way that chance occurrences in the outer world follow significantly upon a particular manifestation of someone's inner life in the form of a dream. The dream-related synchronicities in the stories that follow deepen our understanding of the stories we live by showing us how the plot of our lives lies not just in the external events we live—the entertaining stories of adventure, romance, and intrigue—but in the inner tale of who we are. As in a modern novel, where the plot *is* the character, where the events of the story occur in the inner life of the protagonist, it is the subjective life of our soul that will be the focus in the stories to come.

Our dreams have lives of their own, and more than perhaps any other phenomenon of our inner lives, are utterly private, unique, and subjective. We can share a feeling with an empathic person. We may share an aspiration, hope, or vision with a like-minded person. But only we see, feel, hear, and live our dreams. Regardless of how detailed our descriptions of them are, only we experience the red chair, the smell of our grandmother's cookies, or being late for an examination. The absolute privacy of our dream life is what can be so "vexing," particularly for people whose personalities, histories, and habits lead them to value the "outer" much more than the "inner."

In this private realm, in the life of our soul, we have our own unique way of being, our own special language, our own perspectives and reactions. The liveliness of this inner world is what Montaigne refers to in the quote I have used above, when he notices how we are "awake" when we sleep. Who hasn't had the experience of waking up in the morning feeling drained and exhausted from a hard night of active dreams, frightening nightmares, bothersome, semiconscious anxieties in disturbing shapes and forms and fantasies? Although a quip, Montaigne's observation—that sometimes we are more asleep when awake than we are when we sleep—rings true. A part of us is very much awake when we sleep, and our dreams are proof of it.

Because our inner lives are so completely individual, ours and no one else's, it sometimes seems to me that the psyche could be likened to an island once connected with a larger continent but now isolated. As happens literally in such cases, the plants, animals, and environment of such a place begin to develop their own particularities and rhythms, their own special colors and shapes. Not that the plants and animals of such places have absolutely no resemblance to others—the flora and fauna of a place like, say, Australia have obvious connections to those found elsewhere, and the bearish koala or the rabbity kangaroo are demonstrations of such connections. But there is a different and unique way of doing things in such places. This is the case with our dreams, and it accounts in large measure for the strangeness of our dreams when compared to the daylight world of outer reality.

Given all this, one may well ask what is the purpose of our dreams? What role do they play? While the answer to that question is as varied as the psychologies and philosophies of the world, I find the answer suggested by the results of modern dream research among the most useful.

A number of scientists have recently experimented to discover what animals dream. Anyone with a pet has undoubtedly been intrigued by its quivering paws, heavy grunts, and its unconscious movements while asleep, but only in the last decades have researchers set out to determine what is actually occurring within these animals' brains. By monitoring the brain waves that occur during certain waking activities and while dreaming, scientists have conjectured, on the basis of similarities and differences in brain wave patterns, that animals most likely dream about species-specific survival behaviors, storing and consolidating the memories of waking experiences: cats hunt, rabbits monitor their surroundings, rats explore.[1]

Extrapolating from this research, we might assume that the purpose of the dream in human beings is similar: human beings dream about species-specific survival behaviors, either as practice for confronting situations in outer life or to bring to our consciousness information about ourselves and our environment that is vital for our survival and growth. Because, unlike other mammals, human beings are self-aware, much of the information to which our dreams may be bringing our attention could also be about our inner environment, providing for our emotional growth and health, our spiritual development, or other aspects of our subjective experiences, which are arguably as crucial to our survival as our physical well-being.

Our dreams may well be in charge of the care of our soul, telling us a nightly story, in symbols, of who we are. In this way, we can make sense of what we live day to day. Modern depth psychology presumes, along with dream interpreters from every other culture, period, and religious orientation, that dreams are meaningful, and indeed, the idea that a dream is a text—a story with a narrative structure and purpose— is among the most important contributions psychology has made to human self-understanding.

Are Prophetic Dreams Synchronistic?
Are Synchronistic Dreams Predictive?
Are Psychic or Extrasensory Dreams Prophetic?

Since long before modern psychology, people have held that our dreams, however odd or upsetting, had a significance that wisdom and insight could help us understand. This attitude toward the dream, demonstrated by the myths, tales, and rituals of cultures worldwide and throughout all time, is an acknowledgment that all human beings are, in a manner of speaking, bi-lingual. We speak the language of outer reality, the language others hear and understand, while at the same time we possess our own private, inner language, a language that we ourselves need to listen to in a particular way to comprehend fully. This language, the language of dreams, has always been understood as symbolic in nature. One does not really need to go too far afield to demonstrate that modern psychology has simply espoused a way of looking at dreams that existed long before Freud's *Interpretation of Dreams.*

In Genesis, for example, the first book of the Bible, much is made of Joseph's ability to interpret dreams, both his and others, and the plot of his life story hinges on this ability. At the beginning of his story, Joseph dreams two dreams which in the course of his life come true: while binding sheaves of wheat in the field with his eleven brothers, their sheaves bow down to his, just as, in another dream, Joseph sees the sun, moon, and eleven stars bowing down to him. What his father and brothers make of these dreams—seeing Joseph's exaltation over them in these symbols—is as clear as their jealousy and disgruntlement.

But, as we have already seen, our egos are not always completely in control of events, and in seeking to rid themselves of their gifted brother by selling him as a slave to the Midianites, Joseph's siblings end up unintentionally placing him in a position where yet another pair of dreams brings him, through a coincidence, to the attention of the ruler of all Egypt, the Pharaoh. Imprisoned by sheer chance with the Pharaoh's butler and baker, Joseph hears these two men's dreams—the butler's of a vine with three branches sprouting grapes that he squeezes into the Pharaoh's wine goblet, the baker's of carrying three baskets on his head with birds eating out of the top one. Joseph interprets these dream symbols accurately: that in three days time the butler will be restored to Pharaoh's favor while the baker will be beheaded and hung from a tree for the birds to eat. Years later, the butler, now in Pharaoh's favor, remembers Joseph. The Pharaoh has had two disturbing dreams that baffle and worry him, a dream of "seven cows sleek and fat" beside "seven cows gaunt and thin," and a second dream of "seven ears of grain, plump and good" sprouting on a stalk followed by "seven ears, thin and blighted."

In hearing from his butler of the young Hebrew who from a

dream accurately predicted the butler's restoration to favor, the Pharaoh orders Joseph to be brought to him, but unlike Joseph's father and brothers, the Pharaoh does not resist the events foretold by the dreams. When Joseph tells the Pharaoh that the symbols of his dream indicate seven years of plenty to be followed by seven years of famine, the Pharaoh prepares for the lean times by storing up grain during the time of abundance. Joseph is made governor over the land, fulfilling his rise to prominence predicted long before in the dreams of the sheaves of wheat and the sun, moon, and stars.

This Biblical story, written down for the first time about three thousand years ago though undoubtedly much older than that, can be regarded from a variety of perspectives. For the author of this story, who is telling this tale as part of the sacred history of a people, the point of Joseph's story is to illustrate Joseph's prophetic powers, the wisdom he has been granted as someone chosen by God for a unique purpose in history. After we acknowledge the religious intention of the author, however, we may also notice that this passage in Genesis is indeed relevant to the subject of synchronicity and dream life. Joseph's brothers, the butler, the baker, and the Pharaoh himself all have dreams that come true, dreams whose symbolism has significant parallels to the subsequent external events of the story. To use the modern term, we would describe these situations as synchronistic for these individuals—an unusual chance occurrence in the external world which parallels a subjective state in a way that is significant emotionally and symbolically. Hence, Joseph's story is evidence that, while synchronicity may be a modern concept, it is by no means an exclusively modern experience.

Not all dreams are synchronistic, obviously. Many, if not most of our dreams, are about circumstances that have never occurred and indeed could never occur in the outer world. Our dreams are populated by people who do not exist in reality. In our dreams we have abilities that we do not actually have: to fly, to leap tall buildings in a single bound, to shrink to the size of a pea. Every once in a while, though, we do dream of an event that does occur in reality, either because the dream showed us this event literally or, as in Joseph's story, symbolically. This sort of dream we will be calling synchronistic, a dream in which the inner tale is told before the identical outer story occurs.

Now this phenomenon, as evidenced by Joseph's story in Genesis, has gone by many names over the ages—prophetic, extrasensory, predictive, psychic. What is important to understand is that these terms are not purely descriptive, but in fact they all indicate a certain understanding of the purpose of the synchronistic dream. To call such a coincidence of inner image and outer occurrence "prophetic" is to call attention to the religious nature of its meaning, as the author of Genesis does in order to illustrate his belief in Joseph's holiness and to narrate an important way that he understood God's action in the history of the world. To call such a dream "extrasensory" is again not a simple description but has implicit in it a statement of causality, ascribing the coincidence of dream and event to an ability to perceive reality not accounted for by our ordinary five senses. To call such a coincidence "predictive" or "psychic" is to work from an assumption that the future has an objective reality of which certain people in certain circumstances are granted a vision, as if they were fast-forwarding a video tape or flipping to the back of a mystery novel to read the ending. The terms "predictive" or "psychic" are statements of causality: the putative objective future existence of an event *caused* our vision of it in the present retroactively.

In all of these terms, though, there is an assumption of a *causal* connection between dream image and the subsequent external event. The dream's objective future existence or its occurrence in another dimension *causes* us to see it in a dream through some sort of extraordinary sense or ability. Or, from a religious perspective, God, in His omniscience, may grant us the ability to prophesy, lending us His knowledge of the future for His purposes in the world. Naturally enough, from the perspective of our ego, it is hard *not* to view things causally when an inner vision subsequently comes true.

But, as we already know, Jung's notion of synchronicity concerning such dreams takes a completely different approach to the experience. Rather than applying an objective causal explanation—that the event retrospectively *caused* our dream—it emphasizes that the significance of a coincidence between a dream image and subsequent external event lies in the *subjective meaning* we experience in the event, in its emotional effect, or, as I have been arguing, in the part it plays in the story of our lives. It is from this *acausal* perspective that we will be examining the dreams that follow, from the perspective of the *inner* meaning of the coincidence, its significance *to us*.

Jung, in fact, specifically developed his idea of synchronicity as an *acausal* connecting principle in order to be able to discuss the phenomenon of meaningful coincidences—a universal experience among humans—in a purely descriptive way without obliging himself to make metaphysical statements on the nature and structure of the universe, a theological and philosophical task he considered beyond the purview of an empirical psychology. Even if we do not share the author's perspective on Joseph's role as a prophet, or even if we do, the fact remains that synchronistic dreams—dreams which parallel external events in a significant way—play, and have always played, a part in many people's life stories.

Why all questions of terminology are important, and precisely why I believe limiting oneself to describing such coincidences as synchronistic rather than predictive, extrasensory, or prophetic is a more careful, and ultimately more useful, approach to such events is perhaps best illustrated with a real-life example. The story of a client I will call William will serve well to make my point.

William woke up panicked and anxious one morning after a vivid dream in which his mother was driving along a winding coast road very fast and very dangerously, in the family car remembered from his childhood. He and his mother had never really gotten along very well, and indeed, much of my work as a counselor with him dealt with that relationship. Tragically, the week after this dream, William's mother did in fact die by driving her car off the road and into a ravine, circumstances as likely to be accidental as intentionally suicidal on her part.

This coincidence between a previous dream and subsequent event was certainly synchronistic, in that its emotional impact and its significance to William's life was undeniable. But was it predictive, prophetic, or extrasensory? To say that it was, is to say, in essence, that William's dream had given him knowledge that such an event would occur, is a statement that obviously can only be made after the fact. But at the time of William's dream, he had no knowledge of any such event, because no such event had occurred. William had no sense of himself as a prophet, or of his dream as prophetic. And without such a perspective, the most we are able to observe is that a dream and a subsequent event are strikingly similar and incredibly meaningful.

To see William's dream in any other way than as an acausal, significant coincidence might prompt some people, William himself, perhaps, to assign a certain measure of responsibility to William in her death. Given the knowledge in his dream, which from a "predictive" or "extrasensory" perspective has been made equivalent to perceptions through normal sensory means, he should have warned his mother, or worse still, without an acausal perspective which would acknowledge the completely random nature of the parallel between his dream and the subsequent accident, William might actually have begun to believe that somehow his hostility toward his mother and their poor relationship were somehow responsible for her death, that his ill feelings and wishes had "caused" her fatal accident. It was *his* dream after all, wasn't it?

At times after his mother's death, William indeed felt both of these things, which only demonstrates how hard it is to let go of cause-and-effect ways of thinking that flatter our ego, even when they cause us unnecessary suffering. Because dreams are wholly private and personal, the temptation to think that we are in charge of the reality they depict is strong, especially since dreams can have a ring of truth to them. So it took some work for me to help William see that the coincidence of the dream of his mother's death was, indeed, precisely that—a coincidence, an unusual external event, over which he had no control.

A dream can be synchronistic *after* the fact, however meaningful it might feel at the time. In this case, the significance of the coincidence lay in the way the dream had, before his mother's death, heightened William's feeling of connectedness to his mother, despite an estrangement of many years, and in a different way it even served to prepare him for the eventuality of her death, by presenting it in the dream.

In examining the purpose and nature of dreams, particularly synchronistic dreams, what is especially important to remember is that dreams use a *symbolic* language of images. In Joseph's story, the stars he dreamed of did not, subsequently, literally bow down, nor did three specific vines bloom, or seven specific cows waste away. The dreams Joseph interpreted used *symbols* of situations which subsequently had meaningful parallels in reality. Which is to say that the synchronistic nature of certain dreams may not always reside in a literal dream image that subsequently occurs in external reality, but may find its parallel in a significant symbolic connection between inner image and outer event. For example, if the day after his dream Wiliam himself had been forced through circumstances beyond his control to drive his own car off the side of the road, the parallel between the dream and the subsequent external event would still be significant, only now the synchronistic meaning of the coincidence would lie more clearly within the symbolism of the dream—what it meant to him to find himself in an external situation framed symbolically as one in which his mother found herself. In this case, the temptation to assign an objective cause to the dream would be considerably less.

In conclusion, to look at dreams through the lens of synchronicity is always to examine the *subjective* meaning of a coincidence between a symbolic, imaginative, inner world and a specific, concrete outer event: what we make of such coincidences, what they mean to us in the narrative of our lives. Through synchronistic dreams, we are shown aspects of our stories, portions of our character, that perhaps some of us have not fully appreciated, ways in which the inner plot of our souls have fundamental connections with the world around us.

What Will Be Will Be: "Predictive" Dreams

William's synchronistic dream of his mother's death was dramatic and sad, but it is comforting to know that the coincidence of inner image and subsequent outer event in other synchronistic dreams does not have to be either spectacular, devastating, or even as externally dramatic. Val, whose story about how her unhappiness on the job coincided with the explosion of the train was told in the last chapter, had a different experience of a synchronistic dream, humble in content and simple in effect, but memorable and important for her.

Val's dream occurred at a point in her life that predated even her hardships with her tyrannical boss. At this earlier time, she was, as she put it, "a poor mom on welfare, struggling to get by" but inwardly she was struggling with an extreme poverty of self-esteem as well, feeling herself too stupid to get ahead, not good enough to make it, not smart enough to figure out a way to a more comfortable life. Then she dreamed the following dream:

I was in a large bed in a large room, and felt very strongly that I shouldn't be there. But around the bed were lying various people, all around the bed in such a way that I couldn't figure out how to get out of this bed without stepping on them. Unable to figure this out and pondering the situation, it hit me that the reason I needed to get out of the bed was because this was the Dalai Lama's bed, which only increased my feeling of urgency. Then, the Dalai Lama himself came into the room and, seeing me in his bed, did nothing but look at me compassionately. At this point, a statement came to me in the dream: "Whoever is in the Dalai Lama's bed belongs in the Dalai Lama's bed." The dream ended, without any resolution other than this.

Val awoke from the dream puzzled, with a strange feeling that all would work out for her, and that she was where she needed to be in her life. At that point, she told me, whatever reassurance she felt from the dream did not come from knowing who or what the Dalai Lama was, besides having heard his name and having some vague sense of him as a religious figure. That was, until the night following the dream, when she saw that, in fact, the Dalai Lama had come to town to visit his followers and to teach. Stunned that she could have "predicted" his visit, she sat up and took even more serious notice of what the message of the dream seemed to be.

One does not have to resort to theories of retrospective causality to explain why Val dreamed about the visit of the Tibetan holy man without consciously knowing about his visit. The modern theory of the unconscious allows us a rational, rather than a mystical or metaphysical, explanation in the idea that it could have been a case of subliminal perception on Val's part: she had seen an announcement of the visit in a newspaper or on the news and had forgotten about it, or perhaps someone had mentioned his visit in passing, in a conversation she had overheard but hadn't paid attention to. Yet, her perception remained unconscious, that is, until the unconscious presented it to her in the form of the dream.

However, any theory of causality does not address the significance of this "predictive" dream for Val, which lay quite apart from any cause-and-effect explanations. Her subsequent realization of who the Dalai Lama was and what he stood for was at the core of how the dream affected her, coming to Val at a time when she was feeling considerably less than exalted herself, uncomfortable in her situation and unable to find her way out.

In discussing the dream with her, I suggested to Val, knowing her as a clinician particularly good at working with individuals who found themselves "down and out," that perhaps her own experience of hardship might have been a holy bed of sorts, the place from which her subsequent strength and ability to help people came from. But while the dream itself makes this point symbolically, only the outer event, she said to me in response, really made her appreciate what she was going through then. "It was really amazing to see what I had dreamed come to life that night and know that I had a connection to it, without even knowing it. To feel that I was supposed to be in the Dalai Lama's bed, that I belonged there, that it was okay, was very hopeful."

Though our attention cannot help but be drawn to a synchronistic dream like William's, I have presented Val's dream here to make clear that very often the synchronistic occurrences in our lives, especially in our inner lives, have a simple, day-to-day quality to them, without the high drama and extreme improbabilities of many of the stories I have presented thus far. Dreams are ordinary occurrences, and so synchronistic occurrences around dreams very frequently have an ordinary, but no less important, feel to them.

Indeed, the very everyday quality of some of my own synchronistic dreams has at times lulled me into a lack of appreciation of their meaning for me in the course of my life story. An incident from my days as a counseling intern stands out, involving a young woman with whom I had a very stormy counseling relationship.

Coming from a difficult background, as an only child of parents who were intermittently indulgent and neglectful, this client whom I shall call Grace had a very hard time with relationships and with her own feelings of self-esteem, first idealizing someone, usually an older man, and seeking to merge with him to feel better about herself, only soon to feel lost in the relationship, which would then lead her to end it quickly and ruthlessly so as to preserve her sense of independence. These break-ups, although initiated by her, always led her to feel even more alone than before, and the cycle would begin all over again.

In that Grace did this throughout her teenage and young adult years, the fact that she attempted to live out the same pattern with me, even while entering counseling to understand and change it, was not a source of wonderment. The only difference with me was that when she got the feeling of being engulfed, I managed to make a case for her staying in the counseling relationship which she did for a good solid year, only attacking me every now and then in the relationship to gain distance from me. Naturally, under such circumstances, the relationship she and I had was tumultuous, but, fortunately, far less so than her self-destructive romances.

After many go-rounds of this cycle, Grace terminated counseling abruptly one day, using other commitments as the reason she no longer had the time, energy, or money to continue our work together. I urged her to stay, reiterated that my door was always open, and regretfully saw her go. Months went by, and reassured by my supervisor that her leaving counseling was not necessarily a sign of my incompetence as a counselor but might actually be something she needed to do as a part of her growth, I had a dream of her one night, the first dream that I had ever had of a counseling client.

In the dream, I saw Grace come through the door of the room we generally met in, sit down calmly, and warmly say to me that she was ready to begin again, that she had thought over what had happened between us, wanted to apologize for treating me badly, and was actually grateful that I had stuck with her through the ups and downs of her feelings. The dream felt so natural and lifelike that I didn't even think to mention it to my supervisor, assuming that I was somehow unconsciously trying to make myself feel better for not having been a "good enough" counselor to her and attempting to continue "treating" her in my dreams.

The next week, though, I realized that perhaps more was going on than I was privy to, for Grace had called the agency to schedule an appointment with me, and when she arrived, it was just as it had been in my dream. She was calm and centered, without any of the bristling animosity or neediness that she had always brought to her relationships. She told me that she had gotten a great deal out of our relationship over the year and that my consistency had helped her join a spiritual community by showing her that others could be truthful and committed to her well-being. Since she felt that part of her growth consisted of reviewing her own life and taking responsibility for her behavior, she wanted to come back at least once to tell me that she felt bad for having been so difficult.

At the time, I was stunned at how accurately my own dream had "predicted" the circumstances which eventually came to pass, but now, looking back, of course, the dream's unique meaning to me was attendant upon the fact that the event had actually, coincidentally, occurred. Had the flow of chance events not mirrored my dream back to me in this coincidence, had this client not come back to talk to me a week later, my dream would have been one of many in which the symbolism—what this client meant to me—would have remained strictly subjective.

The synchronistic quality of the event lay in the way the random external event happened at a time so close to the internal image, and this forced me to bring my subjective feelings about this woman into the objective relationship I had with her: the meaning of the synchronicity for me and my professional development was to see that the therapy relationships I had with my clients were in fact *real* relationships, not just artificial constructions or services provided for hire. I realized that I cared about them—they existed for me subjectively—just as they felt genuinely, deeply, connected to me, deeply enough to return for resolution in actual fact, and not just in my dreams. That my first dream of a client should be so synchronistic is still a source of wonder to me.

To see this dream as "predictive" rather than synchronistic is to understand the event in a wholly different, and much less subjective, fashion. If a dream of mine is able to predict the future, then I must certainly be endowed with rather special abilities. It would be these special abilities of mine—my clairvoyance, my psychic talents, my chosenness by God—and not the symbolic subjectiveness of the outer event which would take center stage, a shift in emphasis which, for almost anyone's ego, exerts quite an attraction. To see this dream as predictive would also mean that at times the normal chain of cause and effect, in which present events occur as reactions to past events, is reversed for unknown and indeterminable reasons, so that events yet to occur in the future retroactively cause present events, such as predictive dreams.

Perhaps because I myself struggle so much with my own ego, tempted myself to believe some of the flattering ways such events could be understood, Jung's notion of synchronicity is attractive to me as an exercise in caution, based as it is on what is known rather than what we may speculate to be true. By the same token, to know that some people come upon such appreciation for the synchronistic nature of their dreams quite naturally and without any training except their own experience is gratifying.

Marie, an acquaintance of mine for a number of years, shared with me her own experience of a dream she had following the birth of her son. She and her husband had a number of problems conceiving, trying for some years with little success, thus making infertility an issue around which her life revolved. After her son was born, the family's economic situation required Marie to continue her work as a nurse, even though she felt the need for a change.

Marie had always looked inward for guidance, and she went to bed one night asking to receive some insight concerning her dilemma. If Marie were a different person, she could easily have dismissed the dream she had that night: she dreamed she went to the infertility clinic that she had so often visited as a client, only this time, in her dream, she was going there to work.

Upon waking up and remembering her dream vividly, Marie didn't dare dismiss the possibility that it might have a synchronistic meaning, especially since she had prepared herself before sleeping that night to be open to whatever answer presented itself. Instead, she immediately called the clinic. The receptionist recognized her name, of course, and, a bit puzzled at why she was calling, asked Marie hesitantly if she wanted an appointment. Marie told her that she wasn't looking for an appointment. The baby was fine, she said but added that she was calling to see if there were any job openings, since she was looking for a job.

The receptionist said that in fact just that day she had gotten notice of a school nurse position. Would Marie want the information on that job? Marie said yes and followed up on this lead, getting this job and the change in career focus that she had been wanting to make for some time since the birth of her son. As Marie puts it herself, "It's the perfect job for me. I'm working with school-age kids, so everything I do in my job applies to my family, and everything I do in the family applies to my job. It's just the perfect change that I needed."

One could argue endlessly, I suppose, about the causes of such a coincidence. Did Marie receive a vision from God in the form of a dream? Did she subliminally perceive information the last time she had visited the clinic or overhear a conversation on the street, only to have her unconscious formulate it into the dream she remembered? Is she capable of clairvoyance while sleeping? But while questions such as these will never be resolved and need not be for our purposes, one cannot argue with the synchronistic meaning of the event for Marie, for whom finding this job was quite a meaningful coincidence, nor with the way in which, without reading any books on synchronicity but by simply being open to the connection between her subjective experience and her external reality, Marie went about bringing together disparate elements of her story into a coherent whole.

Dream Symbols and Synchronistic Events

So far, we have focused on dreams whose images have near-literal parallels with subsequent external events. But the symbolic nature of dream images themselves is sometimes echoed, significantly, in the course of one's external life. Bobbie's story from the introduction, in which her series of dreams of Tarot cards coincided with a whimsical gift on the part of her husband of a Tarot deck, is an example of how an inner symbol may be found by chance in outer life. Bobbie had not dreamed that her husband gave her a Tarot deck; the synchronistic connection was instead the symbol which repeated itself, by meaningful chance, in her outer life.

One rainy afternoon in San Francisco, Jonathan, a computer

consultant who is a friend of mine, told me such a story in response to my description of this book. The previous winter, the barber who cut Jonathan's hair for over fifteen years died after a long illness. Though he had known this man for a considerable length of time, Jonathan did not consider the man a friend, even though they had invited each other to parties, occasionally gone to lunch together after a hair cut, and had business and personal friends in common. Because their relationship was neither a close friendship nor a distant acquaintance, his barber's death, Jonathan told me, was very awkward for him to confront. What should he do? What should he feel? What response should he have?

The morning before the man's memorial service, Jonathan dreamed that he was in front of a house that was half-built. The framing was in, but the walls weren't done yet, and he had the feeling that it was now up to him to finish the job. The dream stuck with Jonathan, he said, because the imagery was so clear and the feeling of obligation to finish the job was so vivid. Later that very day, Jonathan found that the principal text from the Bible that the minister had chosen for his barber's memorial service was a series of verses from the book of Proverbs, beginning with "Wisdom has built her house, she has set up her seven pillars," and continuing on with other verses concerning the symbolism of the house, including "the wicked are overthrown and are no more, but the house of the righteous will stand," and "Wisdom builds her house, but folly with her own hands tears it down."

Jonathan cocked his eyebrow, as he told me the story. "I have to say, I was so surprised by the way my dream and the memorial service readings fit together, not to mention how the minister kept referring to my barber's life as a house he had built, a structure in which all of us who had known him helped to build with him. It made me think about my own life, and about the powerful dream I had just had that morning. Was I being wise or foolish? Why was the house in my dream left half-finished? Was this my life?

"It felt to me like the symbol of the house, along with my barber's death, put me on notice that there were certain things I needed to do to put my own house in order, things that I wanted to ignore and have others do for me, things I couldn't 'contract out' to others. I'm not much one to believe in dreams, but if you want meaningful coincidences, that was one."

I asked Jonathan what exactly he was talking about, what sort of things he felt he needed to do to put his house in order.

"Well, for one thing, I made a will. I finally made that appointment I had been putting off with a financial advisor and actually ended up putting money in a retirement account. I had always seen those things as part of my wife's job: I made the money, she managed it for us. But that day in church, when I heard the words from the Bible right on the heels of my dream, it got to me somehow."

"But couldn't you just have been responding to the fact that someone you knew had died?" I pressed him a bit.

"That was definitely part of it, though I have been to plenty of funerals, for people I felt much closer to, and they never had this effect. It was that weird coincidence of the dream and the Bible passages that day. I still recite the words to myself, even now. 'Wisdom has built her house but folly with her own hands tears it down.' Powerful words." And with that, Jonathan shook his head and changed the subject.

Stories such as this one, I confess, are the sort of tales concerning synchronistic dreams that I find the most engaging, for they defy all attempts at placing the dream within a chain of causes and effects. The dream that Jung himself used to illustrate the limits of rationality and the power of our nighttime imagination has become a traditional tale in the annals of synchronicities, and so, is an appropriate story to tell as we end our discussion of "predictive" dreams. I am going to let Jung tell his own story:

The problem of synchronicity has puzzled me for a long time, ever since the middle twenties, when I was investigating the phenomena of the collective unconscious and kept coming across connections which I simply could not explain as chance groupings or "runs." What I found were "coincidences" which were connected so meaningfully that their "chance" occurrence would represent a degree of improbability that would have to be expressed by an astronomical figure. By way of example I shall mention an incident from my own observation . . .

My example concerns a young woman patient who, in spite of efforts made on both sides, proved to be psychologically inaccessible. The difficulty lay in the fact that she always knew better about everything. Her excellent education had provided her with a weapon ideally suited to this purpose, namely a highly polished Cartesian rationality with an impeccably "geometrical" idea of reality. After several fruitless attempts to sweeten her rationalism with a somewhat more human understanding, I had to confine myself to the hope that something unexpected and irrational would turn up, something that would burst the intellectual retort into which she had sealed herself. Well, I was sitting opposite her one day, with my back to the window, listening to her flow of rhetoric. She had had an impressive dream the night before, in which someone had given her a golden scarab—a costly piece of jewelry. While she was still telling me this dream, I heard something behind me gently tapping on the window. I turned round and saw that it was a fairly large flying insect that was knocking against the window-pane from outside in the obvious effort to get into the dark room. This seemed to me very strange. I opened the window immediately and caught the insect in the air as it flew in. It was a scarabaeid beetle or common rose-chafer (*Cetonia aurata*), whose gold-green colour most nearly resembles that of a golden scarab. I handed the beetle to my patient with the words, "Here is your scarab." This experience punctured the desired hole in her rationalism and broke the ice of her intellectual resistance. The treatment could now be continued with satisfactory results.[2]

Admittedly, part of the enduring charm of this story is the flourish with which Jung reports himself giving aid and succor to the synchronicity, making sure that the point of the dream and its parallel event in the outer world is not lost on his recalcitrantly intellectual patient. As I've mentioned earlier, acausal connections can often profit from being presented with the proper style for maximum transformative effect.

Even if every synchronistic experience is in itself unique, there do seem to be patterns in these experiences, particularly for people who resist acknowledging the unconscious, irrational, and symbolic levels of their existence. When Act One of our story consists of our ego digging in, wanting its own way, come hell or high water—as with Kathryn's blind date from hell or Elise's refusal to consider musical comedy—then the stage is set for an acausal accident to bring the curtain up on a very different Act Two later on.

Working for months with a client who claimed he wished to do dreamwork with me but who dismissed, resisted, and denigrated all attempts to discern meanings in the dreams he defiantly reported to me in our sessions, I continued somewhat hopelessly forward with him, taking each dream seriously and yet truly feeling that we were getting nowhere. However, whenever I suggested that perhaps dreamwork was not really being all that productive, he insisted it was, and on and on we would go.

When we finished one session, having spent quite some time on a dream he had of a dog, gathering associations which were then pooh-poohed, spinning possibilities that were then shot down, suggesting possible feelings evoked by the dog in the dream that he would deny, I had to admit that I was relieved. Standing up and opening the door to my office, which is in a professional building in downtown Berkeley, I wish now I had had Jung's grace in presenting what I saw to my client—for in the doorway, sitting obediently and attentively, as if waiting for us to open the door, was a large, well-behaved golden retriever.

Stunned into silence, I looked at my client, who looked at the dog, then at me, then at the dog. And without exchanging a word, but with the air full of uncanny feeling, he left, both of us wondering how in the world a dog had ended up sitting so politely in the doorway of my inside office, staring at our door.

The next week, I was happy to notice, my client was not quite as stubbornly antagonistic about the possibility that his dreams might hold a meaning for him, and the appearance of the dog in the doorway, an occurrence we never discussed, marked the end of the sort of resistance to dreamwork that he had shown throughout the whole first part of our work together. Sometimes a synchronistic event needs no analysis for it to have a transformative effect, just as sometimes a story is so perfectly wrought that it achieves its effect without your even being aware of it.

More Than You Know: "Extrasensory" Dreams

Besides dreams which coincide with subsequent events in a synchronistic way, many dreams seem to disclose not just what will be but what *is* in ways that are impossible to know through normal sensory experience. The word most people would use, "extrasensory," is the simplest description for such dreams, but to employ such a term, I believe, confuses the issues of causality in a way that is not true to the concept of synchronicity.

To give another example related to dogs, when a client of mine told me a dream she had had in which I was playing in the backyard of a house with a large white dog, I experienced initially that familiar hair-raising feel of a synchronicity in the making, for indeed, I have a big white Samoyed at home, well known to friends and family for her extroverted personality and bossy ways.

Containing my thrill, though, I found that it was probably a good thing I didn't follow Jung's lead and make any dramatic statements about this client's "extrasensory" abilities, for as she began to talk about the dream, she was very matter-of-fact about her clairvoyance: "I suppose I dreamt about that white dog of yours because I always see the white hair around the cuffs of your pants. It's either that or you have a Himalayan cat. Which is it?" Sheepishly, I had to admit that perhaps this was less an example of a "sixth sense" on her part and more a case of infrequent dust-busting on mine.

Not that we didn't go forward and work with this dream productively, as my client free-associated to dogs in general and her dream dog in particular, as we explored what the image of my playing with the dog meant about how she felt about me as a person and about our relationship. Obviously, causal connections—she saw the white hair on my pants and dreamed about what it made her think of—can be every bit as meaningful as the acausal connections of synchronicities.

On the other hand, I have had clients report dreams with any number of details about my personal life that they could not possibly have known and which I certainly never revealed to them. One woman dreamed that it was my birthday when it was in fact my birthday. Another repeatedly dreamed of the number 909, which is my unlisted home address. Still another once dreamed of a plot which perfectly paralleled a short story I was in the middle of working on, which I had never told her about.

Were these synchronistic, in the sense that we have come to understand the term, that is, meaningful? To me they were, even if they had none of the high drama of some of the other incidents I have recounted or experienced, in that they served to reinforce the personal element of the relationship I had with these clients. They were like the minor touches a writer gives to the setting in which the main events of the story unfold—the deep violet curtain whose color reflects a character's feeling, the caress of a cheek which creates a feeling of tenderness, the chipper tone of a receptionist's voice to change the mood.

Big or small, dramatic or mundane, synchronistic dreams and their effect on our stories always challenge us to acknowledge the meaningful randomness of the plot line we are living. Like my dream of my former client Grace, the week before she resumed her therapy with me, my experience with Jerry changed the course of my professional biography and serves as an apt, albeit painful, illustration of how hard it can sometimes be not to draw objective causal conclusions about the intersection of dreams and external events.

In my experience, individuals generally seek psychotherapy for two reasons. Some people, who are basically capable of dealing with life on its own terms, come for counseling because unusual circumstances have overwhelmed them and led them to seek help; and some people come because their upbringing and development are insufficient to enable them to deal with the ordinary stresses and strains of everyday life.

Jerry fell squarely in the first category. Well adjusted, productively employed in a creative field, he came to me because of two extraordinary situations that he needed help in handling: being diagnosed with AIDS and caring for his aging father following the death of his mother. Either of these situations would have been cause enough for even the most competent person to seek out support; taken together, they overwhelmed even Jerry's own considerable emotional resources. Fully expecting a short-term counseling relationship, I worked with him for a number of months, giving him support, checking in with him weekly on what actions he had taken regarding his health, exploring with him what he might do to change his relationship with his father so that both of them could have their needs taken care of, and after a period of a little less than a year, all seemed to have gone smoothly. My client's own health was stable due in part to the preventive treatment he was receiving for the HIV, and his father had moved himself, with my client's help and insistence, into a retirement community where many of his social and physical requirements could be attended to without his son's constant vigilance.

Agreeing that he had accomplished what he had come for, which was as I had expected given his essentially firm footing on life, we ended our relationship and I wished him well. A year later, though, out of nowhere, I dreamed of Jerry. He was at a beach house, lying very still in a bed and breathing very slowly. The dream was an anxious one, with a sense that something was wrong, and yet, I was not in the dream and so there was nothing I could do but watch. I woke up unsettled that morning, remembering the dream vividly, and for the rest of the week I thought a great deal about my former client. Many times I came close to picking up the telephone to give him a call, just to check in, but then I would check myself instead, discounting my anxiety and telling myself that Jerry really wasn't the sort of person who would take well to worried phone calls from former counselors. In short, I did what I think most people would do under the circumstances: I ignored the dream as a figment of my imagination.

Months passed before I was made to see how powerful such figments could be. One day, unexpectedly, I got an urgent phone call from Jerry. He came into my office the next day, looking emotionally drained, tired, and obviously depressed. In the course of a difficult relationship that had begun after he had left our work together, all of the feelings he had held down for years and years by managing, by performing, by coping came rearing up, until one day, he told me, months ago, he checked into a hotel near the ocean, where his family had gone on vacation a number of times when he was a child, and following the recipe laid out for him in a book on assisted suicide, took the cocktail of drugs and chemicals suggested in order to kill himself.

Tired of living, certain he would eventually die an agonizing death by AIDS, and feeling forsaken by everyone, he told me that at the time he decided he might as well get it all over with.

"What happened?" I asked, troubled by the situation and remembering with misgivings my own dream of many months before.

"Well, I just lay there for about three days unconscious until I woke up, feeling like shit, but not dead, of course, and went home. No one came to look for me. In fact, no one seemed to miss me at all. They just assumed at work that I had gone on a spur-of-the-moment long weekend. My father and I don't talk all that often, and the woman I had just broken up with was, naturally, not too surprised that I had dropped out of sight for a while."

An ideal therapist, I was taught, is supposed to think through every intervention with every client, but I have to admit that this time if I thought at all it was quickly and intuitively. "When did this happen?" I asked, and he told me the dates.

At the first possible moment after our session, I consulted my dream journal, and indeed, I'd had the dream the week before his suicide attempt. The following week when Jerry came in, I told him what I had dreamed and when I had dreamed it, actually reading my journal entry to him. Wondering more than a little bit how he might take the information that the image I had had bore such an uncanny parallel to what had actually transpired, my hope was that he would recognize, from the fact of my synchronistic dream, that even if he hadn't felt a connection to anyone or anything at the time, such connections nevertheless existed. I am glad to say that Jerry accepted my self-disclosure in the spirit intended, and we continued our relationship for some time after that.

Yet for months I found myself silently reproaching myself for not having called him when I'd had the dream, unconsciously doing what I have seen many people do in the face of such synchronicities, acting as if the dream had been predictive, which is simply another way of putting my ego in the center of things, imagining that I, in my great wisdom, could have—indeed, had been—granted somehow a glimpse of the future, and like God should have intervened to have changed the course of history. The fact is that the dream was not synchronistic for me before the moment when I found out by sheer chance that an external event had an extraordinary parallel to my own inner experience. And this is the danger of seeing such dreams as "predictive" post-facto: one cannot and should not reproach oneself for not having intervened in a situation that, from one's own subjective experience, did not or had not yet existed.

The significance of this event lay not in my action or inaction but in the way that the fact I had been dreaming of him changed many of the assumptions Jerry had been making about how he stood in the hearts and minds of other people. As tends to happen in a synchronistic event, the line between subjective and objective, inner and outer, ourself and others, becomes a meeting point, a place where the plot of what we do and the character of who we are comes together and is, like any good story, resolved at last.

Obviously, the psychotherapy relationship is not the only place where synchronistic dreams figure decisively into the plot, even if the therapy relationship is one of the few places in our culture in which dreams are encouraged, examined, and appreciated. The special bond between mother and child is expectably a relationship in which all sorts of synchronicities occur, including those involving dreams, and my colleague Pete's dream concerning a mother he had never met illustrates just how decisively a synchronistic dream might change our whole life story.

Adopted at birth but without much desire to locate his birth parents, Pete, beginning at the age of twenty-seven, began to have what he described to me as a series of insistent dreams about his birth parents. The dreams, he told me, were vivid enough to hold his attention for several days at a time, and he felt compelled to share many of them with his friends. Feeling quite protective and loyal toward his adoptive parents, he had never considered searching for his birth parents until these dreams continued without abating, and so, in direct response to these dreams, he went forward and got all the non-identifying information he could from the social service agency through which he had been adopted.

That was when Pete discovered just how many of the details about his birth parents had been accurately disclosed to him in his dreams: his ethnic background, for example, as well as the fact that at the time the dreams began he was the same age as his birth mother was when she had given him up. Hoping that now that he had obtained the information the dreams would subside, Pete found instead that they continued, until one night, he had a dream in which he was told, in no uncertain terms, "Your mother's name is Gladys." Upon waking up, Pete considered the dream meaningless, since his *adoptive* mother's name was Gladys. What he told me he had not considered at the time was that the dream might be giving him another message entirely.

After another year or so of such dreams, Pete took seriously the suggestions of those around him who were convinced there was an unconscious reason for them, and he began to contemplate actively searching for his birth parents. The laws of the state where he had been adopted were liberal in this regard, requiring only the consent of the birth parent and adult child to release identifying information. Pete thought it would be an easy process, since the social worker he had previously spoken to had indicated that his birth mother had left such consent. Nevertheless, in contacting the agency again, he was told by the new caseworker that no such consent was on file and that he would have to initiate his own search, which is when, frustrated and upset, he found that his dream came in handy.

In an attempt to persuade the caseworker on the telephone to release at least the name of his birth mother and her last known address to him, he told her that he'd had a dream that her name was Gladys. Stunned into silence, the caseworker took a long moment to catch her breath. "Oh, I see," she said, her voice quivering. "Well, her name *is* Gladys," and, feeling the force of Pete's synchronistic dream, she was persuaded to reveal the information, saying, "If anyone ever asks you, just tell them it came to you in a dream." Two days later, after a search through phone books, Pete located his birth mother and has managed to build a very satisfying relationship with her.

In telling this bit of his biography, Pete himself continues to be amazed not only at the coincidence between the dream and his mother's name, which is significant enough, but at the strange coincidence of both his mothers having the same name. Having been so conflicted from the start about searching for his birth mother, he told me that, once again, the meaning of this coincidence lies in its symbolic value, the coherence it represents concerning his life. It gives his life story that dimension of beauty Kundera spoke of, a small but significant coincidental detail which in a novel, as well as in Pete's biography, we feel fits somehow.

The "extrasensory" dreams we have heard thus far have had mostly to do with an outer event occurring simultaneously with an individual's inner, unconscious image. However, the phenomenon of a shared dream—the same dream shared by two or more people at the same time—is a subgenre in the general category of dream synchronicities which we have been exploring. Introduced to me by a friend who knew I was working on this book, Naomi told me the story of how she experienced a type of synchronistic dream.

Naomi had been part of a tight community of friends throughout her young adulthood. While sitting at home one day telling a new group of friends stories about her old group, one of the old group called her up, just to catch up on old times. Delighted to hear from him in such a synchronistic way, she begged off a long conversation and instead fixed a time to meet with him.

When she and her old friend got together the following week and after all the requisite catching up had been done, they began discussing a friend of theirs who had died, a man so beloved by everyone in the group that they had nicknamed him St. Chris. Feeling a bit sheepish about not having maintained contact with Chris during his last years, Naomi confessed to her friend that she had long had a series of recurring dreams about Chris, seeing him in various places in her dreams, doing various things, only to see an expression of astonishment spread over her friend's face. "You too, huh?" he said to her, launching into his own series of dreams about St. Chris that he had never told anyone, dreams which were identical to Naomi's.

I asked Naomi what she made of this coincidence. She responded by saying that there were really two synchronicities here. First, her old friend had contacted her just at a time when she needed to hear from him, particularly because of her feelings of loss about the old group of friends. Second, the discovery that her grief about Chris and the old group was shared provided her with the very sense of connection she had felt the need to repair.

The feeling I got from speaking with Naomi was one which, in the literature of synchronicity, is sometimes described in terms of an unconscious field being activated, analogous to an electrical or magnetic field, which exerts an influence on a number of people who happen to find themselves within the range of its effect. Another metaphor often used in Jung's works to describe this experience of coincidental simultaneity is that a certain set of archetypal complexes becomes "constellated" by the feelings two people share about an important turn of events in their life stories. As a description of what it feels like to have shared dreams with an old friend, I think the metaphor of an activated unconscious field is a good one, for it sums up quite well the sense of belonging, mutual connection, and group consciousness which, for Naomi, was the meaning of the incident.

The problem, however, with such metaphors is that it is quite tempting to try to use the metaphor concretely as a way to explain what might have "caused" such coincidences, the way it *is* possible to explain why two compasses point toward magnetic north at the same time at different places on the globe. The wonder of Naomi's shared dream, in my opinion, is precisely that it could *not* have been caused by "energetic fields" or "cosmic vibrations," but was beyond anyone's conscious or unconscious control. The extraordinary and ultimately inexplicable quality of the event served to bring to Naomi's awareness just how much Chris and all her friends meant to her as she moved on in her life to another chapter. The subjective result of the coincidence, Naomi's appreciation of her history, is, for me at least, a denouement that does not suffer in significance without a discernible cause.

I Can Dream, Can't I? Working with Dreams

To really appreciate synchronistic dreams, ours or anyone else's, one needs, as I mentioned at the start of this chapter, to be able to work productively with one's dreams, and the first step in doing this is to presume that what we dream is meaningful. At the beginning of modern psychology, this was a bold presumption, but nowadays, bolstered by many years of psychological theories, and even supported by experimental research, we see that the presumption of meaning in dreams is neither naïve nor self-serving.

Nevertheless, to presume the meaningfulness of dreams does not mean that a dream is a message in a bottle from the unconscious, to be

uncoded for secret directions about specific situations, as dream dic-
tionaries displayed at the check-out counter of the supermarket would
have us believe, in which the symbols are listed alphabetically, "aard-
vark" to "zoos," and standard, universal interpretations are given, good
for everyone and for all times.

The meaning that a dream carries is more like the meaning of a
story. As the endless volumes of literary interpretations attest, many
valid meanings can be found in the same story, which can be helpful
in providing insight into ourselves as readers and into the world of the
author who wrote the story. *The Wizard of Oz* by L. Frank Baum, for
example, has been interpreted from a wide variety of perspectives. The
psychological meaning many Jungians, including myself, have found in
the tale, viewing Dorothy as a symbol of the archetypal Feminine and
her journey as a hero's tale concerning the attainment of psychological
maturity, is but one of a number of meanings people have gleaned
from Baum's story. By contrast, I was once treated to an interpretation
by a man who claimed that Baum intended his story as a parable of the
United States' economic situation in the early twentieth century in
which American reliance on a gold standard—the yellow brick road—
would need to change to a reliance on another source of wealth symbolized by the Emerald City and the Wizard of Oz.

My point in citing such widely varying examples of literary interpretation in the context of dreamwork is to caution against taking the
stance that unfortunately many critics feel obliged to take with regard
to their interpretations of a text: my ideas are right, yours are wrong; I
know the true meaning of the work, and you do not. When dealing
with a literary work, there might be some justification for such an
attitude, in view of how completely the interpretation accounts for
what exists in the text. An interpretation of *The Wizard of Oz*, for
example, which has nothing to say about the role of the Wicked Witch
of the West in the tale, would obviously not be a very good interpretation. But with dreams, in which the "text" is wholly subjective, there

can be no absolute rights or wrongs in interpretation; there are merely better or worse interpretations.

As in literary criticism, the usefulness of the dream interpretation depends in part on how well whatever interpretation we advance accounts for the complexity of the imagery of a dream or of a series of dreams. But unlike literary criticism, our interpretation of dreams must always take into account our subjective experience as well—how the dream made us feel, what the dream made us think about, how the dream fits into the overall story of our lives. An interpretation of a dream that accounts for all the imagery but ignores the inner experience or significance to the dreamer is not an interpretation worth much at all, no matter how elegant or comprehensive. And with regard to synchronistic dreams in particular, as I hope I have made clear by now, our ability to value our subjective experience lies at the heart of whether or not such coincidences enrich our lives.

For some of the people who shared their stories with me, these twin attitudes—to presume meaning and to value subjective experiences—came naturally, since they generally went about attending to their inner lives—their feelings, their fantasies, their dreams—with as much seriousness as they did their outer lives—their relationships, their work lives. Indeed, for people like therapists, who spend much of their professional and personal time devoted to the development of their own and others' inner lives, synchronicities might even be called a kind of "stock in trade." But the stories I have recounted show that such people hold no monopoly over dreams; there is nothing inherently special or different or gifted about them that events like this occur to them. Like Jonathan with his dream of finishing his house or Pete with the series of dreams about his birth mother, all it takes is a bit of insistence on the part of one's inner life, along with an attention-grabbing coincidence, and the importance of attending to one's inner life becomes a matter of course.

Since everyone dreams, understanding the dream as an everyday occurrence and examining it with diligence is probably the best way to start working with dreams. Some people keep dream journals, while others only write down their dreams now and then, whenever the spirit (or dream) moves them. Drawing, painting, or sculpting the dream images is a more time-consuming technique, yet for some people, for whom words do not come easily, it is the only way to give the dream life its due.

The point of all these methods of recording dreams is not "how" to do it, since there is no best way, just as there is no best way to read a novel or watch a movie. The best way is what works for you. My friend Yvonne sits down and reads fiction cover-to-cover in one fell swoop, in order to enter into the world the author has created. I like to spread the experience out, taking breaks chapter to chapter, to let my own impressions simmer and bubble to the surface. So, too, with our inner tales. If you presume that dreams have a meaning and spend some time being with your dreams in a way that suits your personality, you will undoubtedly find out more about your inner life than you ever thought possible.

Because dreams are symbolic in nature, when they coincide significantly with events in our external lives, what results is often the same thing that results when a good book has the effect intended by the author: our consciousness is raised, our awareness of who we are and our place in the universe is broadened and deepened. In the next chapter, we will be moving even further inward and upward, from the world of the dream to the realm of our spirituality, where the coincidence of inner life and outer event takes on even greater transpersonal significance.

Chapter Five

Getting in Touch with the Author

Synchronicity and Our Spiritual Lives

The spirit is the true self.

CICERO

Ever since the Enlightenment, that decisive period in Western history when faith in rationality and in empirical science began to challenge religious beliefs and supplant faith in spiritual experience, many have found themselves inwardly adrift, unsure of what to make of experiences that at one time would have simply been seen as God's action in their lives but which, when seen by the light of reason, either make no sense or cannot have happened. Moreover, with the spectacular success the Industrial Revolution has had in transforming life on earth, this scientific faith born of the Enlightenment seems to have been well founded, making it even harder for many people to value those aspects of our lives which are irrational and subjective. Our religious and spiritual experiences, to continue using the central image of this book, are seen as merely "fiction" from the perspective of a rational, empirical approach to life, and because the meanings we assign to such experiences cannot be proven since the "causes" of such phenomena cannot be definitively determined, our modern age has made the "crisis of faith" an especially characteristic affliction.

In outlining the current state of affairs so broadly, as an introduction to our exploration of synchronicity and spirituality, I have no wish to deny the plain fact that many, many modern people have a stable set of religious beliefs and practices, often allied with particular communities, denominations, or traditions, which for them sum up and direct their inner and outer lives. But even within such communities of faith there is a discernible sense of embattlement.

And for others still, this modern "crisis of faith" has taken other forms. In rejecting traditional religious beliefs or acknowledging that such practices or communities do not fit them or help them make sense of their experience, the very words "religion" or "spirituality" are up for grabs and defined in ways that are often quite individual in nature. Indeed, in my experience, the word "religious" is often used quite explicitly to connote institutional religion, with "spirituality" connoting instead "my personal beliefs" or "my own individual experiences," a semantic shift which has as its result the loosely organized set of beliefs and practices that usually goes by the name "New Age."

Whether traditionally religious or more idiosyncratically spiritual in format, the fact remains that these "fictions" of ours, our religious and spiritual experiences, beliefs and practices, are an essential and universal part of being human, regardless of how externally transformative a faith in reason and science has been or will continue to be. To be human is to tell stories, to live and use symbols to make sense of our lives, to search for a deep, direct experience of that which is beyond our own limited mortal existence, and no amount of technology is likely to change these essentials about ourselves. In keeping with the beginnings of the science of psychology, in which a race was on to identify what constituted the basic instincts of the human personality,

Jung did his part by nominating what he called the "religious instinct" on the basis of his observation that all human cultures have always told stories of how things came to be to make meaning of the universe and to live out those meanings through rituals designed to provoke experiences of a transcendent reality.

Nowadays, the tensions run high between the purely scientific way of seeing the world and one which assumes the existence of a power greater than ourselves, and like it or not, we all find ourselves in a state of profound transition around the place of sacred stories in our lives. Are my beliefs "fictions" in the least respectful sense of the term, a set of self-serving fantasies I have formulated or made up about the nature of existence to reassure, comfort, or delude myself? Is it possible to "prove" the existence of God somehow, if all we have are our subjective experiences—what has happened to us individually, what we have felt, what it meant?

As we have seen so far, wherever there are deep questions, wherever there is a story to be told, wherever there are transitions to be made, there, too, we have found synchronistic events very often playing an important and sometimes decisive role. And, with regard to the stories of our spiritual or religious lives, the acausal connecting principle which is at the heart of a synchronistic experience, the way that objective reality is brought into a meaningful relationship with subjective experience, affords one way to bridge the conflicting demands of rationality and belief.

Thus, in this chapter not only will we be looking at the way that meaningful coincidences shaped the stories of particular individuals with regard to their spiritual life but the value placed on the subjective experience of the individual will lead us to discuss basic questions about the nature of religious experience, its relationship to scientific ways of understanding the world, and psychology's perspective on both science and religion. And through the stories we will hear of the synchronicities in people's spiritual lives, we will see more clearly what it means to be human.

How I Met My Spiritual Teacher

As I discovered doing the research for the chapter on love and friendship, ask someone how they met their husband, wife, lover or life partner, and chances are that you will hear a story of synchronicities. I was not surprised to find, therefore, that the same turns out to be the case when I ask people about their spiritual development. Ask someone how they met their spiritual teacher and embarked upon what they consider their spiritual path, and more likely than not, it happened synchronistically. What I didn't expect, however, in talking to people about their spiritual lives, was how few people had ever told anyone else the story of their spiritual awakening, a sign, in my opinion, of just how devalued (or perhaps protective) people have become about these sacred stories which, in other cultures, have a central place in human relationships. I felt very privileged, for this reason, as I listened to tale after tale unfold of how, through sheer chance, people found themselves on the road to higher consciousness.

In retrospect, it should not have seemed strange to me that, as I was about to sit down to begin writing the first draft of this chapter, I got a phone call from a young woman named Ellie. Having been told by a friend of hers that I was writing a book on synchronicity, she thought she would give a call and offer me the story of her spiritual awakening. I had intended to write that day, but I decided to practice what I preach about synchronicity and be open to the potential meaningfulness of this coincidence. I changed my plans in order to meet with her that day, and soon after, in the sunlight of a California spring, we managed to find one another in the crowded shopping mall near her school.

"I've never really sat down and told anyone this," she said, equally shy and self-confident, "but the reason I'm here talking to you, doing what I am doing in my life at all is pure chance." Describing herself as a science major at UCLA without any exposure to spirituality or psychology, Ellie told me that the year before, at age twenty-five, she had undergone a "mid-life crisis," knowing that the scientific career she had always trained for was not what she really wanted to be doing but having no idea what her calling might be.

"It was like I was at the end of my life as I had known it. Not that I ever considered suicide or anything like that, but I just knew that the life I had been living was over." By chance, a friend gave her a copy of one of Marianne Williamson's books, which Ellie read with some interest, the first ever of this sort of reading she had done. Intrigued by Williamson's spiritual perspective, she thought she might like to go hear Williamson talk, but the location of the talks and the fact that Ellie did not have a car made it rather impractical. Upon discovering that Williamson also had a radio show, Ellie took the time to tune in to the show on a regular basis, finding herself over a period of six months more and more drawn to its spiritual message.

Ellie found herself intrigued in particular by Williamson's frequent references to a spiritual community center called the Agape Center and, through directory assistance, she got its phone number, discovering then that it was located by sheer luck only a ten-minute walk away from where she was living. As Ellie began to attend the center's events on a regular basis, at the same time her uncle, who was in training as a hypnotherapist, asked Ellie if she might want to do some hypnotherapy with him, not for psychotherapeutic purposes but rather to help break her of her habit of nail-biting.

"So there I was, really without intending to, going to the Agape

Center and in hypnotherapy," she said to me, proceeding slowly in her story, almost as if it was hard for her to believe herself. One night, as her process of inner awareness continued in both venues, Ellie was sitting in a bookstore, leafing through a magazine when a book left on the table in front of her by someone else caught her eye. Coming across the book by accident, in this way, she took a brief glance through it, and though not overly impressed by it, she nevertheless found in it a reference to Ken Wilbur and transpersonal psychology, neither of which she had previously heard of and about which she knew nothing.

Shortly after this accidental acquaintance with the idea of transpersonal psychology, Ellie had a transformative spiritual experience during her regular meditation which she describes as a "communion with her higher self." During this experience, her long period of confusion and lack of direction was finally brought to a close, for in it she received a vision of what it was that she should be doing in her life, what her purpose was, and how she should go forward. She told me that what she was told in her vision was that transpersonal psychology was the path she was to follow, even though at the time of the vision, she did not know what transpersonal psychology was.

In a café, shortly after this experience, Ellie found herself making eye contact with a young man across the room. After avoiding his eyes numerous times, she instead "went with the flow of the experience," introducing herself to him and beginning a conversation. Toward the end of their talk, learning he was a sociology major, she asked him, on the off-chance, if he knew what transpersonal psychology was. He initially said he had no idea, but then, upon reflection, said that he had had a friend whose mother had gone to some school up north that specialized in psychology, a school named John F. Kennedy University, but that he didn't know much more. Ellie smiled as she continued the story.

"So, the next day I called information and got the number of JFK. I called them and asked them, the way I had been asking lots of people over the months since that moment of clarity, did they know what transpersonal psychology was? The guy laughed at me. 'We only have a whole master's program in it.' And that's how I ended up going to graduate school here, how I ended up deciding to be a psychotherapist. A whole series of chances: Williamson's book given to me out of nowhere, picking up that book in the store by chance, being told by my higher self that transpersonal psychology was my path, and then just happening to meet a man who directed me to JFK, who himself didn't even know what transpersonal psychology was!"

As the result of what looks on the outside to be simply a series of chances, Ellie appeared quite certain that she was doing what she needed to be doing, both for her spiritual life and her vocation, and the role that chance seemed to play in moving her toward where she felt she needed to be obviously imparted an element of wonder to her story, as is always the case in synchronistic experiences.

Now, many of us could probably tell similar stories of how we ended up doing what we needed to be doing in our lives, inwardly or outwardly, and Ellie's story, with its random occurrences, has none of the drama or astronomically remote improbabilities that some of the other stories of meaningful coincidences we have heard have. What it is important to see, though, is the meaning which Ellie made of the random occurrences: that a series of external chance coincidences felt as though they led her, geographically and spiritually, to a place where she found what she considers her spiritual vocation. She did not set out to find JFK. She did not decide to become a psychotherapist. She did not sit herself down one day and say, "I am going to do something about my spiritual emptiness" and begin attending church deliberately and consciously in a search for spiritual fulfillment. In fact, at the beginning of what she came to see as her spiritual awakening, she had no idea what to do or where to go to resolve her disenchantment with the scienitific career she had been pursuing.

The connections that occurred for Ellie indeed *occurred to* her, without her causing them, and yet, they took on great meaning and import for the direction of her inner and outer life. Did she interpret the events of her life in this way in retrospect? Did she "make up" this story, in the sense that she read meanings into these chance events? Yes and no. As she tells the story, the external opportunities of the Agape Center, hypnotherapy, and transpersonal psychology happened by chance to enter her life at a point of openness to transformation, to which she responded by taking action. As with all the stories we have seen, a coincidence can hold meaning or not, depending on the attitude we bring to it.

Another woman, Roberta, happened upon her own spiritual path by a more unlikely but no less transformative coincidence. Driving across country by car and tiring of the endless interstate around about Ohio, Roberta followed an impulse and turned off the highway to make her way west, at least for a little while, by country roads. Off in the distance, in the middle of the fields and fields of farmland, she spotted a clump of buildings and people, all of whom seemed to be busy, in the midst of a colorful celebration or parade of sorts. Intrigued at finding a festival this far off the beaten track, she followed her nose and went to investigate, discovering a spiritual community organized around a guru, whose founding of the community was being celebrated this very day and whose tradition of welcoming the visiting stranger on this day was seen as an auspicious sign.

Roberta was more than taken by the sheer coincidence of it all, reminiscent of the sort of feeling that Pete had when coming upon Mary in the motel in the Mojave desert or my friend John had when meeting the man who would become his mentor in a remote ashram in India. Staying to learn more about the community, its teacher, and its practices, Roberta told me that she counts her own spiritual awakening as having begun on that day, when she happened upon that community in the midst of celebration in the middle of nowhere. If there is a moral to this story, it is, I suppose, that even the road to nowhere leads somewhere.

For another synchronistic coincidence involving wandering the world and following one's intuitions, Naomi recounted to me a story that took place when she was seventeen years old and living in an ashram in Nepal. For a very long time, she had suffered from an illness for which none of the Eastern nor Western medical practitioners she consulted could find either the cause or the cure. After a very affecting dream one night of a man she had never met but whose image she could see in her mind quite clearly, she left the ashram, though sick, and decided to travel.

Difficult as this was, since she was suffering from a chronic illness, Naomi, like Roberta, followed no particular route in her travels and by chance and intuition, felt drawn to a particular town in India. There, seeing a naturepathic clinic and thinking that perhaps the people there might be able to help her with her declining health, to her amazement she met the man she had dreamed of so many months before, whose face was still as fresh in her mind as the night she had dreamed of him. Clearly feeling that both the dream and her finding him were a sign of importance not to be ignored, she underwent the treatment he prescribed and was eventually cured of her illness, staying on at the clinic for three years afterward to be trained by the man whose spiritual and medical expertise opened her eyes to the connection between body, mind, and spirit at a formative time in her youth.

• • •

How Barry met his astrology teacher is a story which began with a synchronicity and ended by teaching Barry a lesson wholly different from that which he thought he would be learning. In his own words:

"In 1981, while I was at the University of Chicago, I had gotten a fellowship to study Bengali in Calcutta. As Hindu astrology was going to be the subject for my dissertation, I made inquiries and I found an astrologer, an old Bengali man who agreed to teach me the rudiments of Hindu astrology. Named Prodip, he was an interesting man and had led quite an eventful life. At some point, during the middle of my stay there that first visit, he suggested that I meet with his son, who was also an astrologer and a palmist, who was named Torun.

"Now astrologers and palmists in India usually contract a space with a jewelry shop, as they prescribe stones. So, later on, when I eventually decided to look Torun up, I found this small jewelry store tucked away between other stores on a very quaint street in Calcutta, where everything was falling apart in that evocative way it does in India. I knocked on the door to Torun's chamber—they call them chambers there—and upon entering I found a man sitting behind his desk in a very cramped little cubicle, rather paunchy, in his mid-forties, dark-faced with very intense eyes. I introduced myself, telling him that his father had sent me to meet him, but I did not feel drawn to him, and the short reading he gave me did not move me, so I just got up, thanked him, and left.

"Back in Chicago, after that year, I finished my written exams, and when the fellowship I expected to get to go back to India didn't come through, I wondered whether or not I was meant to go back to India at all. But then at the last minute, I got another fellowship and away I went in the beginning of 1983. That year I discovered that a part of my soul is in Calcutta. It's really a fascinating city, one of the most fascinating cities in the entire world, and certainly in India. It's extremely cosmopolitan, but very traditional and tribal, with moldering, decaying buildings. It's quite beautiful in its decadence, and every conceivable misfortune and vice under the sun is found there, and so are tremendous warmth and richness of culture.

"Since I now knew Bengali very well, I thought I would go back to Prodip and resume my lessons. But when I approached him, he said he was sorry but that he was too old, he couldn't take on any pupils anymore. I was very disheartened. I pleaded with him, but he continued to say no, saying that I should study with his son. 'Did you meet my son?' he asked. Yes, I said off-handedly, without much interest, but Prodip urged me to go and see him and talk with him further. I left, discouraged, really without much intention of following up on meeting with his son.

"I meandered away another week or so, thinking about who I was going to study with. One day I was walking to the Institute where I was studying, strolling jauntily, having made my mind up to look for an astrology teacher that day, and as I turned the corner down the block from the Institute, down a long dirt road, I saw two men standing on my left. I looked at them, turned, then looked again, doing a double-take, seeing that these two men were looking at me. The younger of the two was suddenly very excited to see me, but I didn't recognize him at all, and he came up to me with lots of enthusiasm, saying, 'Hi, how are you?' and so forth, to which I responded hesitantly, asking, 'Do I know you?' As it turned out, I actually had never met him. But the man with him just stood and looked at me with intense eyes, so intense that I ended up ignoring the other man who was fawning over me. I smiled at him, though I didn't really know why, and he smiled at me. I didn't remember him, but I walked up to him anyway and said, 'Hello.'

"He asked, 'Do you remember who I am?'

"I said, 'No but you do seem familiar to me.'

"He replied, 'I am Prodip's son Torun.'

" 'Oh, *hello,*' I said. 'I've been meaning to meet with you. I would like to talk to you about the possibility of studying with you.'

"He became genuinely welcoming all of a sudden. 'Very fine,' he said. 'Come with me,' and he took my hand, and from that moment we were inseparable. Something suddenly shifted in that chance encounter with him on the street, from being totally uninterested in him I suddenly felt drawn to him like a magnet and I didn't understand why, but as soon as it happened I had the feeling that this relationship was meant to be. I finally found the person I was going to study with, though I had no preconception that this was going to be the case."

From this chance meeting with a man whom Barry had already met but whom he didn't even recognize on the street grew a lifelong relationship. At first with Torun's help, Barry expanded his knowledge of astrology, Hinduism, and his own spiritual path, but over time, the relationship grew more complex and difficult, as Torun revealed his own shortcomings, spurring Barry to see that he needed to follow his own path and not get hooked so thoroughly into relying on a teacher to show him the way forward.

The story Lisa tells of her spiritual development, strewn with synchronicities as well, demonstrates the truth of what Barry learned through his long relationship with Torun: spiritual insight comes through paying attention to the movement of one's own soul and not always through outer reliance on teachers and teachings. Nature, in Lisa's story, served as her spiritual teacher by way of coincidences which had significant impact on how she approached the world around her.

From a strong southern Protestant tradition, Lisa had spent her life involved in church, both as a participant and a leader. Married, with three children, to a traveling salesman, she told me that for many years, however much she loved her husband, his repeated absences were problematic and eventually she began to see that he was a man incapable of the kind of intimacy she had always sought. When her children grew up and became more independent, and after she had gone back to school to fulfill her dream of becoming a physical thera-pist, she and her husband by mutual consent decided to separate rather than to continue in their emotionally distant, unfulfilling rela-tionship.

What Lisa didn't count on was how the news of her divorce would be received by the church she and her husband had long at-tended. She found that many of the members of her church, to whom she had once been close, were far more sympathetic to her husband, who as a salesman was able to put his side of the story across to them in a way that gained sympathy and understanding, and certain people explicitly blamed the separation on Lisa's independence and self-asser-tiveness. This experience of being judged and the acute lack of support she experienced from what had been her religious community were a watershed experience for her, placing her in that situation we have come to see as characteristic of synchronistic events—a period of tran-sition.

During this period, Lisa told me, she began to have dreams and visions of a sort that at the time were utterly unprecedented for her. One series of dreams involved Native American rituals and religious figures, such as healing circles, medicine men, and shamans, and dur-ing the day, when Lisa found her attention wandering, she had re-peated waking experiences of these figures appearing and speaking to her. Another set of dreams and visions involved figures which at the time Lisa was unfamiliar with, but which she subsequently discovered were Hindu deities, the elephant-god Ganesha and the powerful male deity Shiva with whom she had had a vision of herself making love. A little shocked by such "pagan" imagery, from the standpoint of her own strictly Christian upbringing, she told me that she was encouraged by her counselor at the time—to whom she had gone mostly for support around the breakup of her marriage—to follow the thread of these visions and see where they led.

Where they led, Lisa found, was into nature. As the individual figures she was seeing began to fade into the background, what she found occurring in her spiritual life were repeated appearances of what she called "animal guides." This phase of her spiritual path was inaugurated by an especially powerful synchronicity. Having had a vision of an enormous snake, so big in fact that she could see neither its head nor its tail, lying on an altar before her like a sacred object to be revered, she found herself later that week resting on a log in a nearby wilderness area where she had taken to going for personal meditation during the time of her divorce. She heard a rustle in the leaves and looked down to see, slithering through the brush, the body of a beautiful snake slowly making its way past her until it disappeared. This moment, in which outer reality mirrored her own inner life, was a moment of synchronistic confirmation for her, leading her to feel more certain about the lonely and strange process of spiritual growth she had been experiencing in recent months through dreams and visions.

From then on, Lisa began her own personal vision quest, making a practice of coming to this same spot in the forest, developing a ritual based on her own visions and on some of her readings in nature spirituality. She would draw a ritual circle around her on the earth, to symbolize wholeness and protection, offer food and other tokens to the animal spirits of the area as symbols of respect and relationship, and then would settle in and wait to see what came to her. Almost without fail, Lisa found herself visited by the animal residents of the area. Birds, lizards, snakes, and insects all appeared before her, sometimes in response to her specific requests for guidance, sometimes simply to keep her company.

The similarity of Lisa's spontaneous spiritual practices to Native American rituals struck me as she told me her story, and I wondered what she made of it. For her part, she said, she had the feeling that once freed from a constricting marriage and a traditional religious attitude she had been able to get in touch with the more natural spirit of the land upon which she was living and which, of course, had been occupied for thousands of years by the very people whose rituals she seemed to be recreating for herself. Though living at the time in a recently constructed suburb outside a major city in the South, her family's history in the area went back for over two hundred years, and Lisa came to explain her experiences to herself as an acknowledgment of her own deep connection to the land she lived on.

Unlike the previous stories where, through a series of chance events, people met spiritual teachers or had their consciousness expanded, this story of how Lisa met her spiritual teacher, so to speak, in the form of nature and the living past of the land represents a synchronicity of yet another sort. Her spontaneous creation of rituals, whose similarity to traditional practices of which she was wholly unaware at the time, based on visions of guides and deities with astonishing parallels to specific religious figures, seems to demonstrate that sychronicities need not be single, dramatic incidents but can also take the form of a slow process of emerging wholeness in a person's life story.

Is Everything a Synchronicity? On the Perception of Meaning in Events

By now, if I have done my job, the reader of this book, having heard such a grand variety of synchronistic experiences—dramatic as well as humble, externally significant as well as internally transformative—may well be asking the question, "Well, what *isn't* a synchronicity?"—a question that may feel especially appropriate in the area of spirituality or religion. The foregoing examples of how people perceived chance events in their lives as meaningful, not because they resulted in specific external changes, like a job, a love affair, or a friendship, but because of specific *internal* changes that influenced their understanding of themselves, changes that obviously can neither be confirmed nor denied by anyone else, bring up a key issue: how people perceive meaning in their lives.

Didn't Lisa simply go about reading spiritual meaning into the animal appearances to make herself feel better? Couldn't it be that Ellie retrospectively tells the story of how she went to graduate school to make it seem like she was led there by a spiritual force beyond her control? Can't you draw sweeping philosophical or religious conclusions from nearly anything that happens to you? Might we not invest our lives with such significance because it makes us feel important or even chosen? Voltaire, that quintessential Enlightenment thinker, wrote his marvelous satire *Candide* specifically to make fun of the indiscriminate, facile, and therefore silly ways some people go about seeing meaning in everything and to respond to questions such as those above.

The hero of his story, Candide, is followed about, through catastrophe after catastrophe, by his teacher Dr. Pangloss who, despite the apparent reality, maintains that all is for the best in this best of all possible worlds. Voltaire ends his novel with Pangloss babbling at Candide, "All the events in this best of possible worlds are admirably connected. If a single link in the great chain were omitted, the entire harmony of the universe would be destroyed. If you had not been expelled from that beautiful castle, with those cruel kicks, for your love for Miss Cunegonde; if you had not been imprisoned by the Inquisition; if you had not plunged your sword through the baron; if you had not lost all the sheep you brought from that fine country, Eldorado, together with the riches with which they were laden, you would not be here today, eating preserved citrons and pistachio nuts."

Indeed, in a book on synchronicity, story after story of chance events is presented by the people who experienced them as meaningful and transformative, in a presentation that may be sounding by now a great deal like Pangloss's, where almost anything—the appearance of a snake, the fact I met an astrology teacher, how I came to go to grad school—is given overwhelming and life-transforming significance. Voltaire's satire, however, as with all satire, comes from exaggeration, and I know very few people who like Pangloss feel an unswerving certainty in the meaningfulness of the events that occur to them or would make the claim that, had they not seen a snake or met their husband, the entire harmony of the universe would be destroyed.

I would like to draw the reader's attention to the way in which most of the stories presented so far, including the ones just told, involve people very much at a loss as to what to make of their lives, people who do not know where to go or what to do, who do not approach the events of their lives with the philosophical position that "all is for the best in this best of all possible worlds." Indeed, much of the meaning of synchronistic events appears in direct contradiction to what people wanted to believe about the direction of their lives. A lifelong churchgoer, Lisa found herself quite troubled when her friends at church turned their backs on her, and certainly the last thing she wanted was to leave behind the community which she had been so long a part of. Likewise, with Ellie, whose mid-life crisis occurred when she had no way to avoid acknowledging that what she wanted to believe would be meaningful—a career in science—was in fact not fulfilling or satisfying.

What occurred in many, if not most, of the synchronistic events as told to me was that what people in fact wanted to believe about themselves and their lives—emotionally, professionally, psychologically, and spiritually—was revealed to them, against their will by sheer coincidence, as not at all what it seemed. The fact that in a book we must tell these stories after the events have happened and after people have articulated their meaning for themselves, has a tendency to obscure for the reader that when the events actually occurred their significance—what they would come to mean in the course of these people's life stories—was not at all as clear and concise as it now appears.

So, if the Panglossian facility with which some of these people seem, in these stories, to be assigning great, even at times cosmic, significance to minor events is troubling, I suggest that this is an effect of hearing the stories after the fact and to remind the reader to pay attention to what the subjective experience of the person living the event must have been at the time. If our lives are stories, what I was told and what I am presenting are the revised and edited versions. The rough draft, that is, the original experience, is where the experience of meaning lies most fully for the people involved.

But even then, the issue is not entirely resolved, for what of the objection that people have "read into" events retrospectively what they wanted to? I find this objection an interesting one, because it poses a question that may seem at odds with the subjective-objective balance that psychology tries to strike: is our subjective experience more important than our objective experience? Or, to use the central image of this book, are we, then, the authors of our stories? If meaning is a wholly subjective phenomenon, wherein we tell ourselves stories about our lives to make sense of it all, wouldn't we *have* to be the authors?

Yet, what is noteworthy, as we have heard time and again in the stories people tell of synchronistic events, is that the narrators do not feel at all that they are the authors of the experience. When a coincidence occurs between an internal state and a chance external event, which we ourselves did not cause or seek out, it feels not as if we wrote the story but as if some objective, external force, some divine principle of order, God or Fate, has a plan in mind for us and our lives. At the time of such an event or when we look back upon a series of such events, we see an organization and intention that *seems* objective, that seems like a story written by someone else, and certainly not at all what we ourselves would have written. In fact, sometimes the wonder of the event is that it happened at all, so unlikely and improbable as some of the coincidences were.

Who then *is* the author? Where does the meaning come from in the stories of our lives? For people with a religious faith, whose subjective experiences posit the existence of an objective God, then clearly God is the author. In any of the stories so far, someone with this sort of faith in a God who is involved in one's everyday life probably would not have called the events that occurred to them synchronistic but would simply have said, "God led me to my husband," "I was divinely called to the job I took," or "It was God's plan for my life that I was where I was when it happened."

But what if I do not or cannot share your religious perspective, your belief in the objective existence of God? The resolution to this question of where meaning comes from, of who *is* the author of our stories, reminds me of a quip from none other than Voltaire, when he said in his typically irreverent way, "If God did not exist, it would be necessary to invent him." This observation about human beings, our necessity to invent God, was one which Jung in his own turn provided a far more developed and serious explanation for, perceiving not that we, as Voltaire would have it, deliberately and speciously "invent" God, but rather that all human beings share a capacity to see or imagine wholeness.

Jung's notion of the archetype, as I mentioned in my introduction, is defined as a typical mode of apprehension, a pattern of psychological perception and understanding common to all human beings. One such mode of perception, and perhaps one of the most important that Jung identified, is the archetype of wholeness, the ability to perceive the fundamental unity of the disparate parts of our experience. As we have seen from the various synchronistic experiences recounted so far, the perception of wholeness in these incidents derives not from our ego, our conscious sense of self, but instead from the way in which the meaning unites *all* of who we are, parts of our experience we were unaware of, potentials we have that have lain dormant or undeveloped, elements of our personality that we didn't know existed.

For this reason, Jung called this archetype of wholeness the Self, for indeed the experience of this archetype is very much one of a supraordinate personality, the whole of ourselves brought together into a coherent structure, as if in a story in which all things have their place and significance. According to Jung, this sort of experience, in which an event activates our archetypal capacity to perceive wholeness, is responsible for the way it feels to our ego that the meaning of such events comes from without, from an external source, from an objective principle of order in the universe. When we perceive such wholeness, it does not feel as if we, our egos, our everyday selves, are the author of the significance, but as if there is an Author, a Self with a capital S, whose plan for our lives seems wondrous and comprehensive in its structure and coherence.

This archetype of wholeness is responsible for what Jung called the God-image in the human psyche. His phrase, the God-image, rather than God, is an observation meant neither to deny the possibility of an objective God nor to denigrate the beliefs and experiences of those who feel able to make such objective assertions about ultimate realities. It is merely to observe the particular qualities in human experience which allow some of us to perceive God's action in our lives, and for others, who do not believe in God, to understand why the God-image is so powerful, universal, and important, why, as Voltaire said, "If God didn't exist, it would be necessary to invent him."

Our capacity to perceive wholeness, the archetype of the Self, is therefore the author of our stories, the means by which chance events are connected through their subjective significance. For those of us for whom God is the first cause in the entire chain of causality, the result of which is the universe, as for Thomas Aquinas, there are no accidents, for God is the Author of all our stories. For others of us, whose faith in an objective principle of order in the universe is not quite as certain, whose notion of God's role in our everyday lives is unclear, or whose belief in an objective God does not preclude an interest in what it is about *humans* that allows us to perceive and know God, Jung's notion of the Self provides a non-theological way of speaking about and understanding such meaningful coincidences.

Through the psychological principle of synchronicity, value is placed on our subjective realities, a value that is not permitted by either religious or scientific viewpoints concerning the nature of objective reality. In the idea that our innate human capacity to perceive wholeness accounts for the meaning we experience in random events, Jung has provided us with a way to speak of the transformation we undergo through the coincidences of our lives and the myths that they reveal to us about who we are most deeply.

When Worlds Collide: Mystical Experiences as Synchronistic Events

With an understanding of Jung's concept of the Self to address the important questions that tend to arise around spirituality and synchronicity, let us now push even further into the thicket, into the realm of what are traditionally called mystical experiences. In the ordinary sense of the term, every synchronistic experience is mystical, in that it defies the usual way we go about understanding our lives as a chain of causes and effects. But while synchronistic experiences are frequently mystifying, they are not necessarily "mystical" in the sense that the term has been traditionally used in Western religion: an individual's direct, conscious experience of God.

Given this definition, obviously, every mystical experience is not necessarily synchronistic, for many involve no coincidence between inner state and outer event but instead are wholly inward, transformative experiences that bring us to a higher consciousness. In Ellie's story, for example, the spiritual awakening she experienced in her meditative practice was not itself a synchronistic event, in that it was not a coincidence between inner and outer, even though it was indeed an example of a mystical experience—a direct experience of a higher level of consciousness which changed her inner life. What she experienced as synchronistic were the series of chance events that occurred afterward, which led her to the place where she felt she could fulfill what had become, by way of her mystical experience, her vocation to transpersonal psychology.

The stories which follow concern mystical experiences which *were* synchronistic in nature. These stories are meaningful coincidences between inner vision and outer event which either had a specific religious or spiritual content to it, or which had an important effect on the development of an individual's spiritual awareness. They illustrate the role that synchronistic events can play even in our relationship to God, however God is understood.

The story which Stuart told me of how he found his own vocation as a therapist is one example of a mystical experience that was synchronistic. As has been the case for many of the individuals who shared their stories with me, Stuart found himself unhappy in his situation as an actor in New York City, scrambling for jobs, "terminally self-absorbed," to use his own description, and feeling very much in need of a major change of life. A series of events then occurred in which this change of life, with all its excitement and disruption, came to pass. Offered an acting job out of state with a troupe that worked with kids to raise consciousness about issues of abuse, just as his partner was falling ill in the terminal stages of AIDS, he became acquainted with the woman who would become his mentor when she impulsively offered him a room in her own house, not knowing he was in need of housing at the time. During all of these events, however, Stuart's own feeling was not the "Aha" sort of experience others have had but rather a continuing sense of questioning: "Why is this happening to me? Why not? Where is this going?" He had the vague feeling of being led somewhere for something, but without really knowing what or where.

It wasn't until after his partner's death that an utterly unique inner experience occurred to Stuart and synchronistically clarified what he needed to do next. While he was folding his laundry in a laundromat in Manhattan, his mind wandering, a voice in his head said clearly, distinctly, and simply: "San Francisco." At this point in telling me his story, Stuart laughed. "I don't know how to describe it. It wasn't my voice. It wasn't as if I was talking to myself or anything like that. It was just very clear and that's all it said. Just 'San Francisco.' "

Now in the course of his work with kids which, it turned out, was far more psychotherapeutic in focus than a mere acting gig, Stuart had grown in insight and had learned to heed such messages. So when, coincidentally, he discovered that friends of his were going to take a trip to San Francisco, he invited himself along, and that is where he now lives and pursues his career as a psychotherapist. As he said to me, "This is where I need to be. This is the place I was supposed to go," I could see the resolution in his face of all the many questions he had been asking himself about his direction in life. Like stories we have already heard of people being seemingly guided to the right place at the right time, Stuart's story involves a direct, immediate, conscious, and transformative experience of hearing a specific voice tell him to do a specific thing, which ultimately ended in his making the transition he had been searching for in his life.

The natural question raised by this incident is, who or what was that voice? Was it Stuart himself? Stuart says it wasn't. The way he describes the experience is *not* as an ordinary coming to consciousness about his desire to move to the West Coast but as an entirely random and very specific inner event that led him to change his life.

Was it God? Unlike Ellie, who was more comfortable using religious language to describe her experience of an inner voice, Stuart seemed quite wary of concluding that God had told him to go to San Francisco. And yet, he felt convinced that were it not for the mystical experience of being told where he should go he would not have the life he has in San Francisco, a place he had not really anticipated ever living in.

As with dreams, the synchronistic direction of mystical experiences such as this one is from the "inside out"; the acausal element is the inner event which comes from nowhere, certainly not from the individual's conscious sense of self. The very use of the word "mystical" to describe such happenings indicates that *who* the voice is might never be objectively determined. But the subjective meaning of the event, confirmed by Stuart's subsequent external satisfaction in this new chapter of his life, makes Stuart's story a synchronistic one—for this inner voice led him directly but coincidentally to an important change of life.

All ages and cultures are rife with stories of physical healing that synchronistically coincided with mystical revelations or instructions. I will confine myself here to one told to me personally, to illustrate how what from traditional religious perspective is a mystical healing could also be called a synchronistic event.

Juanita, who came with her family to the United States from Puerto Rico, had suffered most of her life with psoriasis on her hands, for which doctors had long been able to do nothing. She had tried all sorts of standard medical treatments, such as drugs and lotions, and, these failing, Juanita turned to less standard forms of treatment, native herbal remedies prepared by friends and the like, also without avail.

One day, during prayer in which, she says, her condition was not the focus, she, like Stuart, heard the voice of a woman whom she immediately identified as the Virgin Mary, who told her that she should immerse her hands in water and give thanks to God for her healing. Juanita remembers the sweetness in the voice as its most outstanding characteristic, a loving, maternal tone which Juanita said made her instantly feel very good all over. She did as the voice said, filling her sink in the bathroom and putting her hands into the basin while offering thanks to God. In a week, her life-long psoriasis was gone.

It has become a bit of a hobby to adduce causal explanations for such events as Juanita's, explanations usually based on the notion of psychosomatic illnesses or, to use an older term, conversion disorders, where emotional conflict manifests or is converted into physical symptomatology. When spontaneous healings occur, therefore, they are explained as some obscure unconscious conflict that is resolved so that the person can "give up" the illness or affliction. In theological or religious terms, obviously, the explanation is a good deal different, and the idea that the Virgin Mary visited Juanita as mediator for a specific and very concrete manifestation of God's generosity—which is Juanita's own interpretation of events—in itself explains the resolution of her psoriasis. Nowadays, in the midst of New Age consciousness, the so-called mind-body connection, shorn of any notion of the unconscious as well as of any specific doctrinal affiliation, is taken for granted to be *de facto* the cause of such events. And of course, any of these causal explanations could be persuasive, given your own background, intellectual habit, and personal experiences.

If one refrains, though, from attempting to ascertain the causality of the specific physical event and appreciates instead Juanita's own subjective experience—out of nowhere a loving voice promises a physical healing which does in fact subsequently take place, apparently attendant upon Juanita's obedience to the instructions she is given—then, what we see is what we have been calling synchronistic thus far: an internal event which to the individual is experienced not as herself but as Someone Else delivering her instructions, guidance, or advice that, when followed, coincides with meaningful external developments in the person's life.

My point is that by calling such a mystical experience synchronistic, we are not attempting to explain what happened in religious or psychological terms. All we are doing is commenting on the structure of the incident, in which a chance internal event coincides with meaningful outer events, and stating that this event has been incorporated as an important incident in the story Juanita tells of her life. Because our purpose in this book has consistently been to explore how people make sense of their lives, how random occurrences are woven into a story that gives our lives coherence, when it comes to mystical experiences especially, the content of the event—what it meant—must always be the individual's own to interpret and live.

Unlike Juanita, Val tells the story of a mystical experience which resulted synchronistically in a healing that was emotional, rather than physical, in nature. During her father's long illness, Val and the rest of her siblings had kept a distance from him. Abusive during their childhood and not having mellowed with age, he had become in this latter part of his life entirely dependent upon Val's mother to cope with his steady decline in health. So when Val's mother called her one day to ask if she might come and stay with them to give her some respite, Val went with heavy heart and much resistance.

When she arrived, the scene was as bad as she had imagined it would be. She was uncomfortable sleeping in the house she had all but fled many years earlier. Her father, in chronic pain, went in and out of consciousness, and her mother was distraught, exhausted, and dependent on her. After a few days there, Val suddenly woke up one morning and felt what she described as a "powerful message" to get in the car. She obeyed and drove as guided by an unknown force to an area of town she had never been to before and found herself in a shopping center she had never previously visited. Her conscious mind, mystified as to why she was doing any of this and yet feeling compelled to do so, she entered a bookstore and without browsing at all went straight to the back, to a shelf of books on natural healing treatments, picking one particular book off the shelf from all the others and opening it to the specific page in which a treatment for the relief of pain was described entailing the use of camphor oil and flannel. Stupefied, she bought the book, went to a nearby store where she bought the camphor oil and flannel she had been directed to buy, and brought them home, where her mother was sitting, eating breakfast in the kitchen downstairs.

Feeling certain she had gone off the deep end, Val told her

mother of her experience, and the two of them went over the treatment for pain described in the book. Wondering if perhaps she herself was meant to do the healing described, Val handed the chore over to her mother, unable to face the sort of contact with her father that it entailed.

"Their relationship had always been bad, and the illness hadn't helped," Val told me, as I listened to the juke box near us begin to play the music from the final scene of Wagner's *Tristan und Isolde*, a synchronistic touch providing a real-world soundtrack for the story I was hearing. "But, you know, that massage with the camphor oil and flannel changed their whole relationship. I don't know whether it relieved his pain physically, I suppose it did somewhat, but the real healing took place emotionally, because after this massage, which only happened because I happened to follow an extremely weird inner message of astounding specificity, my mother and father actually fell in love with each other again. I left soon after this incident, since I was really no longer needed, and their second honeymoon continued for the whole last year of his life. They were really sweet to one another. I would call to talk to them, and both of them were like different people. It was truly amazing. It was like I had been the vehicle for an emotional healing, though don't ask me why or how. I don't know. All I know was that the message I had gotten, like instructions from the universe, changed everything. It was really something."

In the mystical experiences of Stuart, Val, and Juanita, an inner experience of an entirely different character than any previous experience they had ever had led them to actions in the outer world which changed their lives or those of people around them, actions they would never have otherwise taken. Less awesome, perhaps, but no less mystical is Tony d'Aguanno's story of his vision quest. (The reader may remember Tony from his story of the "magic bill," which he had given his friend in lieu of a job.) During a Native American ritual in which the participants were urged to choose a power object for themselves from a pile of rocks that stood in the middle of a circle, Tony volunteered to go first. He had planned to examine each rock in the pile to select the one that felt most right to him, but then, on the periphery of his vision, he saw a particular rock shaped like a mountain with a wolf's head on top, "pulsating," in his words. Without thinking, he chose this rock and took it home with him at the end of the ritual.

Tony was preparing to leave for a two-month trek around the country, but the week before his departure date, his car began to give him trouble, and his mechanic told him that the engine seals were all but shot. She urged him to plan on using another car, in that it was all but certain the engine would not last, but Tony ignored her advice and set out anyway, thinking at the last moment: "I better take that rock with me."

In the foothills of the Sierras, the inevitable came to pass. The temperature gauge of the car went through the roof, and Tony was forced to pull off to the side of the road to camp for the night. In the morning, receiving a message from somewhere, someone, or something, Tony did a sort of spontaneous ritual with the rock over the engine of the car, feeling a little foolish and yet feeling just as impelled to carry out his actions. The car started up that morning, and even though it continued to have intermittent problems throughout the rest of his journey, it nonetheless got him home.

When Tony took the car right away to his mechanic for the repairs that he had put off for months, she looked at him in amazement. "I've never seen this before. The seals are fine," she said, unable to believe her eyes or Tony, when he swore to her that he'd not had any work done on the car.

Whether or not his own "power object" in the form of the rock he had chosen or the ritual he had performed over the engine magically "caused" the healing is most certainly beyond determination. But such mystical experiences as Val's and Tony's, in which individuals feel themselves guided, forced, or drawn inwardly to perform particular rituals that dramatically coincide with external events illustrate another way that we come in contact with a sense of wholeness, the Self we are part of, that gives shape and coherence to our story.

The lives of mystics are always punctuated, if not almost wholly structured, by stories of amazing incidents of the sort presented in the last section, generally referred to in religious language as miracles, signs of God's direct intervention in human history. Indeed, for one's sainthood to be recognized by the Roman Catholic Church, a specific number of certified miracles connected with the individual is required, and such things as healings, bilocation (appearing in two places simultaneously), and the physical transformation of objects form the general corpus of miraculous feats that give evidence of one's holiness.

In contrast to stories of healing, in some religious traditions, wounding and suffering are the essence of the mystical synchronicity instead, as is the case for the men and women in the Christian tradition who are reported to have received the wounds of Jesus Christ on their own bodies. Stigmatics, as they are called, starting with Saint Francis of Assisi who received the marks of Christ during an ecstatic experience toward the end of his life, are from one point of view living examples of synchronicity, the physical wounds in their hands, feet, and sides coinciding with the wounds of the crucified Christ described in the New Testament. Though it is easy to call such stories mere legends when they date from the Middle Ages, more recent, extremely well-documented examples of this particular form of mystical experience, such as Padre Pio from Pietrelcina, are harder to ignore.

Born in a small southern Italian town in 1887, Francesco For-gione was by all accounts pious even by the standards of his time and place. He entered the priesthood and quickly evinced an intensity of religious devotion. In 1918, after a celebration of St. Francis's reception of the stigmata, Padre Pio, as Forgione was now called as a priest, awoke the next morning from an ecstatic state of union with God that had left him on the floor of the choir loft of the church, bleeding profusely and painfully from his hands, feet, and side. These wounds never healed throughout the following fifty years of his life.

Mystics and mystical experiences by their very nature bring forth strong responses from believers and nonbelievers alike. In contrast to what some anticlerical types might believe about organized religion— that such mystical experiences are used and promoted by the church to advance claims the church supposedly has on the ultimate truth of existence—the reality is that the institutional church hierarchy of the Roman Catholic Church has consistently shown itself as hostile and suspicious toward mystical experiences such as appearances of the Virgin Mary, spontaneous healings, and phenomena like the stigmata. In part due to fears of hoaxes being perpetrated to discredit the church or dupe credulous believers into scams of a spiritual, financial, or psychological nature, and in part due to the general anxiety any bu-reaucrat feels when faced with irrational challenges to his or her au-thority, those within the church may not be any more likely to believe in the appearance of such mystical phenomena than the most hardcore rationalist outside the faith.

For example, following the appearance of Padre Pio's wounds, which during his long life no medical treatment was ever able to cure nor psychological examination to explain, Padre Pio's own superiors placed him virtually under "house arrest," forbidding him to appear in public, to say mass, to have any prolonged interaction with anyone outside a small, immediate circle. Nevertheless, as one can imagine,

Padre Pio developed quite a following, and the stories of healings effected by him, of visionary appearances he made to people in turmoil or need, and of the wisdom of his teachings quickly became legion. Because he lived in the twentieth century, Padre Pio's story has been examined with all the thoroughness of modern science, and while one can debate whether the cause of his stigmata was psychological, spiritual, mystical, physical, or self-inflicted, or argue about whether or not he was a saint or a hysteric, one element of Padre Pio's story lies beyond doubt: his wounds were real.

Not knowing any of this story, during high school I developed a very close friendship with the captain of our high-school soccer team, Vince, whose family had been born in Pietrelcina and had personally known Padre Pio. My own background is thoroughly Protestant of a very down-to-earth American sort, so I knew nothing of mystics, and certainly nothing about Padro Pio except that Vince had been baptized by him and actually carried a scab from one of Padre Pio's wounds in his wallet. Like most teenagers in New Jersey would have, I thought Vince's scab thing was strange, but southern Italian Catholicism was, as I've said, more or less another world for me at the time, and of mystics, saints, stigmata, miracles, and cures, I was completely ignorant.

Vince and I continued our friendship into college, and the week before I was to leave for a year to study abroad in Italy, we went to mass together in a church near his dorm at the University of Pennsylvania. It was an early mass and the enormous church was all but deserted. Sitting right in the middle of it, with no one around us, three distinct times during the service I smelled the overwhelming scent of roses, once during the sermon, once during the consecration of the Host, and once at the benediction at the end. The odor was a peculiar one, very penetrating, like roses in decline, and very strong, washing over me in waves. I looked around and saw there were no roses in the church, no women close by who might be wearing perfume, and no incense burning.

On our way back to Vince's dorm room, Vince asked me simply, "Did you smell anything strange in church today?"

"Well, actually, I did—" I responded, but before I was able to tell him what it was, he silenced me.

"Don't say anything to me about it, okay. Just, when you go home tonight, go over to my parents' house and tell them that you smelled something at mass today."

Mystified, I did as I was told, going to Vince's parents that night and merely saying that I had smelled something in church. Vince's father, to my astonishment, described what I had smelled: "Roses, very strong, and three times, after the sermon, during the consecration, and at the end of the service."

Quite taken aback, I must have looked dumb-founded when I said, "That's right. That was exactly it. How could you possibly know?"

He acted completely calm and matter-of-fact, smiling slightly at my befuddlement. "That was the odor of Padre Pio's spirit which was with the two of you today, just before you leave for Italy. He was bestowing a blessing on your journey and on your friendship."

Indeed, as I have subsequently found out, the odor of roses is among one of the most frequently reported phenomena in connection with Padre Pio, but my own experience of it, a sort of mystical experience I had had without really even knowing I was having one, most certainly falls within the realm of the mystical synchronicities we have been discussing, though the direction here is reversed—an utterly unique outer event in the course of my life meaningfully coincided with an inner emotional situation to create in me a very different attitude toward such phenomena than the one I grew up with in my own religion, an openness toward the mysterious and unexplainable that I hadn't had before then. Though I have taken a staunchly agnostic stance toward this incident, not feeling as confident as Vince's father of placing a religious interpretation on the coincidence, I have still told the story many times to many people, just as Val or Stuart or Juanita have told their stories, a sign of just how significant such coincidences can be in the course of our life history.

When Worldviews Collide: Are Miracles Synchronistic?

What Padre Pio's story raises is a question that has often been posed to me, usually by people with an active religious faith: "Are miracles examples of synchronicity?" Though the answer to this question once again requires a thorough discussion of terms and premises, I believe the question is an important one, as we apply a psychological concept such as synchronicity in relationship to phenomena generally understood as part of the religious or sacred stories of a culture or of individuals.

What one needs to be clear about first is what the term "miracle" means, a word often used quite loosely in informal conversation. Derived from the Latin word *mirari*, to look at in wonder, in its most general meaning, a miracle is anything at all which excites our amazement. In this broad sense, therefore, anything extraordinary at all that makes us gape in astonishment—Luciano Pavarotti's high C, the stunning purple of an autumn sunset, the fact the Chicago Cubs won the World Series—could be called miraculous. But, within a religious context, the term "miracle" has a more precise meaning and is applied to events normally considered impossible in the physical world but which have come to pass through divine intervention: God parting the Red Sea for the Israelites, Jesus of Nazareth turning the water into wine at the wedding at Cana, Padre Pio healing a man of an illness every medical expert has declared incurable.

As mentioned before in our discussion concerning where meaning comes from and who the author of our stories is, this narrower religious use of the word "miracle" describes an event that from a religious perspective is not really "acausal," for after all, in such a view, God is the cause of miracles. But the word "acausal" as we have been using the term with reference to synchronicity refers to human cause and intentionality, to an event that the person himself or herself could not have made happen and did not intend to have happen. Obviously, when Stephen's car blew up in the accident that led to his job as a cameraman, the explosion had a cause—the car's radiator had a leak, the oil was low, and so forth. When we notice the coincidental nature of the event and describe it as an acausal occurrence, we are saying that Stephen himself did not will this event to occur and did not act consciously and deliberately to make it happen.

According to this understanding of the use of the word "acausal," therefore, we see that miracles are indeed, from our human perspective, acausal events, for in ascribing their cause to divine forces beyond human comprehension or control, miracles are *defined* as acausal. Otherwise, miracles would simply be "magic," a word we use to denote causality that is not empirically provable. In magic, we stick pins in an effigy of our boss and believe that this action will kill him—when he dies, it is to our own deliberate magical action that we ascribe the cause of his death, although we have no rational, empirical, or discernible reasons upon which to base our belief that we are the cause. In magic, *we* cause the impossible to happen through an occult sort of causality, through forces and powers unseen by most people but which magicians can manipulate for their own purposes.

In religious systems such as Christianity, Judaism, or Islam, however, miracles are the antithesis of magic, for, however much we may have sacrificed goats, prayed to St. Jude, or sent someone good or bad vibrations, only through the grace of divine intervention do miracles occur. Whatever actions we may have taken—prayer, sacrifices, and the like—are simply to ready ourselves to receive the generosity which God, Allah, the Great Spirit, or the Breath of Creation bestows in the form of an event impossible in human terms. God has granted our prayers through His grace, not because we prayed to St. Jude, sacrificed a lamb on the altar of the temple, or walked seven times around the Kaaba in Mecca. Miracles are, thus, acausal events in two senses: first, in the sense that their physical causes cannot be determined, and second, in the sense that *we* do not cause them.

In conclusion, then, "Are miracles synchronistic?" Indeed, they are, though the meaning of a miracle for a religious person is going to be quite a bit different for that of a nonbeliever. Here, we need only appreciate the difference between my response to the scent of roses in an empty church and that of my friend Vincent's parents. Mr. and Mrs. Mandato understood my amazing experience as a miracle, seeing in it the standard religious meaning—that God, through Padre Pio, was with us that day in church. I, however, have been able to accept this irrational experience as real by viewing it through the lens of what it meant to me, subjectively, emotionally, and symbolically. For me, refraining from absolute statements of objective reality, I can nevertheless term the event synchronistic—a coincidence whose significance lay in the difference it made in my hitherto very practical religious attitude by opening me to the possibility that God may be working in mysterious ways in my life. The spontaneous healing of Juanita's hands means one thing to her and quite another to her astounded doctor. In both cases, the event has emotional and symbolic significance as an acausal ocurrence, but in each case the meaning is different.

What of the opposite question, "Are synchronicities miracles?" Indeed, they can be, but again only for those whose religious faith leads them to perceive the action of God in this particular episode of their lives. To call a coincidence a miracle is to place a religious interpretation on the event, but even after you have explained a synchronistic event of a miraculous cast in terms of ordinary causality, a popular pastime since the advent of modern science—the Star of Bethlehem was an unusual conjunction of planets, the Israelites' passage through the Red Sea was made possible through drought conditions and a freakish wind pattern that blew the shallow water aside—one still has to reckon with the subjective significance of the event for those who experienced it as a random but transformative event in their stories of who they are. For some, the word "miracle" fits best to describe this significance, for others, the description "synchronicity" allows for a language that neither affirms a particular theological position nor dismisses the occurrence as nothing but unusual natural phenomena.

Telling Fortunes: Purposeful Luck and Meaningful Chance

The mystical experiences we have been discussing seem simply to happen to people, often without their willing it, sometimes, as in my case, without even their knowledge. Yet, in the realm of spirituality and religion, throughout time and cultures, the principle of synchronicity has been used actively and purposefully. By believing that outer events and inner experiences can coincide meaningfully, virtually all peoples everywhere have used this insight to develop ways of gaining spiritual direction for themselves, to discover the stories of their souls.

Having made so much of the acausal nature of synchronicity, the idea of divination, an active and intentional use of synchronistic events, might appear to be a contradiction: how can one set about *using* an occurrence that happens by chance? One way, a poor way, in my opinion, is to drag cause-and-effect ways of thinking into divinatory work, in which case the divination will look more or less like stereotypical fortune-telling: asking the cards, the tea leaves, the crystal ball, or the lots to tell us about specific future events, which numbers to play on Saturday's lottery, which horses to bet on, which of our boyfriends will be the most successful and so which we should marry. Such materialistic and concrete attitudes around predicting the future through mystical means are based on a presumption that the chain of cause and effect throughout time is immutable—*this* cause will have *that* effect predictably—and that if we know about these causes and effects in advance we will be able to "cause" another "effect" ourselves, i.e., win the lottery, become a millionaire, be happy.

As common and as universal as such an attitude might be among us all (modern people are hardly worse in this regard than the ancients, who sometimes used the oracles and necromancy just as materalistically as any modern-day bookie), the fact remains that a less crass and more meaningful way of approaching synchronicity exists. All methods of divination presume that chance *can be* meaningful, though not always or definitely, and if it *is* meaningful, it is usually considered meaningful with respect to the state of one's spiritual development rather than the spread of tomorrow's horse race. This approach to divination is not prediction but exploration, and when we look at the many methods of divination throughout time and culture, we find an endless variety, from familiar and everyday to esoteric and elaborate.

Some of these methods are folkloric and quaint, such as Sharon's grandmother's belief in the predictive power of the apple peel from Chapter 2. Some of them are idiosyncratic, as when Lisa scrutinized the various actions of the animals that appeared to her in the wilderness in response to various questions she had in mind at the time. And yet they can also include as elaborate a discipline as astrology, in which the positions of the stars at various points in an individual's life are understood to hold meaning.

On the other hand, some methods of divination are explicitly spiritual or philosophical in nature, for example, the throwing of the sticks as an indication of which passage to read in the book of Chinese wisdom called *I Ching* or the Book of Changes, or the common Christian practice of opening the Bible at random to whatever passage the eye happens to catch first. Even so, both of these divinatory practices involve the manipulation of material objects, and indeed, some methods of divination consist of nothing but such manipulations and examinations, seeing messages in the matter itself: Etruscan necromancers, on the Italian peninsula before the Roman Empire, examined the livers of chickens, seeing in their markings and shape omens for the future and meanings concerning the present, just as the pattern discerned in the bottom of a cup of tea leaves is consulted for the shape of things to come or the order of the universe at a particular moment.

Various symbolic methods, which use images and pictures, have had long and venerable histories, such as the Nordic runes, in which various tiles with letters are chosen at random and examined for meaning. In this same category of symbolic methods, a primary form of divination for Westerners is the Tarot, whose history is traced by some as far back as ancient Egypt but which in all likelihood dates to the European Middle Ages. That psychologists would be shocked to see such tests as the Rohrschach with its inkblots or the Thematic Apperception Test with its open-ended drawings as the modern-day descendants of the Tarot does not change the principle behind symbolic modes of divination: in encountering an external reality—an inkblot, a picture, a symbolic card, a chicken liver, a random passage, or a pattern in nature—we can better encounter and see our inner spiritual reality.

Why is this true? Why does divination work? Why have people always and everywhere developed such methods and used them? Again, those who believe in an objective divinity would assert that it is because God or the gods send us messages through external patterns, objects, and signs. But if we refrain from such ontological assertions and stay strictly within the realm of human experience, we can see that divinatory methods allow us to use the very same capacity as we use to create art, write fiction, or imagine anything significant into being. In approaching external reality with an assumption that meaning is possible, we allow the archetype of the Self the ability to manifest itself, not externally or causally but subjectively and symbolically. The only difference between a divinatory process and the other synchronistic events we've heard so far is that the latter tend to take us by surprise, seeming to present us with a coherence to our stories that we had been unconscious of, while during divination we are conscious and deliberate in being open to the meaning of what we are presented with in the random patterns of the cards, runes, tea leaves, yarrow stalks, or coins.

Such is the case with the very conscious and deliberate method the Chinese monks at Kuei-yuan use to elect an abbot as head of their community. As reported by Holmes Welch and Robert Aziz, these monks choose an abbot by drawing lots from among the names of hundreds of candidates: after prayer and ritual, a senior member of the community uses chopsticks to pick out a name from a metal tube, and the person whose name is drawn three times in a row—from among the hundreds possible—is acknowledged as the abbot. As one might imagine, this time-consuming process, which the community continues for as long as it takes until the thrice-chosen name appears, can sometimes eventuate in the selection of a person whom the community initially perceives as a bad or problematic candidate. But even when almost universally acknowledged inferior individuals have been chosen, this method nevertheless seems consistently to have worked: to the community's surprise, such "inferior" individuals have proven themselves capable leaders, which points up the elegance of such a method in which pure chance—free from the influences of human prejudice, envy, malice, and ambition—is better at providing for the community's leadership than any mortal could have been.[1]

This example of a "deliberate synchronicity" serves well for us to examine just what conditions are necessary for such chance to lead to insight and significance. First, like the monks at Kuei-yuan, one needs to take seriously what is being presented. Like Marie who did not question her dream after she asked for guidance, when one uses a method of divination, one needs to listen to the answer presented. Synchronicity always relativizes the ego, and whether accidental or deliberate, the synchronistic result of a divinitory process may be one which we initially do not want to accept or are not yet capable of seeing.

Second, one needs to keep in mind that the result of the divinitory process is going to be subjective in nature, in the realm of the inner meaning of the story of our lives, rather than physical or material in the basest sense. Many people, in my experience, approach methods of divination with the idea that they are going to be told what to do, as if the pattern in the Tarot cards or in the stars is a secret code to be broken in which an explicit action-oriented suggestion is going to be made, as if an objective meaning out there in some way is going to be radioed in through the receptor of the cards or the astrological chart. In appreciating how meaning is made in our lives, from the inside out rather than from the outside in through the capacity of our Self to order the disparate parts of our lives into a coherent, symbolically profound narrative, the random pattern presents us with an opportunity to explore the meaning of what already exists in that specific moment, rather than to tell us what will be in the future.

Randomness is the essential difference between projective psychological tests and traditional methods of divination. Tests like the Rohrschach or the TAT have been standardized so that the patterns are always the same, which enables comparisons from person to person and the collection and organization of data on groups of people's psychological constitutions. In divination, by contrast, the patterns created by the stars, the Tarot cards, the sticks, or the tea leaves are always uniquely different and time-specific, meaning that divination is an individual process, unable to be replicated, as singular as a story or a work of art.

My client Bobbie, whose story about being synchronistically given a Tarot deck by her husband appeared in the introduction to this book, initially approached using the cards with the typical "give me an answer" attitude until gradually she found her attitude changing into one of exploration and openness. In one funny incident that helped change her approach, she told me she had asked for a specific suggestion about what to do in a certain situation. At the time, she used a very simple layout of five cards in a cross, a pattern she had been shown in a dream, in which the top card represented what she was aware of in the situation in question, the bottom card what she was unaware of, the cards on the right and left what was in conflict in the situation, and the center card the resolution.

However, after Bobbie dealt the cards, the answer she felt she received from the cards was one she didn't particularly care for—the cards and their symbols seemed to suggest that she should take no action at all, since they were all images of people sitting and contemplating situations. Bobbie felt that strong action was needed in this situation, so she decided that rather than listen to the spread she would do another layout, hopeful that a second reading would give her a more palatable answer.

She dealt the cards again, only to find to her amazement that all the cards were upside down, that is, facing away from her, as if they didn't want to talk to her. When she told me about this incident, feeling equally sheepish and enlightened, she and I both drew the same conclusion from the occurrence: having ignored the message of the first layout, the second layout confronted her resistance to listening to what she had already been told.

In synchronistic events like this one, it almost seems that the cards had a will of their own, that they were offended. Yet, it is possible to pay attention and derive meaning from the random event without placing such an anthropomorphizing construction on an occurrence. Again the story of the monks is instructive: when faced with an abbot who is wholly unlike what they imagined, they do not start all over until "chance" chooses someone they consider more suitable. Rather they presume the meaningfulness of the chance occurrence and work with it in a process of inward, spiritual exploration.

Sometimes though such modes of divination have the same "predictive" feel as some of the dreams did in the previous chapter, and to see such coincidences as examples of inward meaning rather than "fortune-telling" can be quite a psychological challenge. For all my interest in synchronicity, I am not immune to the habitual temptation of applying retrospective causality to the story of my life.

On a lark in Italy on the last night of my vacation with friends, my best friend from college, Michael, and I consulted a card reader whose methods I had never seen before. We asked, "What does the future hold for our friendship?" and the woman, dressed up in fake gypsy turban and all, began flipping over cards, one after another into a pile, until after a dozen or so cards she stopped, pulled out three, and said, "A woman will come between the two of you," in dramatic fashion designed for tourists like ourselves.

Now it was hard to take such a prediction seriously. First, it sounded like the sort of stock prediction you could make to any two men, except that we were two gay men and the likelihood of a woman coming between us was slim to none. Second, it looked very much like the woman had simply rifled through the cards until she found two cards with male figures separated by one with a female figure, ostensibly to support her prediction and prove to us that it was in the cards. We laughed and thought nothing more about it.

Michael was scheduled to fly back home the next day, in the early afternoon, and I had made an early-morning appointment with the owner of the wine estate where we all had been staying to see what the other houses on the estate were like. The property wasn't big and the plan was for me to get home in time to drive Michael to the airport in Pisa an hour away. However, fate intervened, and the car that Benedetta, the property manager, was driving repeatedly broke down on the far side of the estate, so that by the time I got back home, Michael had left, afraid of missing his plane. I didn't think much of it even then, for the two of us spoke that night by phone.

Since he went to Germany and I returned to the States, when Michael died a year later, the story that had been told by the card-reader in Florence that night had been the story that we had lived. A woman, Benedetta, *had* come between Michael and me on our last day in Italy, and that night in Florence was the last time I was with Michael during his life. I had not gotten a chance to say goodbye to Michael in person: a woman had come between us.

As always in synchronistic events, as we have seen, only after the fact can the significance of what happened be discerned and appreciated. In this case, more moving than the card-reader's prediction coming true was for me the poignancy of the coincidence, the unexpected way my best friend and I took our final leave from each other, a story which has since become a permanent part of my history. The prediction in itself was useless at the time, after all—neither of us could conceive of what she had told us actually happening; its importance lies wholly in the way that the subsequent events affected me. What is important in a divinatory process is really not the predictions or the revelations, the signs or omens in themselves, but rather how our capacity to perceive the wholeness of our lives—the Self—may bring inward and outward aspects of our lives into a relationship with each other with the result that the story of our lives is written simultaneously for us and with us.

Synchronicity and a Psychology of Our Sacred Stories

As we have seen in this chapter, three different worldviews can collide in the stories of synchronicities in people's spiritual lives. One, upholding rationality, science, and causality, often calls such stories "myths" in a derogatory sense and tosses their reality aside, placing them on par with tall tales and other entertaining bits of fiction: they did not happen and could not have happened. The second, upholding God's objective reality, also calls such events "myths" but uses the term affirmingly, in the sense of a "sacred story" whose reality is important to appreciate: such things did occur, they occurred by the will of God, and their significance is religious in nature. The third viewpoint, the one we have seen applied to such synchronicities, is that of psychology, which refrains from taking such sides and limits itself to noting how important such "myths" are to humankind: coincidences such as these do occur and they mean something.

To answer seemingly simple questions about meaningful coincidences has therefore demanded that we understand what premises lie beneath the questions and spend some time untangling the threads of terms and presumptions. Regardless of our approach, though, the examples given here of synchronicity in people's spiritual and religious lives, the most inward and sacred parts of our life stories, indicate to me that our capacity to find meaning is what gives our lives the quality of a single, unified story. It is meaning which structures our lives into a coherent narrative, and in synchronistic events, occurrences fraught with meaning, we contact the Author, a higher Self, upon which we, like the people whose stories we have heard in this chapter, might rely for orientation, inspiration, and wholeness.

Chapter Six

Every Story
Has a Beginning
and an Ending

Synchronicity
and Matters of Life
and Death

Sweet breezes have awoken
Day and night they stir and whisper;
Everywhere they are at work.
Oh fresh perfume, oh new music!
Now, poor heart, fear no longer,
Now, all things must change.

The world grows more beautiful each day,
And what may yet happen, one cannot tell.
The flowering will not end, and
Even the deepest, most distant valley is blooming.
Now, my poor heart, forget your pain.
Now, all things must change

LUDWIG UHLAND
"Faith in Springtime" (Frühlingsglaube)

Of the four aspects of synchronicity pre-
sented at the start of this book, the fact that such coincidences always
happen at points of transition is the aspect which most informs the

tale of our life as a whole. We have thus far been looking for the most part at stories *in* people's lives—who they love, what they do, how they grow, what they believe. In this final chapter, we will be looking at the bigger picture: the story *of* our life, and how synchronistic events occur in the two most momentous and universal of transitions—our births and our deaths.

That our birth and death frame our life stories so significantly seems at first almost too obvious to mention, except perhaps to stress, in light of what we have indicated concerning synchronicity so far, that the literal transitions into and out of existence we each experience have acquired for humans a very important symbolic meaning. Not only do theologians and scholars of religion, with some justification, put the archetypal cycle of birth, death, and rebirth as the very center of all religious rituals throughout time and across cultures, but, as we have seen in the stories already recounted, the symbolic aspect of birth and death informs the story of each transition we make throughout our lives, such that throughout our lives we experience many little deaths and many recurrent births again and again.

In this final chapter, we will be focusing on those specific stories I am tempted to call our autobiographies, and even more specifically on the beginnings and endings of these stories. I am sure that by now, given all the stories we have already heard, the notion that synchronistic events occur around birth and death will hardly surprise anyone. Expectably such occurrences show us what they have shown us in other areas of our life, namely, the narrative coherence of our stories, the potential wholeness beneath the lives we live.

In dealing with our actual transition into and out of life, however, our literal birth and our literal death, synchronistic events often intervene to underscore the deeply symbolic aspect of these transitions which people too often overlook. So, in the stories of pregnancy, birth, death, and bereavement that follow, it was a meaningful coincidence that served to remind the person involved of what the archetypal images of religious ritual and myth have always shown: that our life is a cycle, in which death follows birth, and rebirth follows death, and how, as in Uhland's poem above, all things must change.

In Due Time: Pregnancy, Birth, and Synchronicity

Almost thirty years ago, Mary Williams, a Jungian analyst in London, submitted an article to the *Journal of Analytical Psychology* concerning an experience with a patient of hers whose story presents so many of the themes that I, too, discovered when I heard women's stories concerning their pregnancies. The timing of conception, the circumstances surrounding the pregnancy and birth, and women's feelings and reactions to this central experience are so often rife with synchronistic elements that after a while one almost stops being amazed by the presence of such coincidences and begins to expect the unexpected.

The woman in Mary Williams's story began psychotherapeutic treatment due to deep conflicts about her womanhood. Thirty-eight years old and married, she suffered from a lack of sexual responsiveness and fits of crying which she traced back to the beginning of her menstruation; her mother had reacted to her first period as if it were a catastrophe. Under the care of a domineering mother and aunts, this woman, an only child, grew up fearful and unsure of herself. Although she had married her husband for convenience, he nevertheless seemed to view his wife as a "fine mother for his children."

In such a situation, where the woman in question obviously needs to make a transition in her life and in her feelings about herself, a dream with prophetic and hopeful overtones not unlike many we have already heard came to her. In this dream, the woman said:

"I was in a room like yours [the therapist's]. There was a crash. A picture in a brown mahogany frame had fallen off the wall. When

Your nearest Church of Scientology

Drugs, toxins and radiation destroy your life.
Get rid of them!

Do the

Scientology® Purification® Program

❑ **YES!** Send me more information about how to start the Purification Program.

❑ **YES!** Send me a FREE catalog of books, lectures and videos by L. Ron Hubbard.

Name _____

Address _____

City _____

State/Province _____ Zip/Postal code _____

Phone _____

e-mail address _____

Fill in this card on both sides and send it to
your nearest Scientology organization.
(Find addresses at the back of *Clear Body, Clear Mind*.)

Visit our web site: www.clearbodyclearmind.com

BUSINESS REPLY MAIL
FIRST CLASS MAIL   PERMIT NO. 62688   LOS ANGELES, CA

POSTAGE WILL BE PAID BY ADDRESSEE

BRIDGE PUBLICATIONS, INC.

4751 FOUNTAIN AVE.

LOS ANGELES, CA 90029

How Toxic are you?

Drugs, toxins and radiation block a person's ability to think clearly. How much are they affecting you? Get your FREE Toxic Test and find out.

❏ **YES!** Send me a FREE Toxic Test.

❏ **YES!** I want more information about the Purification® Program. And send me a FREE catalog of books, lectures and videos by L. Ron Hubbard.

Name _____

Address _____

City _____

State/Province _____ Zip/Postal code _____

Phone _____

e-mail address _____

MAIL IN THIS CARD TODAY
Take the test online at www.clearbodyclearmind.com

I went to look at it, the picture fell out. It was like a nest of boxes. As I looked, they came out one after the other. And then, deep inside, I saw a baby doll. Its hands were raised and it seemed to be smiling at me."

Familiar with an English superstition in which a picture falling off the wall is a harbinger of imminent death, the woman marveled at the juxtaposition of this prophecy of death and what seemed, at the time, the remote possibility that she might be pregnant, symbolized by her discovery "deep inside" of the baby doll with its hands raised toward her. Williams goes on to describe the synchronicities which then occurred in this woman's life subsequent to the dream.

"The first intimation of the 'prophetic' nature of the dream occurred three weeks later with the sudden death of [her] mother. The patient was absent for four months settling the estate and looking after her father. On [her] return, she appeared to be pregnant (and this was shortly confirmed) but had not considered the possibility as her periods had continued, though they had been abnormal ones. . . . There were no more mysterious crying fits. Her reaction to her pregnancy was ambivalent, intense pleasure coupled with resentment against fate for forcing the issue before she felt ready for it.

"The synchronicities were by no means at an end. Her doctor became anxious because the foetal head had not descended into the pelvis at the expected time, so [he] sent the patient to a specialist. There was a discrepancy of about six weeks between their forecasts [of the birth date] which threw the patient into a state of anxiety as she had many arrangements to make. . . . She then appealed to the analyst who unthinkingly fell into the role of oracle and, taking the date of the dream as the date of conception, counted up two hundred and eighty days and gave the answer [as to when the baby would be born]. This made the doctor's forecast three weeks early and the specialist's three weeks late. The oracle appeared confounded as nothing happened on the predicted date. Three weeks later, [the woman] was admitted to hospital with an induction in view. By that time, however, the size of the foetus compared with the size of the opening made a cesarian section advisable. The baby, a fine boy, was slightly dehydrated and from his condition, the dream date was confirmed.

"We cannot speculate as to what held up the onset of labour, but two further meaningful coincidences must be mentioned. The patient's mother died three weeks after the dream and the baby was delivered three weeks after term. Had she unconsciously equated the two events in time? Then, as the patient herself remarked, 'Cesarian babies look like dolls and not like new-born babies at all!' an observation of fact which again linked the outer and inner reality in a meaningful manner. What seemed to be psychically true was that the child and the new self had not yet become sufficiently real to her.

"Mother and baby were seen two months later and from her expression there was no doubt that the infant had become a reality. It was noted that her household now consisted of three males, her father, her husband, and her son; a significant change of pattern from that of her former setting [that is, her family of origin dominated by women]."[1]

So, this woman's dream of her pregnancy had the additional synchronicity of coinciding with her mother's death as well in a set of circumstances which indeed came to pass in the outer world. But the synchronistic timing of the pregnancy is what is most striking here: being released by her mother's death from the very unhealthy emotional relationship which had sent her to analysis in the first place, this woman found herself almost immediately able to "conceive," literally as well as figuratively, of being a mother herself, a mature, adult woman.

Judy, an acquaintance of mine, told me a nearly identical story of synchronistic timing, with her own first pregnancy occurring in conjunction with her mother's death. "I had been trying for quite a long time to get pregnant through artificial insemination, and nothing seemed to be working. I had been through many, many procedures, which, as you may know, have an ever decreasing probability of effectiveness. That is to say, if it hasn't worked the first, second, and third time, it is less likely that further fertility drugs are going to work. It really is a case of diminishing returns, and I knew that. My doctor at the time was very frank with me, setting the odds of having a healthy baby at about 20 to 1 under the circumstances, but I figured I would try one more cycle of drugs and see what happened, and after that, would make my peace with not getting pregnant.

"Meanwhile, my mother had been ailing, which was an additional stress, and so I am dealing with this, as well as the insemination, the drugs, the timing of it all. Then my mother dies, not unexpected, but how can you ever prepare for it really? And the very next ovulation after her death, I get pregnant, and so does my sister."

The conjunction of birth and death here in Judy's story mirrors the story Williams tells of the predictive dream of her patient (though without the emotional difficulties of Williams's patient), and also underlines the odd way that pregnancies occur with a timing that in itself may be an example of meaningful chance. Certainly the symbolism of the previous generation passing on to make room for the next is inherent in these stories, recalling the many myths and fairy tales from around the world in which the connection between birth and death is also presented: the older king or queen needs to be deposed, killed, or removed in order for creativity and fertility to be restored to the land. In these synchronistic stories which link birth and death so closely, we see that indeed fiction often reflects the truth of the stories people live.

The element of timing in these stories, the fact that pregnancies can synchronistically occur at an especially significant juncture in one's life, is reflected in yet another story told to me, this time by Marie, whose dream of the infertility clinic leading to a job was also told in Chapter 4. As Marie tells her story:

"Hank, my husband, and I were trying to get pregnant for about two years. And during that whole time, I was working the most, and Hank was going through his master's program. So there were a lot of financial worries around getting pregnant, but we knew it was time and we were ready. And what happened was that the month he got a good job, I got pregnant. But the thing was, of course, I didn't know that I was pregnant. So he got the job and we were all excited, and then a week later—and remember, this was after two years of trying—I got the news that I was pregnant. It was just at the time I could relax into it."

Though one might say that getting pregnant is a causal event— sperm meets egg, conception occurs, cause and effect—Marie's story emphasizes that pregnancy is indeed one of the chancier events in our lives, as the unreliability of birth control and the frustrations of many people who want children can attest to. Whether or not we get preg- nant is a matter of such uncertainty, even nowadays with amazing technology at our disposal, that *when* it does occur, it can be a mean- ingful coincidence of the most singular sort in a couple's life. For Marie, the timing of her pregnancy, coinciding with the resolution of outer-world anxieties, enabled her to relax and enjoy the experience.

Likewise, my friend Jacqueline's anxieties about her second child were resolved in an unusual and synchronistic way, enabling her, too, to relax and enjoy the experience. Her first child, a wonderful little girl, was born with a genetic birth defect, and as a consequence she and her husband had decided not to risk having another baby. So, when she found herself pregnant again, it was as much a cause for concern as for celebration. Jacqueline tells the story herself:

"I was set up to worry about this pregnancy. I didn't want to be, of course, but I couldn't help it. So my husband and I went in one Friday, about five months into my pregnancy, to get an ultrasound, in order to make sure everything was going well. Later that night, after watching the pictures of Joseph inside me, it hit me that we had spent an hour looking at him and recording the images on videotape, but during all that time I never saw the baby's arms or hands. I sat bolt upright in bed, really scared, and told my husband about it. He reassured me, of course, and even though I felt ridiculous, I spent that whole weekend worrying that I was going to have a kid without any arms or hands. My friends would tell me that the doctors would have told me if they had seen anything, and so on, and I would nod, and act like I was calmer, but inside, I was saying to myself, 'They don't know. It could happen. It happened before.'

"As anxious as I was, I still was able to wait until Monday, and then, I called the doctor and said, 'I want you to call the hospital testing department, find out that my ultrasound was normal, and call me back.' He called me back immediately, he was a really great guy, and said, 'I am so sorry you spent the weekend worrying about this, you should have called me. The reason it took so long on Friday is that you have an unusually shaped uterus and everyone wanted to look at it. But the baby is fine. You know, I have a new ultrasound unit being set up right now, and I need someone so I can check how it functions. Why don't you come in and you can put your mind at ease, take another look at the baby and then you'll really know he's okay.'

"So in I went that day, to get the second ultrasound done, and just as I am looking at the screen with that thing on my belly, thinking, 'I hope he's okay, I hope he's okay,' there he is, inside of me, putting his thumb and forefinger together, making an OK sign at me! I'm just astonished, and the doctor bursts out laughing. 'See, mom, he's telling you he's okay.'

"Now babies do this, it's a reflex, but what was synchronistic, if you want to use that word, was that it happened at the exact moment during the ultrasound that I'm saying, 'I hope he's okay.' That's what I think is the great part. And it's no lie. In fact, I have had a picture made of that moment, taken from the tape of the ultrasound, Joseph making the OK sign. From then on, I relaxed. I knew he'd be fine and, you know what, he was."

What's interesting in this story is not just how Jacqueline's quite rational fears about her second child were calmed, but incidentally, how the doctor, too, sensed the synchronistic character of her unborn son's gesture, presenting it to her a bit like Jung in the story of the scarab beetle. Though reflexes explain *that* such an action occurred, the timing and meaning of the coincidence has a central place in the story of Jacqueline's family.

Synchronistic events often become a part of the story an individual family tells about itself, its lore. For Rena, following her own intuitions regarding the timing of the birth ended up being a synchronistic matter of life and death, and she tells her story with a great deal of feeling, as one might tell a legend or a myth:

"I was three weeks from my due date, and we were camping on an island with two other couples. One of the guys we were with was a doctor. The whole time we were there, which was supposed to be a week or so, I kept thinking to myself, 'Rena, something's not right,' and I would have the doctor friend of ours examine me, but everyone kept telling me I was okay. Still, I couldn't shake the feeling, so my husband and I left one day early, paddling our way back off the island, and we got home without incident. Bob, my husband, is really reassuring and he kept repeating that everything was going to be okay, that I should just relax, it would be fine. But I knew something wasn't right. I just knew it.

"I waited until the next day. Bob was gone, he was at the playground with the other two kids, and so I just decided, I'm going to the hospital, by myself. That's it. I left him a message, trying to sound casual, 'I'm going to the hospital, See you in an hour.' I got to the hospital and I asked the resident there to call my doctor, but she kept asking me all these questions, to assess me: 'Why do you think anything's wrong? Do you do any street drugs? Alcohol?' that sort of thing, to which I answered no, of course. 'Well, then,' she told me, 'I think this can wait till tomorrow morning.' And I said, 'No. I need you to call my doctor now,' which she did, thank God, and my doctor told the resident, 'If Rena is there, it's for a good reason.' He told me to wait until he got there, and when he came, they did a portable ultrasound, but the result was very poor. Consequently, they monitored me throughout the night.

"Then the next day, after an exam which indicated something wasn't right, they induced my labor and my daughter was born. Now, it turns out she had the umbilical cord around her neck, not once but twice, which is really unusual, and had I not come in when I did, she would have strangled to death inside me. I have always felt really amazed to have stuck to my feeling. There was a reason. And you know how they say that people's birth experience affects them later in life. To this day, Katie, my daughter, will not wear a turtleneck." Rena stuck to her guns only to have her intuition about her baby's danger, a situation she could not have possibly known about, synchronistically confirmed for her.

However, the timing of events may not be the sole element that carries synchronistic significance in conception and birth. Rena's intuition about her delivery finds a parallel in the even more dramatic story of my friend Gail's dream. Gail's first pregnancy had proceeded uneventfully, and with contented anticipation, she and her husband prepared for a home birth with a midwife, "like all good hippies," as she put it.

Thus, the vividly detailed dream of her son's birth that she had shortly before going into labor seemed unlikely, more the product of unconscious fears than of reasonable expectations: Gail dreamed that Sam was born but wasn't breathing, that she had to push away the midwife to give him mouth-to-mouth resuscitation herself because the umbilical cord hadn't been working, that he was turning blue and then finally began to breathe the moment her husband touched him. However, Gail is not the sort of woman to dismiss such dreams, and when she went into labor, she stayed on her guard, and in fact, all that she had dreamed did in fact come to pass. Sam wasn't breathing when he was born. The gentle procedures the midwife was performing weren't working. Gail had to push her away to provide mouth-to-mouth and Sam took his first breath, to everyone's enormous relief, the moment his father touched him for the first time.

Sensing both the inner physical situation as well as what actions would need to be taken, Gail exemplifies how much easier life can be when one is open to the possibility that inner images may indeed find parallels in outer events. "It didn't feel frightening to me as it was happening, for I had already dreamed it all in advance. It was just happening the way I saw it, and I did what I needed to." In preparing her for the unlikely event of a complicated birth, Gail's ability to consider the possibility that her dream might be synchronistically paralleled by the events of her son's birth actually helped her to save his life.

Pregnancies and births happen in their own time, regardless of our conscious wishes, hopes, efforts, and fantasies. We may decide we want a child and make every effort to have one, and yet, whether it happens or not is beyond the control of even the most desirous and diligent of couples. And even when a pregnancy does occur, when the surprise moment of conception is confirmed, doctors give us a due date which can only be an approximation, for when and how the baby arrives is also a matter beyond determination. For this reason, in my opinion, almost nothing more than a pregnancy and birth deserve to be called synchronistic: the random coincidence of one of millions of sperm meeting a particular egg, yet from this coincidence, which we do not ultimately control, grows all of life. Is there any more significant coincidence that we experience?

Why We Have the Children We Have: Synchronistic Lessons

Whether we get pregnant is a matter of chance and when and how we give birth is most of the time beyond our conscious control, but the potential synchronicities in the experience of parenthood do not end with just our children's arrival. The significance of the coincidence between who we are and who our child is as a person also carries synchronistic aspects for many parents, sometimes making parents confront their own egotistical fantasies of who they wanted their child to be, and at other times and for other parents, providing synchronistic confirmation of what is important in their own life stories.

From a woman who has served as midwife to many births, including that of her sister Janet who is at the center of this story, comes a tale which makes one wonder, in the way that so many synchronicities do, just how acausal one's psychological attitude is and evokes the question of why we are given what we are given in our children:

"When my sister Janet had Jeannie, her husband, Kefir, really wanted a boy. He's from Mali, in northern Africa, and comes out of a culture where having a first-born son is really important. So throughout the pregnancy, he called the baby inside her 'him' all the time, and made no bones about it. He had decided it was going to be a boy; it had to be. So the moment arrived, and Janet went into labor. We had planned a home birth, but after a long time laboring and laboring, we eventually went to the hospital, but still no baby. Finally, all the doctors decided to prep her for a cesarean section.

"At this moment, Kefir gave in. He put his hand on Janet's stomach and said to the baby, 'Okay, you can be a girl.' And that was the moment, after all this intense, drawn-out labor, that she came out!"

This story of Kefir's change of heart about having a girl, an internal shift synchronistically coinciding with his daughter's delivery after hours of labor, indicates how this man was confronted by the real meaning of what it is to be a parent, an experience far less about gender and far more about the sacredness of life itself, about loving the children we have and not demanding that they serve our ego's idea of the perfect life. On the other hand, Williams's story of her patient who, raised by domineering women, finds herself surrounded by men for the first time in her life after the birth of her son, was experienced as a synchronistic event that complemented rather than confronted her, as it provided her with an experience of masculinity she sorely needed.

The issue raised by the meanings that these parents place on why they have the children they have serves once again to refine and deepen an understanding of synchronicity. Don't all parents, you might ask, eventually come to grips with who their children are? Don't we all want to love the children we have? Is it so surprising that Solomon should come to love his daughter as much as he would his son or that Williams's patient perceives significance in the family she has and would have perceived significance anyway, even if she had all girls? While these reflections have some merit and may in fact be true about many, if not most, parents, they miss the point of *these* stories.

For these two parents, the gender of their child had a synchronis-

tic significance because of the story that emerged from their experience: who their children turned out to be was a coincidence that led
them to understand the story of their lives in a way that reveals not
some objective truth about their lives but a subjective one. Undoubtedly, had Kefir had a boy or had Williams's patient had nothing but
girls, we of course would be hearing another story—just as we would
in any of the cases in this book had what occurred to the individuals
not happened. What happened to Kefir and to Williams's patient was
what happens in all meaningful coincidences: our ego meets random
chance in a way that is symbolically and emotionally transformative for
our life story. The issue of accepting what happens to us and appreciating its meaning is never more significant when what happens is a
new life. Yet, for many parents, whose histories, personalities, or life
stories get in the way of such openness, *who* their child is sometimes
takes on a synchronistic significance.

Helen was a client who came to counseling at a point of transition in her life, making a shift from the very introverted life of an
accountant, which had grown stale, to try her hand at the more extroverted and potentially lucrative field of real estate. In exploring her
family relationships with her as part of my process of getting to know
her, I was initially struck by the way in which she and her twenty-
something daughter Hannah seemed, from her description, to have a
great deal of difficulty with one another. "We don't really get along,"
she said. "I have always had a very hard time dealing with her. Ever
since she was little, she was difficult. Very active, constantly pushing
the limits, always needing attention. My husband, who is a much more
outgoing person, and Hannah have always had a better relationship
with each other than she and I have."

Filing this information for future use, as therapists are wont to
do, I found that much of my work with Helen centered upon the issue
of developing her extroversion and overcoming her difficulties with

being outgoing, ambitious, and self-directed enough to make a success of her work in real estate. It was not me, though, but her husband who made the comment that she found so transformative, when one day, after one of our sessions in which I had been talking to her about introversion and extroversion, he told her that it sounded as if she should be taking lessons from Hannah. The moment crystallized into a synchronistic event for Helen.

"I was floored. My whole life I had always had so much trouble with Hannah. I loved her, of course, the way every mother does, I guess, but I never really understood her, and Lord knows, I had a hard time appreciating her as a person. But then, when my husband said that to me, it was as if the whole puzzle fit together. That was it: Hannah's personality was what I needed. It was from her that I needed to learn what I need to learn at this point in my life."

Helen's ability to see a meaning in *who* her daughter was as a person, something which had long been difficult for her, came together in a moment of synchronistic understanding where her inner process met the accident of her daughter's particular gifts in a coincidence that eventually changed both their lives. With my full support, Helen began to "consult" with Hannah on how Hannah might behave in certain situations and over time, the breach between them slowly closed.

This compensatory synchronicity between parent and child has its counterpart in the story of my colleague Jack, who was raised by a man whose ideas about who and what Jack should be had had long-term and disastrous effects. A sports fanatic his whole life, Jack's father had decided early on that his only son would be, come hell or high water, a professional athlete, and so that was how Jack was raised, in a boot-camp atmosphere where all activities were directed to the goal of athletic excellence. Unfortunately, the coincidence of Jack's almost non-existent athletic talents and his father's ego was a synchronicity that had none of the sanguine results of the ones recounted above, and the meaning it had for Jack in his life was that of a curse rather than a blessing. Indeed, as one might well imagine, the rebelliousness and rage that Jack felt from such an upbringing dogged him most of his life, though not always with terrible results. For example, his "don't tell me what to do" attitude was instrumental in enabling him to build himself a very successful business, however limiting and painful it might have been in other areas of his life.

Then Jack himself had a son who, as luck would have it, not only physically resembled Jack's much-hated father but who, as he matured, seemed to have inherited all of his grandfather's interest in athletics. "Do these things skip a generation? Isn't that what they say?" Jack said to me one day on our way to a meeting when I asked how the family was. "I spent my whole life trying to get away from sports, because it was crammed down my throat day and night, and what happens but I'm living in a house filled with baseball cards and Monday night football. He's even inviting friends over and they sit there screaming at the TV, just like Pop. It's driving me crazy."

Mere coincidence or synchronicity? The coincidental aspect of the parallel between his son and his father is certainly not lost on Jack, but the meaning of it, how he, Jack, fits it into his life is still in the making. While my ideas, or yours, could make some sense from the outside of this striking coincidence between the very thing Jack had sought to flee his whole life and what by sheer luck of the draw came to him in the form of his son, it is not we who write Jack's biography but Jack who must write his own autobiography. And up to now, it has been a coincidence without that defining inner moment of insight which would, despite its glaring self-evidence to you or me, make it synchronistic for Jack.

It may be that, for most parents, who their children happen to be as people is not experienced as particularly synchronistic, in the sense that our children frequently tend to resemble us and that much of who they are results not from sheer happenstance but from how we have raised them, what we have done or not done—in other words, causal factors rather than chance. Parents without big egos, agendas, or conflicts have few experiences of synchronicity around who their children are because the meaning of their children in their lives grows not out of a chance encounter with fate but out of their very natural ability to accept, love, and appreciate them. But all parents are not created equal, and the synchronistic encounter that many have with their children, at birth or throughout their lives, is the stuff of which literature as well as our lives is made. At those times and for those parents, children, the symbolic future of all our life histories, confront people with what their lives have meant and may well be a unique locus of insight and growth in the course of their stories.

Laboring into Death and Beyond: Synchronicity and the Ultimate Transition

I have borrowed an image from a friend of mine who is a professional hospice nurse to frame the following stories, the last in our book. As she has attended to the dying of so many individuals, watching their families come to grips with the impending loss, seeing the individuals themselves slowly let go of all the things they hold dear about themselves and their lives, she has come to speak of the dying process with a great deal of wisdom and insight. Her image, that we labor into death much in the same way we labor into birth, has a truth that so many of the stories I gathered from people who have had intimate contact with death can confirm.

Death is a process of detachment from the concerns, investments, and connections with this world, and, not unlike labor, is a process that has its own time and rhythm over which we have little control. As the former client I mentioned in the chapter on dreams discovered in his own suicide attempt, even when we take every possible measure to die, we go when it is our time to go and not before; this is a lesson that any family who has attended to the death of a loved one knows, and it is a lesson that many, many stories of synchronistic occurrences seem to drive home.

In a mirror image of the story of Kefir, the African father who at the moment of making peace with the daughter he didn't want seemed to give her permission to be born, Linda tells the story of her partner Jane's final day. Their daughter Annie, who was only two years old when Jane's cancer entered a terminal phase, had conspicuously avoided going into Jane's room during her last week, an avoidance which Linda noticed as she went about attending to Jane throughout the dying process but which she wisely let be. Gathering her friends around her, once Jane had slipped into a coma, Linda and her community did a ritual around the body late that night, during which Annie, in another room, asleep, was heard to burst into tears.

Thinking that death would more than likely happen that day and continuing to respect Annie's need to keep her distance from Jane, Linda sent Annie next door to spend the day with friends. As Jane's breathing grew heavy, Linda knew the end of the long dying process was near, and as she crawled into bed with Jane to be with her, she heard Annie come home, wanting for the first time to be with Jane in over a week. Annie entered the room, came into bed with them, and no more than a minute later, Jane died.

"It was as if either Jane was waiting for Annie to come to be with her or somehow that Annie's peace with Jane's dying allowed her to finally let go," Linda told me, marveling at her two-year-old daughter's timing and moved at how much meaning it had for her to have the whole family together as Jane was delivered into death.

Predictions of death form a large part of what people generally call superstitions, like the one from the first story in this chapter in which a picture falling off a wall means someone close will die, or my own grandmother's belief that a bird flying into the house is a similar portent. The word "superstition" literally means "survival," referring to the way that these folk beliefs have survived the onslaught of modernity to still remain fresh in the imagination as signs of a time when synchronistic events were better understood and appreciated.

Jung recounted quite a number of stories from his own life in which his premonitions were synchronistically paralleled by subsequent events. During the Second World War, on a train, he reported himself "overpowered by the image of someone drowning," a recollection of an incident that occurred during his days in the military, and he found he could not get this memory get out of his mind during the entire trip home. When he at last arrived home, he found the place in turmoil, for at the exact moment this memory had begun to plague him, his grandson Adrian had almost drowned in the lake behind his home. Likewise, having dreamed of a classically antique grave out of which floated a figure resembling his wife, Jung awoke the next morning to find that his wife's cousin had died that night.

However, for a mixture of the amusing and the chilling, Jung's tale of the dream he had in 1922 presaging his mother's death can hardly be surpassed. "I had not dreamed of my father since his death in 1896," Jung writes in his autobiography. "Now he once more appeared in the dream, as if he had returned from a distant journey. He looked rejuvenated, and had shed his appearance of paternal authoritarianism. I went into my library with him, and was greatly pleased at the prospect of finding out what he had been up to. I was also looking forward with particular joy to introducing my wife and children to him, to showing him my house. . . . But I quickly saw that all this would be inopportune, for my father looked preoccupied. Apparently he wanted something from me. I felt that plainly. . . . He then said to me that since I was after all a psychologist, he would like to consult me about marital psychology. I made ready to give him a lengthy lecture on the complexities of marriage, but at this point I awoke. I could not properly understand the dream, for it never occurred to me that it might refer to my mother's death. I realized that only when she died suddenly in January 1923.

"My parents' marriage was not a happy one, but full of trials and difficulties and tests of patience. Both made the mistakes typical of many couples. My dream was a forecast of my mother's death, for here was my father who, after an absence of twenty-six years, wished to ask a psychologist about the newest insights and information on marital problems, since he would soon have to resume this relationship again. Evidently he had acquired no better understanding in his timeless state and therefore had to appeal to someone among the living who, enjoying the benefits of changed times, might have a fresh approach to the whole thing."[2]

While speaking of his father as if the dream were indeed a literal visitation from beyond, Jung's tone is clearly also that of a person quite familiar with the ordinary extraordinariness of synchronistic events, treating the vision of his father from the other side with all the nonchalance that he would have any other familiar visitor to his home. This vision, though, which Jung subsequently understood as a presage of his mother's death, is an example of the sort of synchronistic occurrences which tend to happen as our stories, or the stories of our loved ones, draw to a close.

In the many other stories people have shared with me, however, I find little of Jung's jaunty familiarity with ghosts. Frances, for example, found herself completely spooked when, throughout the course of her husband's lingering death in the hospital, she would find her favorite picture of the two of them showing up in various places throughout her house, places she knew she herself hadn't left it, and furthermore, she lived alone and no one else had the key to the house. She came home the first day to find the picture facedown on the sofa in the living room, somehow having moved off its central place on the mantel. She put it on the nearby coffee table and woke up the next morning with it once again facedown in the bathroom sink. Returning from her visit to the hospital that day, she discovered the picture had moved somehow from the bathroom to the corner of the hallway, propped up facing the wall.

"If it had only happened while I was asleep," she said, "I might have been able to explain it through sleepwalking or something. You know, I was in a state of great upset with Frank's illness and impending death, and I suppose I could have been wandering around asleep or absentmindedly moving it myself, hypnotized or like that. But I couldn't figure out how to explain it moving around the apartment when I was out altogether, and after Frank died, the photograph never moved again. It just sits on the mantelpiece, like a rock."

What effect on Frances did this series of improbable and ultimately unexplainable movements of the photograph have? My impression from speaking with her was that it served to make the reality of her husband's death "come home" to her, integrating her experience in the hospital at the time with her life at the house she had shared for many years with her husband. When objects in outer reality begin to move about seemingly in response to emotional unpheaval and grief, the synchronistic connection makes the subjective reality painfully, unavoidably obvious. But, for all the weirdness of the event, I also got the feeling that such visible effects of his death were gratifying in a certain way, as if his dying were important enough to have such tangible results.

In keeping with various folktales and superstitions regarding omens of death, tragedy and loss can be signaled synchronistically by the unusual appearance of animals, particularly those with markings or characteristics that symbolically link them to the afterlife, such as birds who, as flying creatures, are often associated with the spirit or soul, or black cats and dogs whose dark color links them with the unseen and unknown.

My friend Michael, before his death six years ago, had the uncanny experience of sitting at his living room window in Berlin, Germany, quietly reading, when a huge bang on the wall of the house startled him. As he lived on the third story of an apartment house, he opened the window to look out into the inner courtyard below where he could see the small body of a crow flapping its wings more and more slowly until it died of its injuries. Full of pigeons, this inner courtyard was an odd place for a crow to meet its death, so the whole incident stuck in his mind as being quite uncanny. The following week, he received a call from his mother: his younger brother had that morning been found dead in his bed, of causes unknown at the time and which following two autopsies were never discovered. Looking back, Michael saw the dead crow as a synchronistic prefiguration of the completely unexpected death of his healthy, twenty-four-year-old brother. Here a synchronistic, rather than predictive, interpretation puts the emphasis on how Michael's experience of his brother's death subjectively changed his own vision of his life, incorporating into his story the symbol of the crow as a marker of the importance of his subsequent experience.

Synchronistic phenomena at the moment of death are common enough to give rise to explanations of a causal nature—that an individual's death somehow releases her "life energy," which is why pictures move about an apartment, or that our interconnectedness as a species or a family enables us to feel or sense what the dying person feels or senses, which is why Jung or Michael can have prefigurative dreams and experiences. These explanations have given rise to all sorts of ritual measures, such as the opening of windows to let the soul fly out, holding a wake or vigil over the dead body to ensure its passage, and so on.

Whether the phenomena at death are caused by energy, the soul, or other factors yet to be determined, the fact that synchronistic occurrences tend to occur at the moment of death is beyond doubt. My grandmother, mother, and great-aunt all confirm that at the moment of my great-grandmother's death, during which she seemed to see Jesus coming off a cross in the corner of the room to take her with him, a bright light illuminated the room from an unknown source and extinguished itself when she died. As the story is told in my family, the synchronistic significance of what they experienced lies in the great comfort they feel was given to them by God in knowing that my great-grandmother was being taken into heaven through her death.

Paul, a skeptical philosophy professor of my acquaintance, for whom the entire subject of this book as I described it to him was a cause for much indulgent amusement, nevertheless contributed a story of his own along these lines. Resistant to facing the upcoming death of a friend whom he had employed as a gardener at his house during the man's slow decline from Hodgkin's disease, Paul had successfully managed to avoid visiting his friend at the hospice during his final month there, until feeling guilty, he screwed up his courage and overcame his resistance. The nurses took him aside after the visit and told him that his friend seemed to be rallying a bit and that what looked like a precipitous death might not be as swift after all.

In the middle of that night, half-asleep, Paul saw his friend come to him, all dressed in white. He chatted briefly about this and that with Paul, in this dream-like vision, and then went on his way with a salutation. "See you. I've got to get going." The next day, on calling the hospice, Paul found out that his friend had died at the time of his dream. This was truly the first such experience of this kind that Paul himself had had, and what struck me as he told the story was the way it tempered a bit of his amusement and skepticism at some of the ways others in this book, including me, approach the story of our lives.

For some people, though, the synchronistic experience connected with death is even more dramatic, as they undergo an actual physical experience of the death itself. A former advisor of mine used to tell the story of how she was awakened with a horrible pain in her back and chest the night of her father's violent murder by stabbing. Her pain at the time was so acute that only her stubbornness stopped her from calling 911 for an ambulance. The grim knowledge the next day of what had happened that night, across the country, to her father, made sense of what she had felt. "He and I had always been close, and I chose to believe that I was given an opportunity to share in his death as well."

All these synchronistic experiences, which defy anyone's ability to understand them in a cause-and-effect fashion, carry an important symbolic similarity to one another. Just as we experience death as an obliteration, a tearing apart, a dissolution of the world we have known and lived, so, too, it seems, the symbolism in such synchronicities as those above is that of a kind of dissolution or obliteration of the laws that generally govern our experience in the daylight world. It is as if natural principles do not apply during the process of death, as if causality and matter are suspended. For some people, this suspension of natural law inspires terror, but for others such coincidences hold an important meaning, reaffirming at moments of extreme sorrow and helplessness the connections that we have with those around us whom we love and with whom we have shared our lives. At times, the synchronistic meaning of a coincidence seems almost capable of repairing and making whole what death has torn asunder.

The Synchronicity of Continuity: When the End Is Not the Ending

Anyone who has ever lost a loved one to death knows that our connections do not end after death, certainly, and synchronistic events sometimes appear as reminders of this fact. I remember a conversation I had over brunch years ago, when I was an intern counselor, with a friend of mine whose sister had met a very untimely death following the birth of her first child. I found myself at the time troubled by my friend's lack of dismay over the situation, but looking back now, I see that I was suffering from that dreaded infection that counselors in training often come down with—the Know-It-All virus. With all my reading on grief, mourning, and bereavement but without the life experience to back it up, I began to push at my friend concerning the anger I believed she must have been feeling about her sister's death. My friend kept telling me that her spiritual beliefs had helped her come to terms with the tragedy, that she felt her sister had gone to be with God, and that God had had a plan in mind that none of us understood, all of which, given my certainty that she was in denial, simply made me push further for the anger and grief she was obviously "repressing." The irony here was that I had just gotten a degree in pastoral counseling and would never have tolerated such pushing on the part of a counselor.

Finally my friend's patience wore thin, and showing her irritation, she said, "You need to let this go," at which point we both heard a loud bang nearby. Caught up in the moment, neither of us really thought much about it at the time, we were more concerned with recovering a bit of civility between us. Only later on that evening, when cleaning up the brunch dishes, did I find what had happened: the china dish between us on the table had split down the middle into two pieces.

Now, there can be multiple interpretations of this event. Two causal explanations could be that my friend's repressed anger once expressed had split the dish with its "energy" or that some sort of life force from my friend's dead sister had "manifested" itself in the broken dish. A synchronistic view, though, would hold that the dish breaking was meaningful to me because it was an apt symbol of how my own pushiness had broken our relationship in a certain way. In either case, the conjunction of death, feeling, symbolism, and material reality makes this event one of the more uncanny synchronicities I have experienced.

That the symbolic power of death persists, sometimes for quite a while after the actual death, came home to me in the story of Rachel who told me of preparing very consciously for a personal and private commemoration of the one-year anniversary of her husband Steve's death. Despite numerous invitations from understanding friends to spend the day and evening with them, she thought it would be better for her to be by herself, performing a ritual she had created for herself, taking all their albums out, going through them slowly, turning off all the lights in the house and lighting candles, and trying as much as possible to recreate his presence with her that night.

"So, there I am, the house is all dark, with nothing but candles, and it is approaching seven o'clock in the evening, which is when he died the year before, and suddenly the phone next to me rings. Thinking it is a friend of mine calling, I pick it up instead of letting the answering machine get it. On the other end of the line, I hear this weird little voice, like an adult pretending to be a little kid, really creepy. He asks me, 'Is Steve there?' I am just floored, too shocked really to even think, you know, that it might be some sort of cruel joke or something. So, I just say back, 'No, he's not.' But the voice doesn't stop, and just asks again, real calmly, 'Is Steve there?' Again, I say, 'No, he's not. Who are you? What do you want?' to which this little kid says, 'I was just wondering if Steve might want to come over and play,' which is when I was sure that in fact this was a little kid after all and not a prankster. So I said, 'No, Steve's not here.' And the little kid says one more time, 'Are you sure? Where is he?' And since the coincidence was so weird and I was feeling so out of it, I just said, kind of in a panic, 'Steve's dead,' and hung up the phone. I sat there, freaked out, and then turned on all the lights, blew out the candles, and called up friends, saying, 'Put on dinner, I'm coming over.' Only later did I think how I might have traumatized some little kid somewhere, telling him his friend was dead, but it was just too uncanny and I wasn't really thinking."

When I asked Rachel what she made of this strange coincidence, she raised her eyebrows and lifted her palms up in the air to suggest she didn't really know what it meant. "People have suggested that it was Steve himself calling me, as if my ritual had been effective in conjuring up his spirit or something like that, which I myself don't believe. But, since you asked, I wonder if the meaning might not be more something like that I shouldn't have been alone that night. Didn't Freud say that the unconscious intention of an action is revealed in the result? I look at the result, mainly that I hightailed it to friends that night and foresook my private little ritual, and maybe that's what I was meant to do, you know, spend time with the living rather than continue to dwell among the dead. If so, the event certainly was effective." Knowing Rachel, and especially how important her circle of friends were to her during her bereavement, I think that perhaps the weirdness of the coincidence had overshadowed the meaning of it for her, which I needed to dig a bit to uncover, namely, how it seemed to be time for her to move on and affirm her ability to live.

If the presence of death can be the focus of such synchronistic phenomena, then it can be equally the case that the absence or avoidance

of death, under certain amazing circumstances, may be just as significant and synchronistic. One famous story of this type, first reported in
Life magazine in 1950 and repeated in various other places, tells the
story of a church choir in the small town of Beatrice, Nebraska, who
were due at choir practice at 7:20 P.M. on March 1. That evening every
member of the choir—fifteen people all told—came late for one reason or another. The minister's family was delayed due to finishing up
the laundry, someone else's car wouldn't start, another person was
engrossed in a radio program, still another was finishing her school
work, a pair of mother and daughter were delayed because the daughter was difficult to wake up from a nap. Each of them had a reason to
miss the beginning of practice, which, as it happened, was a stroke of
luck: due to an undetected fault in the heating system, the church
exploded at 7:25 P.M. This chain of occurrences, so improbable that the
chance of it happening was later calculated by a mathematician at
literally one in a million, had more than just a mathematical impact on
the lives of these fortunate parishioners who in *Life* magazine at the
time wondered if indeed this synchronicity was an "act of God."[3]

Another more frankly spiritual story of an accident with a purpose is that of the nineteenth-century Chinese monk Hsu Yun who on
his way to a monastery fell into a river and only narrowly escaped
losing his life. Managing to get himself to his destination somehow, he
lay in meditation, awaiting death. In his own words, Hsu Yun writes in
his spiritual autobiography:

"My concentration became so pure that I did not know I had a
body. After a little over twenty days, all my ailments were suddenly
cured. . . . One night during the rest from meditation, I opened my
eyes and suddenly there was a great radiance like broad daylight. I
could see through everything, inside and out. . . . In my whole life I
had never felt such joy. It was like waking from a dream. I thought of
the many decades of wandering since I had become a monk. . . .

And now if I had not fallen into the water and gotten very ill, if I had not been through easy times and hard times that taught me lessons and changed my understanding, I might have almost missed my chance in this life and how could this day have ever come."[4]

What is of interest concerning Hsu Yun's and the Beatrice, Nebraska, church choir's stories is the similar meaning they both draw from their brush with death. Both see a spiritual reason behind their "good fortune," and experienced their random luck as having a significance concerning the action of God or divine providence in their lives. The synchronistic meaning each found in not dying became a defining and transformative moment in their lives in which the continuity of life was made clear to them, just as it was to Rachel. Sometimes, whether we frame the message in religious terms or not, such synchronistic brushes with death are quite effective in deepening our appreciation for the life we have.

Reflections on Tragedy: On Finding Meaning in Suffering

The "what if" character of these last two stories in which people's lives are saved by sheer chance frequently brings out the skeptical and dismissive side of people. Like Voltaire who had Pangloss go on at great length about "If you hadn't done this, or that, or the other thing, you would not be where you are today," one woman said to me in the course of my telling one of these stories, "So what? For every plane that crashes there is someone who missed it. It happens every day." But as I continue to point out, in all resistance to seeing the synchronistic character of events, mostly what is overlooked or not fully appreciated is the subjective meaning of the events to the people involved. To them, such coincidences—in which they barely missed losing their lives—most emphatically do *not* happen every day.

When I skipped a long-standing meeting for the first time in my new job on the afternoon of October 17, 1989, and missed the collapse of the Oakland–San Francisco Bay Bridge during the earthquake, I can assure skeptics that my synchronistic good fortune meant a great deal to me. The point of a synchronistic story, when we see later on how mere chance has spared us from catastrophe, is that it happened *to us*. These stories are not about the raw data of who died or who did not, but rather they are about the way that death, that ultimate experience over which we have no control, can make us acutely aware of what our life means, to us personally and to those around us.

And yet, the resistance some feel to the often facile or self-absorbed way the meaning of events in our lives is construed may not just be due to a lack of empathy, but may involve some quite legitimate moral qualms. For not all stories end happily. People died in the 1989 earthquake, even if I did not. The skeptics, Voltaire among them, are not, I believe, just being obstinate but are seeing a shadow that the happy endings of so many of the stories in this book often do not present.

If so many of the stories in this book seem to have a positive ending, it is because a synchronistic experience has by definition a significance, and that perception of significance imparts a feeling of order, coherence, and wholeness to our lives. But when we encounter death, we encounter a limit placed on our lives, from which none of us escapes and for which there is no happy ending. The process of dying itself is, for all its potential meaningfulness in the long run, a very painful, often agonizing experience of loss, fragmentation, and disorientation.

Then there is the experience of surviving the death of a loved one, an experience akin to dying ourselves, where our lives as we know them are shattered, and the careful meanings, rituals, and pleasures we shared are gone forever. We may turn over in our minds and hearts again and again what might have been, how we wish we had said this or done that as if thinking differently about what happened might assuage the loss. But it doesn't, and we suffer.

The title of this book, *There Are No Accidents*, has a hopeful ring to it, implying that nothing occurs by chance and that everything has the potential to be meaningful. And yet, the word "accident" refers most often to events we fear and at all costs attempt to prevent or avoid. Accidents kill people. Accidents disrupt lives.

To insist that there are most certainly accidents in this world, and that tragedy strikes on a small and large scale to all of us in the course of our lives, is not merely to be argumentative; it is true. Some of us do not meet the love of our life and ride off into the sunset. Many of us find ourselves alienated, alone and friendless, sometimes for a brief period, and sometimes for longer. Some of us do not feel called to do something which uses our talents and gifts, or we may be prevented socially, economically, or psychologically from developing our potentials. Some of our most important dreams and plans for ourselves are never realized. Our businesses fail, and no synchronistic silver lining of good fortune hides within the dark cloud: we go broke, lose our families, and suffer breakdowns. We are unable to have children, or the children we have become ill or are killed in a random act of violence. The people we love most in the world are taken from us by illness, by war, by natural disaster, by bad luck. Airplanes crash. Earthquakes, hurricanes, fires, and floods destroy all that is precious to us. Just as no one alive escapes death, no life story unfolds without accidents, tragic occurrences of suffering, pain, loss, and disruption.

Tragedies are a particular form of story that human beings have always told, bequeathed to us in the West in definitive form by the ancient Greeks. These tragedies, in which the downfall and destruction of great men and women were depicted in dramatic form, were the focal point of the religious practices of ancient Greece: staged in festivals honoring the gods, these stories gave ritual life to the terrible destinies of individuals portrayed. Through the medium of live theater, the ancient Greeks actually relived Oedipus's self-deception, Antigone's futile rebellion, or Orestes's self-destructive vengeance. "Theater," remember, comes from the same Greek word as theology—*theos* or "god"—and the tragedies of ancient Greece were seen and experienced as sacred truths, not as mere entertainment.

We might wonder, we who do all we can to protect ourselves against tragedies—fastening our safety belts, installing smoke alarms, teaching our children to say no, taking self-defense classes, and praying for good fortune—why would people attend such gruesome rites? For the same reason that we pack the theater to see disaster films or tune into reality-based programming on television? What archetypal hold does tragedy, as a form of story, exert on our souls?

The answer can be found, I think, in the sacred nature of the Greek tragedies. The scenes of personal destruction given form in these plays make sense of suffering without necessarily relieving it, denying it, or removing it, and so give form to a universal truth we all come to know in the course of our lives: that suffering is inevitable and yet has its place and its reasons for being. This was the purpose of tragedy in ancient Greece and why, even today, we continue to re-enact these ancient stories.

Throughout this book we have looked at our lives as stories. Tragedy is a form of story that puts suffering into a coherent structure while being at the same time faithful to its reality. For, to find meaning in suffering, to understand the unhappy ending of so many of our stories, does not require that we minimize or ignore the pain. To see the tragic dimension of our darkest experiences, to be able to tell this part of our story, is rather to make sense of it.

So many of the difficulties individuals encountered in the stories we have heard up to now occurred when their egos were confronted and defeated by circumstances they could not control: real estate deals falling through, relationships ending, plans for one's life meeting insurmountable obstacles. But I think it is useful to move beyond the personal stories to consider catastrophes of larger, almost incomprehensible, dimensions when grappling with our ability to make meaning from suffering. The sad fact of twentieth-century history is, as Einstein remarked, that the development of our technology has outstripped the development of our humanity to the extent that an unparalleled destruction of human life was made possible in the form of the Holocaust. Not that mass destruction has not always been the shadow of human history; indeed, the sacred history of the Jewish people themselves, the primary victims of Nazi genocide, is a story of continual oppression and enslavement. But the difference in scale and the utterly overwhelming complicity of so many "civilized" nations in the mass murder of six million people has presented all of us since with a moral question for which there is no simple answer.

Among the more difficult aspects which any individual confronts in such an event is the sheer randomness of the destruction, the way in which many millions of innocent people were destroyed, not because of anything they did, but simply because of who they were. The abhorrent insanity of the Holocaust is its curse to us who survive, for its irrationality makes it almost incomprehensible. Is it possible to make meaning from such an event? If so, how?

In his tragic novel *Sophie's Choice*, William Styron presents in painful detail what happened to one woman who was unable to find a meaning when confronted with the irrationality of her suffering during the Holocaust. The choice referred to in the book's title, Sophie's being forced by the whim of a camp guard to choose which one of her children will live and which will die during a selection in the concentration camp where she was sent, is a symbol of the capriciousness of her suffering. What she is forced to do is not a choice at all, but is instead a torture without rational foundation, and her experience, as depicted in Styron's story, permanently and irrevocably erodes her sanity and her ability to continue living.

Elie Wiesel's first-hand account of his own experience in the camps, *Night*, chronicles a similar failure to make the meaninglessness of the Holocaust meaningful in any standard religious or philosophical way. A fellow inmate in Buchenwald, Akiba Drumer, whose traditional faith was eventually destroyed by the suffering around him, pronounces, "It's the end. God is no longer with us," and offers himself to the executioner when the selection comes. The result of Wiesel's own confrontation with the horror of what is being done to him and to his people can only be expressed in a contradiction: "In spite of myself, a prayer rose in my heart to that God in whom I no longer believed."[5]

The horror which so overcomes us in the insanity of the Holocaust, however, does not preclude the responses that writers like Styron along with survivors like Wiesel and many others have made to the incomprehensibility of such evil. And perhaps this is the only response possible in such a situation: to remember what happened, both in the sense of using one's memory as well as in the sense of re-member, to put back together. In remembering the story of our suffering, the story of our lives is told, and if the content of the story cannot resolve the irrationality of such suffering, of any suffering, the act of telling the story can be the one valid moral response, the sole way to give what happened a meaning. This is the purpose of tragedy—to tell the story of suffering and in the act of telling it, to give suffering an ultimate significance, to impart some meaning to the experience of a destruction of meaning.

We have already perceived how our innate capacity to use symbols, to tell a story, is responsible for the meaning we experience in random events. Suffering, too, is a random event. By telling the stories of our suffering, we bind together the chaos and fragmentation we feel into a coherence that does not and cannot always redeem the experience. The reality of death, whether it is our own, our loved one's, those of innocent people, or that of faceless millions, does not change by telling our stories. As in synchronistic experiences, it is *we* who change in relationship to the random, tragic event by seeing its place in our history, by telling our stories of what happened, by remembering.

Rebirth and the Cycle of Life

At the end of this section on the end of our lives, and at the end of this book, the following questions seem apt to ask: What is really the end of our story? *Is* there really an end? While definitive, empirical proof of a life beyond this one is and may ever remain out of our ken, we have seen that synchronistic events around death so frequently aid us to see the continuity of our lives. What we do know from our own stories is that our lives here, bounded by birth and death, follow cycles of growth, maturity, decline, and ending. We are born and reborn many times in our lifetime, and we die many a death to many things before we die that final time. Even when we face some of our darkest moments, though, a synchronistic event may occur that helps us turn that darkness into an experience of rebirth and continuation, a chance to remember and tell who we are once again.

I have heard (and now told) many a strange story about amazing and meaningful coincidences, so I am cautious in ranking Charlotte's story as among the strangest or more improbable. However, her story sticks in my mind as a perfect example of how a synchronistic event might give us back a measure of what we feel we have lost through death and how in life, a rebirth of meaning is always possible.

Charlotte's son Todd, a vital and active young college student, was killed near his school on New Year's Eve by a drunk driver, and the physical damage his body suffered in the accident, along with Charlotte's shock and overwhelming grief, made it impossible for her to bring herself to view her son's body. Her husband, distraught but more functional during this tragedy, agreed that it was not a good idea for Charlotte to be confronted with the gruesome reality of what had happened, and following a closed-casket funeral and cremation, Charlotte's son was put to rest.

In the course of my work with survivors of grief, I have come to see that as painful and horrible as it is, the opportunity to view the body of a loved one who has died can be quite instrumental in the process of letting go and moving forward, and Charlotte's story makes that clear. "For months afterward, even though at the time I really could not have done anything else, I was tormented by the fact that I would never see Todd again. In hindsight, I felt worse and worse about not having had a chance to say goodbye, not having been courageous enough to face what had happened. My husband kept telling me that I had done the right thing, that it was better for me to remember Todd the way he was, but I had to say that I began to feel unfinished. I would sit sometimes and just go over and over our photo albums, looking at all the pictures we had taken, thinking to myself, 'No more, Charlotte. No more. Todd's gone. No more memories.'

"And it began to wear at both of us, my inability to go on. You hear that, how people's marriages break up after the death of a child, but until it happens to you, you can't imagine. But now, talking about this years after, I see I was just stuck in my grief and, I have to say, quite a burden on my husband. So, one day, I am sitting at home, crying over the photo albums, saying what I usually said to myself, 'If only I could see him one more time,' when I hear the mailman come. I go to the mailbox and there, unbelievably, is a big manila envelope from Todd. All the hair on my head stood up and I was covered in chills. The envelope was pretty beat up and when I looked at it, I saw that it was mailed the day Todd was killed, December 31. And inside there is a short note from Todd himself, with a bunch of pictures from our last Christmas together that he'd had developed and sent to me that day, only he hadn't put the right postage on it, and it was returned, and forwarded, and passed here and there for months.

"You can imagine my reaction. It was really like the universe had given me the greatest gift, as if I was being told, 'See, he's still here. You can go on. Who Todd was to everyone continues. His life isn't over. Here he is. He's dead but he still is living, in a way.' At least that's what I made of it. Amazing, really." Charlotte paused a long time with a bittersweet smile on her face. "I don't know what would have shook me out of it, if I hadn't gotten that letter and those pictures from him, if I hadn't had the chance to see him again. Things got a lot better after that. Never good. I don't think you can ever really recover from something like that, but the coincidence of those pictures brought his death and his life together for me in a way that was like completing a circle. I was able to go on from there. Still, I can't believe it . . . "

Just as Charlotte's story of a meaningful coincidence illustrates the cycles of birth, death, and rebirth, a final story with the same significance was told to me, synchronistically enough, while I was half-way through writing this chapter about death. In a conversation about business matters with my agent, Candice, she told me, unprompted by me, that a very lovely synchronicity had just happened to her. Her husband had died the year before, indeed, the very week that she and I were putting the finishing touches on the proposal of this very book, and, without him, she said, the remote house in the midst of the hills that they had shared seemed no longer right, no longer where she belonged.

Once upon a time, when her daughter was just a child, they had all lived in another house. In the course of her bereavement, Candice told me, she had thought a great deal about that other house. It was, she said, nothing special, smallish but pleasant, a place that they had rented early on in their marriage but full of good memories of better times. When they were in a position to buy a house, rather than continue to rent, they had approached the owner with the possibility of buying it, but at the time he was not interested and so the family left that house behind.

On a hike with her now-adult daughter, Candice was reminiscing about the old house, sharing how fondly she still thought of it, especially now that she was widowed and felt she needed a change. On a whim, her daughter suggested that they go by and look at the old place, something they hadn't done since they had left it fifteen years earlier. To their delight, when they arrived, they saw a For Sale sign outside, and, counting themselves unbelievably lucky, discovered that it had just gone on the market the day before. Candice made an offer immediately, and the deal was quickly done: the house which had held so many good memories was synchronistically, suddenly, theirs, and the move into a new life, after a period of mourning, a move which in some ways was a move into an old life as well, happened in a way that Candice herself could not have planned or executed more efficiently. Synchronicities like this one show us that even from death, a new life is possible, and not just in a mythic realm beyond this life, but in our own, present, everyday existence as well.

Conclusion

Our lives are full of meaningful events which we deliberately and consciously set out to cause for ourselves: pursuing a relationship with someone we are attracted to, applying for a job we have always hoped for, writing a book, interpreting a dream, naming our children, deciding how we would like to die when the hour is upon us. Such events are not accidental or acausal. They are intentional actions.

Synchronistic events, however, in their very accidental nature urge upon us another truth about our lives, a truth many of us are in the habit of ignoring: that the meaning of our lives, the plot of our life stories, is not written simply by what we know about ourselves but comes from a much deeper place, from our innately human capacity to experience wholeness through living a symbolic life. As with fiction, synchronicities come in many different genres, and indeed, there is no area of our life that is not, at one time or another, touched by chance. All the stories I have told make that abundantly clear; the issue is what we do when an accidental twist of fate reorganizes our lives and shows us something we did not expect. Do we shrug it off and deny its reality? Or do we approach that which we did not cause or create in our lives in a spirit of openness, interest, and seriousness?

My hope is that this book and its many real-life stories have by now fostered an attitude of psychological, emotional, and symbolic curiosity about the chance events that happen to us, good or bad, painful or happy, sweet or sour. The next time, therefore, that something unexpected comes our way—a phone call, a meeting, a dream, a stroke of good luck or bad—I urge us all to remember some of the stories presented here and be open to considering that this chance encounter, this random occurrence, may well be a turning point in the story we are living every day. If we bring a symbolic attitude to our lives, searching out the meaning of what happens to us and thereby allowing our own capacity to make wholeness out of the random and disparate events of our lives, then, as this book has shown, no matter what happens in the plot, wherever the setting, whoever the characters, major or minor, we will see that indeed, there are no accidents in the stories of our lives.

Notes

Chapter One

1. C. G. Jung, *The Collected Works of C. G. Jung*, vol. 8 (Princeton: Princeton University Press, 1960), p. 441.

2. Marie-Louise von Franz, *On Divination and Synchronicity: The Psychology of Meaningful Chance* (Toronto: Inner City Books, 1980), p. 48.

3. C. G. Jung, op.cit., p. 441.

4. Jean Shinoda Bolen, *The Tao of Psychology: Synchronicity and the Self* (San Francisco: Harper and Row Publishers, 1979), p. 37.

Chapter Four

1. Jonathan Winson, "The Meaning of Dreams," *Scientific American* (November 1990), pp. 86–96; June Kinoshita, "The Dreams of a Rat," *Discover* (July 1992), pp. 34–41; Doug Stewart, "Do Fish Sleep? And What's That on Your Eyelash?" *National Wildlife* (April/May 1994), pp. 50–59.

2. C. G. Jung, *The Collected Works of C. G Jung*, vol. 8 (Princeton: Princeton University Press, 1960), pp. 437–38, 525–26.

Chapter Five

1. Robert Aziz, *C. G. Jung's Psychology of Religion and Synchronicity* (Albany, NY: State University of New York Press, 1990), pp. 153–54.

Chapter Six

1. Mary Williams, "Short Communication," *Journal of Analytical Psychology*, vol. 2, no. 1 (1957), pp. 93–94.

2. C. G. Jung, *Memories, Dreams, Reflections* (New York: Vintage Books, 1965), p. 316.

3. Alan Vaughan, *Incredible Coincidence* (New York: J. B. Lippincott, 1979), pp. 167-68.

4. Robert Aziz, *C. G. Jung's Psychology of Religion and Synchronicity* (Albany, NY: State University of New York Press, 1990), pp. 141–42.

5. Elie Wiesel, *Night* (New York: Avon Books, 1969), p. 104.

Adler, Gerhard. "Reflections on 'Chance,' 'Fate,' and Synchronicity," *Psychological Perspectives*, vol. 20, no. 1 (1989), pp. 16–33.

Aziz, Robert. *C. G. Jung's Psychology of Religion and Synchronicity*. Albany, NY: State University of New York Press, 1990.

Carty, Charles Mortimer. *Padre Pio: The Stigmatist*. Rockford, IL: TAN Books and Publishers, 1973.

Combs, Allan, and Mark Holland. *Synchronicity: Science, Myth and the Trickster*. New York: Paragon House, 1990.

Bolen, Jean Shinoda. *The Tao of Psychology: Synchronicity and the Self*. New York: Harper & Row, 1979.

Fordham, Michael. "Reflections on the Archetypes and Synchronicity," in *New Developments in Analytical Psychology*. London: Routledge & Kegan Paul, 1957.

Franz, Marie-Louise von. *On Divination and Synchronicity: The Psychology of Meaningful Chance*. Toronto: Inner City Books, 1980.

Freud, Sigmund. "Dreams and Telepathy," in vol. 18 of *Standard Edition of Freud's Works*, 1922.

———. "Dreams and Occultism," in vol. 22 of *Standard Edition of Freud's Works*, 1933.

———. "The Occult Significance of Dreams," in vol. 19 of *Standard Edition of Freud's Works*, 1925.

———. "Psychoanalysis and Telepathy," in vol. 18 of *Standard Edition of Freud's Works*, 1941/1921.

Frey-Wehrlin, C. T. "Reflections on C. G. Jung's Concept of Synchronicity," *Journal of Analytical Psychology*, vol. 21, no. 1 (1976), pp. 37–49.

Gordon, Rosemary. "Reflections on Jung's Concept of Synchronicity," *Harvest* (August 1962).

Hopcke, Robert H. "Synchronicity in Analysis: Various Types and Their Various Roles for Patient and Analyst," *Quadrant*, vol. 21, no. 1 (1988), pp. 54–64.

————. "The Barker: A Synchronistic Event in Analysis," *The Journal of Analytical Psychology*, vol. 35, no. 4 (1990), pp. 459–73.

————. "On the Threshold of Change: Symbolization and Transitional Space," *Chiron* (1991), pp. 115–32.

I Ching or Book of Changes, third edition, translated by Richard Wilhelm. Princeton: Princeton University Press, 1967.

Jaworski, Joseph. *Synchronicity: The Inner Path of Leadership*. San Francisco: Berrett-Koehler Publishers, 1996.

Jung, C. G. "Synchronicity: An Acausal Connecting Principle," 1952, in vol. 8 of *The Collected Works of C. G. Jung*. Princeton: Princeton University Press, 1960.

————. "An Astrological Experiment," 1958, in vol. 18 of *The Collected Works of C. G. Jung*. Princeton: Princeton University Press, 1980.

————. "Foreword to the *I Ching*," 1950, in vol. 11 of *The Collected Works of C. G. Jung*. Princeton: Princeton University Press, 1975.

————. "Letters on Synchronicity," 1950, 1954, 1955, in vol. 18 of *The Collected Works of C. G. Jung*. Princeton: Princeton University Press, 1980.

————. "On Synchronicity," 1952, in vol. 8 of *The Collected Works of C. G. Jung*. Princeton: Princeton University Press, 1960.

————. "On the Psychology and Pathology of So-Called Occult Phenomena," 1902, in vol. 1 of *The Collected Works of C. G. Jung*. Princeton: Princeton University Press, 1978.

————. *Memories, Dreams, Reflections*. New York: Vintage Books, 1965.

Kelly, Sean. "A Trip Through Lower Town: Reflections on a Case of Double Synchronicity," *Journal of Analytical Psychology*, vol. 38, no. 2 (1993), pp. 191–98.

Koestler, Arthur. *The Roots of Coincidence: An Excursion in Parapsychology*. New York: Vintage Books/Random House, 1972.

Kreutzer, Carolin S. "Synchronicity in Psychotherapy," *Journal of Analytical Psychology*, vol. 29, no. 4 (1984), pp. 373–81.

Kundera, Milan. *The Unbearable Lightness of Being*. New York: Harper and Row, 1984.

Nichols, Sallie. *Jung and Tarot: An Archetypal Journey*. New York: Samuel Weiser, 1980.

North, Carolyn. *Synchronicity: The Anatomy of Coincidence*. Berkeley, CA: Regent Press, 1994.

Peat, David F. *Synchronicity: The Bridge Between Matter and Mind*. Toronto: Bantam Books, 1987.

Progoff, Ira. *Jung, Synchronicity and Human Destiny: Noncausal Dimensions of Human Experience*. New York: Dell Publishing Co., 1973.

Sinetar, Marsha. *Do What You Love and the Money Will Follow*. New York: Paulist Press, 1987.

Styron, William. *Sophie's Choice*. New York: Random House, 1979.

Vaughan, Alan. *Incredible Coincidence: The Baffling World of Synchronicity*. New York: J. B. Lippincott, 1979.

Voltaire. *Candide ou l'optimisme, La princesse de Babylone et autres contes*. Librairie Générale Française, 1983.

Wharton, Barbara. "Deintegration and Two Synchronistic Events," *Journal of Analytical Psychology*, vol. 31, no. 3 (1986), pp. 281–85.

Wiesel, Elie. *Night*. New York: Avon Books, 1969.

Williams, Mary. "An Example of Synchronicity," *Journal of Analytical Psychology*, vol. 2, no. 1 (1957), pp. 93–95.

———. "The Poltergeist Man," *Journal of Analytical Psychology*, vol. 8, no. 2 (1963), pp. 123–43.

Robert H. Hopcke is a psychotherapist and the director of the Center for Symbolic Studies, an institute for training in psychoanalytic and Jungian-oriented psychotherapy. He has led workshops across the country, and lives in Berkeley, California.